Treasury of Favorite Poems

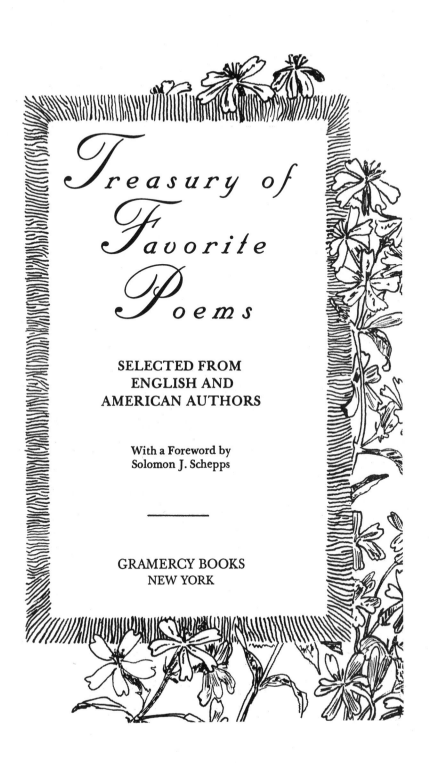

Treasury of Favorite Poems

SELECTED FROM ENGLISH AND AMERICAN AUTHORS

With a Foreword by
Solomon J. Schepps

GRAMERCY BOOKS
NEW YORK

This 2000 edition is published by Gramercy Books™,
an imprint of Random House Value Publishing, Inc.
280 Park Avenue, New York, N.Y. 10017.

Gramercy Books™ and design are trademarks of
Random House Value Publishing, Inc.

Random House
New York • Toronto • London • Sydney • Auckland
http://www.randomhouse.com/

Printed and bound in the United States of America.

Library of Congress Cataloging in Publication Data
[Head, Joseph H.] comp.
A little treasury of favorite poems.
First published 1883 by T. Y. Crowell, New York,
under title: Favorite poems.
1. English poetry. 2. American poetry.
I. Title
PR1175.H4   1978   821'.008   78-15584
ISBN 0-517-26298-3

9 8 7 6 5 4 3 2 1

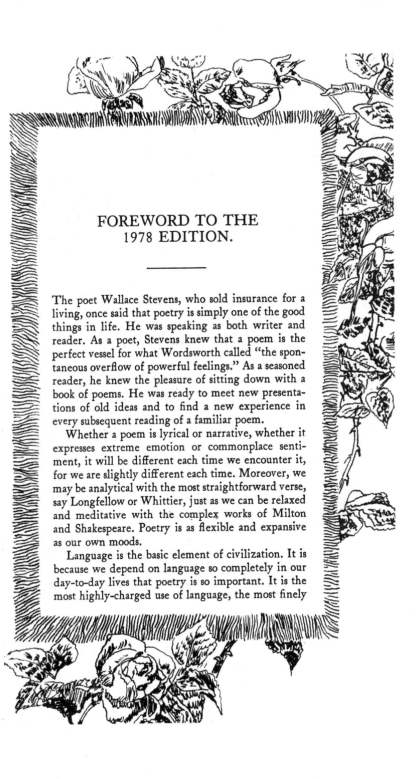

FOREWORD TO THE
1978 EDITION.

The poet Wallace Stevens, who sold insurance for a living, once said that poetry is simply one of the good things in life. He was speaking as both writer and reader. As a poet, Stevens knew that a poem is the perfect vessel for what Wordsworth called "the spontaneous overflow of powerful feelings." As a seasoned reader, he knew the pleasure of sitting down with a book of poems. He was ready to meet new presentations of old ideas and to find a new experience in every subsequent reading of a familiar poem.

Whether a poem is lyrical or narrative, whether it expresses extreme emotion or commonplace sentiment, it will be different each time we encounter it, for we are slightly different each time. Moreover, we may be analytical with the most straightforward verse, say Longfellow or Whittier, just as we can be relaxed and meditative with the complex works of Milton and Shakespeare. Poetry is as flexible and expansive as our own moods.

Language is the basic element of civilization. It is because we depend on language so completely in our day-to-day lives that poetry is so important. It is the most highly-charged use of language, the most finely honed, and the most permanently shaped. Small wonder, then, that so many poems have been written about poetry, that poetry so often describes itself. Lovers strengthen their love by professing it, and so does poetry champion itself. Like a lover, the reader accepts the poem for what it is, delighting in the uniqueness of the object. We admire poetry so much because the stuff of which it is made is so familiar to us: our language and feelings.

SOLOMON J. SCHEPPS

PREFACE.

IT has been the object of the compiler, in issuing this volume, to unite a collection that will afford a well-selected variety for the lovers of poetry, and form an appropriate present for all seasons and occasions. Most of the selections are the brightest gems from American and English authors, and will live as long as a love of the beautiful and the true spirit of poetry find an abiding-place in the human heart. It is submitted to the public, with the hope that it will be found to be an acceptable gift.

CONTENTS.

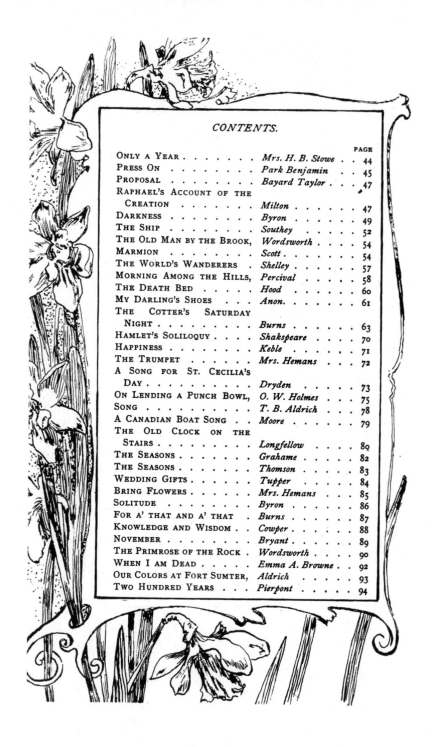

CONTENTS.

CONTENTS.

CONTENTS.

CONTENTS.

CONTENTS.

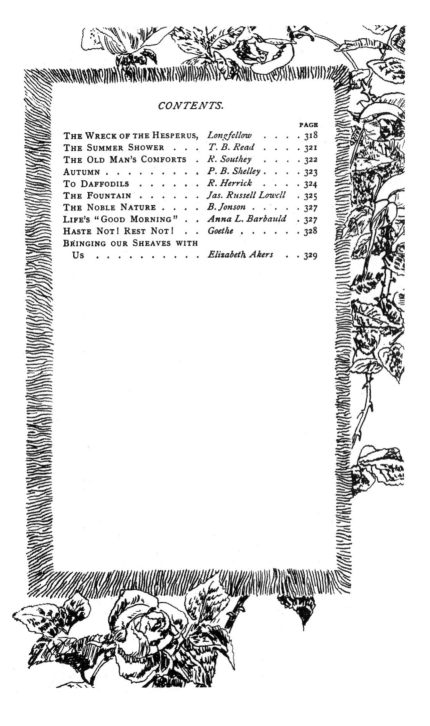

CONTENTS.

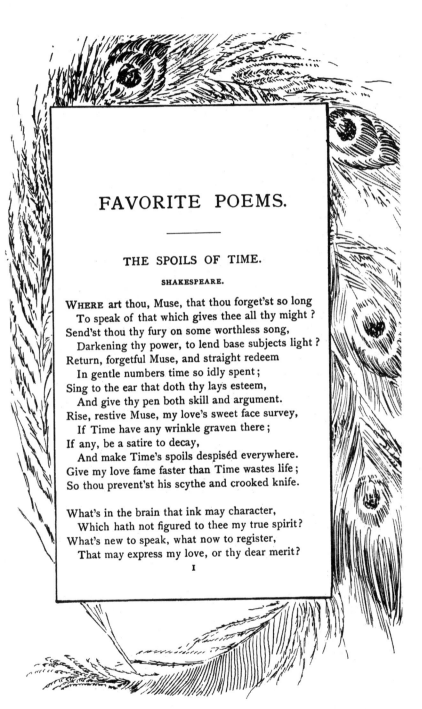

FAVORITE POEMS.

THE SPOILS OF TIME.

SHAKESPEARE.

WHERE art thou, Muse, that thou forget'st so long
  To speak of that which gives thee all thy might?
Send'st thou thy fury on some worthless song,
  Darkening thy power, to lend base subjects light?
Return, forgetful Muse, and straight redeem
  In gentle numbers time so idly spent;
Sing to the ear that doth thy lays esteem,
  And give thy pen both skill and argument.
Rise, restive Muse, my love's sweet face survey,
  If Time have any wrinkle graven there;
If any, be a satire to decay,
  And make Time's spoils despiséd everywhere.
Give my love fame faster than Time wastes life;
So thou prevent'st his scythe and crooked knife.

What's in the brain that ink may character,
  Which hath not figured to thee my true spirit?
What's new to speak, what now to register,
  That may express my love, or thy dear merit?

I

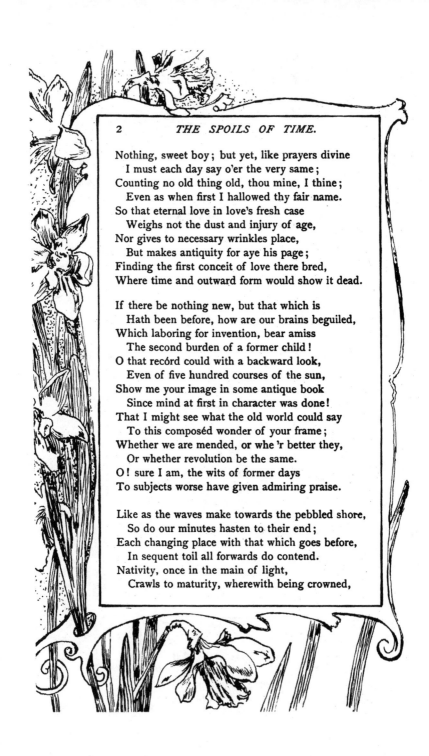

Nothing, sweet boy; but yet, like prayers divine
   I must each day say o'er the very same;
Counting no old thing old, thou mine, I thine;
   Even as when first I hallowed thy fair name.
So that eternal love in love's fresh case
   Weighs not the dust and injury of age,
Nor gives to necessary wrinkles place,
   But makes antiquity for aye his page;
Finding the first conceit of love there bred,
Where time and outward form would show it dead.

If there be nothing new, but that which is
   Hath been before, how are our brains beguiled,
Which laboring for invention, bear amiss
   The second burden of a former child!
O that recórd could with a backward look,
   Even of five hundred courses of the sun,
Show me your image in some antique book
   Since mind at first in character was done!
That I might see what the old world could say
   To this composéd wonder of your frame;
Whether we are mended, or whe 'r better they,
   Or whether revolution be the same.
O! sure I am, the wits of former days
To subjects worse have given admiring praise.

Like as the waves make towards the pebbled shore,
   So do our minutes hasten to their end;
Each changing place with that which goes before,
   In sequent toil all forwards do contend.
Nativity, once in the main of light,
   Crawls to maturity, wherewith being crowned,

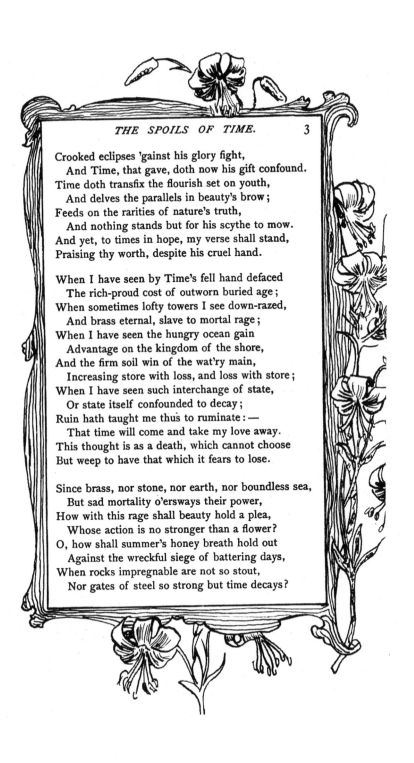

Crooked eclipses 'gainst his glory fight,
  And Time, that gave, doth now his gift confound.
Time doth transfix the flourish set on youth,
  And delves the parallels in beauty's brow;
Feeds on the rarities of nature's truth,
  And nothing stands but for his scythe to mow.
And yet, to times in hope, my verse shall stand,
Praising thy worth, despite his cruel hand.

When I have seen by Time's fell hand defaced
  The rich-proud cost of outworn buried age;
When sometimes lofty towers I see down-razed,
  And brass eternal, slave to mortal rage;
When I have seen the hungry ocean gain
  Advantage on the kingdom of the shore,
And the firm soil win of the wat'ry main,
  Increasing store with loss, and loss with store;
When I have seen such interchange of state,
  Or state itself confounded to decay;
Ruin hath taught me thus to ruminate:—
  That time will come and take my love away.
This thought is as a death, which cannot choose
But weep to have that which it fears to lose.

Since brass, nor stone, nor earth, nor boundless sea,
  But sad mortality o'ersways their power,
How with this rage shall beauty hold a plea,
  Whose action is no stronger than a flower?
O, how shall summer's honey breath hold out
  Against the wreckful siege of battering days,
When rocks impregnable are not so stout,
  Nor gates of steel so strong but time decays?

O, fearful meditation! where, alack!
  Shall Time's best jewel from Time's chest lie hid,
Or what strong hand can hold his swift foot back?
  Or who his spoil of beauty can forbid?
O, none — unless this miracle have might,
That in black ink my love may still shine bright.

MANFRED'S SOLILOQUY.

BYRON.

THE stars are forth, the moon above the tops
Of the snow-shining mountains. — Beautiful!
I linger yet with Nature, for the night
Hath been to me a more familiar face
Than that of man; and in her starry shade
Of dim and solitary loveliness,
I learned the language of another world.
I do remember me, that in my youth,
When I was wandering, — upon such a night
I stood within the Coliseum's wall,
Midst the chief relics of almighty Rome;
The trees which grew along the broken arches
Waved dark in the blue midnight, and the stars
Shone through the rents of ruin; from afar
The watch-dog bayed beyond the Tiber; and
More near from out the Cæsars' palace came
The owl's long cry, and, interruptedly,
Of distant sentinels the fitful song

Begun and died upon the gentle wind.
Some cypresses beyond the time-worn breach
Appeared to skirt th' horizon, yet they stood
Within a bowshot — where the Cæsars dwelt,
And dwell the tuneless birds of night, amidst
A grove which springs through levelled battlements
And twines its roots with the imperial hearths :
Ivy usurps the laurel's place of growth ; —
But the gladiators' bloody Circus stands,
A noble wreck in ruinous perfection !
While Cæsars' chambers and the Augustan halls
Grovel on earth in indistinct decay. —
And thou didst shine, thou rolling moon, upon
All this, and cast a wide and tender light,
Which softened down the hoar austerity
Of rugged desolation, and filled up,
As 'twere anew, the gaps of centuries,
Leaving that beautiful which still was so,
And making that which was not, till the place
Became religion, and the heart ran o'er
With silent worship of the great of old ! —
The dead, but sceptred sovereigns, who still rule
Our spirits from their urns. — 'Twas such a night —
'Tis strange that I recall it at this time ;
But I have found our thoughts take wildest flight
E'en at the moment when they should array
Themselves in pensive order.

MUSIC OF NATURE.

PIERPONT.

In what rich harmony, what polished lays,
Should man address thy throne, when Nature pays
Her wild, her tuneful tribute to the sky!
Yes, Lord, she sings thee, but she knows not why.
The fountain's gush, the long-responding shore,
The zephyr's whisper, and the tempest's roar,
The rustling leaf, in autumn's fading woods,
The wintry storm, the rush of vernal floods,
The summer bower, by cooling breezes fanned,
The torrent's fall, by dancing rainbows spanned,
The streamlet, gurgling through its rocky glen,
The long grass, sighing o'er the graves of men,
The bird that crests yon dew-bespangled tree,
Shakes his bright plumes, and trills his descant free,
The scorching bolt, that, from thine armory hurled,
Burns its red path, and cleaves a shrinking world, —
All these are music to Religion's ear : —
Music, thy hand awakes, for man to hear.

REMEMBRANCE.

SOUTHEY.

Man hath a weary pilgrimage,
    As through the world he wends;
On every stage from youth to age
    Still discontent attends;

With heaviness he casts his eye
  Upon the road before,
And still remembers with a sigh
  The days that are no more.

To school the little exile goes,
  Torn from his mother's arms, —
What then shall soothe his earliest woes,
  When novelty hath lost its charms?
Condemned to suffer through the day
Restraints which no rewards repay,
  And cares where love has no concern,
Hope lengthens as she counts the hours
  Before his wished return.
From hard control and tyrant rules,
The unfeeling discipline of schools,
  In thought he loves to roam,
And tears will struggle in his eye
While he remembers with a sigh
  The comforts of his home.

Youth comes; the toils and cares of life
  Torment the restless mind;
Where shall the tired and harassed heart
  Its consolation find?
Then is not Youth, as Fancy tells,
  Life's summer prime of joy?
Ah, no! for hopes too long delayed,
And feelings blasted or betrayed,
  Its fabled bliss destroy;
And Youth remembers with a sigh,
  The careless days of Infancy.

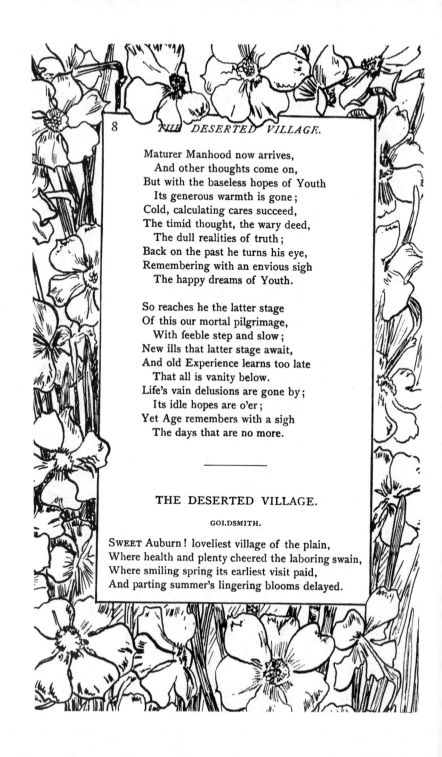

Maturer Manhood now arrives,
  And other thoughts come on,
But with the baseless hopes of Youth
  Its generous warmth is gone;
Cold, calculating cares succeed,
The timid thought, the wary deed,
  The dull realities of truth;
Back on the past he turns his eye,
Remembering with an envious sigh
  The happy dreams of Youth.

So reaches he the latter stage
Of this our mortal pilgrimage,
  With feeble step and slow;
New ills that latter stage await,
And old Experience learns too late
  That all is vanity below.
Life's vain delusions are gone by;
  Its idle hopes are o'er;
Yet Age remembers with a sigh
  The days that are no more.

THE DESERTED VILLAGE.

GOLDSMITH.

SWEET Auburn! loveliest village of the plain,
Where health and plenty cheered the laboring swain,
Where smiling spring its earliest visit paid,
And parting summer's lingering blooms delayed.

Dear, lovely bowers of innocence and ease,
Seats of my youth, when every sport could please,
How often have I loitered o'er thy green,
Where humble happiness endeared each scene!
How often have I paused on every charm, —
The sheltered cot, the cultivated farm,
The never-failing brook, the busy mill,
The decent church that topped the neighboring hill,
The hawthorn bush, with seats beneath the shade
For talking age, and whispering lovers made!
  How often have I blessed the coming day,
When toil remitting lent its aid to play,
And all the village train, from labor free,
Led up their sports beneath the spreading tree!
While many a pastime circled in the shade!
The young, contending, as the old surveyed;
And many a gambol frolicked o'er the ground,
And sleights of art and feats of strength went round
  Sweet, smiling village, loveliest of the lawn;
Thy sports are fled, and all thy charms withdrawn;
Amid thy bowers, the tyrant's hand is seen,
And desolation saddens all thy green:
No more thy glassy brook reflects the day,
But, choked with sedges, works its weedy way;
Along thy glades, a solitary guest,
The hollow-sounding bittern guards its nest.
  Ill fares the land, to hastening ills a prey,
Where wealth accumulates, and men decay;
Princes and lords may flourish, or may fade;
A breath can make them, as a breath has made;
But a bold peasantry, their country's pride,
When once destroyed, can never be supplied.

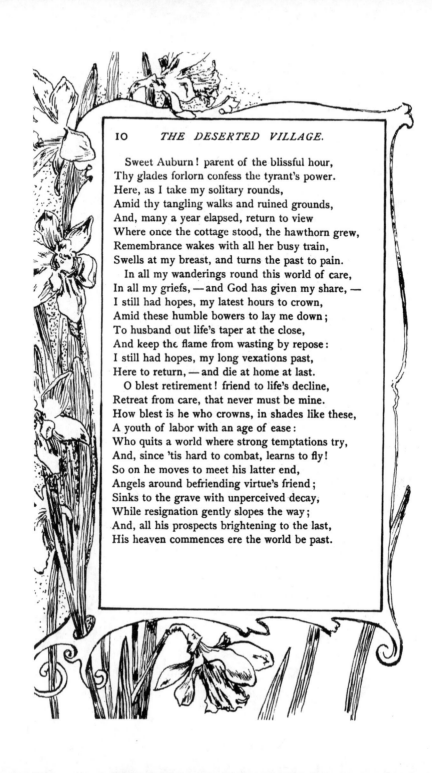

Sweet Auburn! parent of the blissful hour,
Thy glades forlorn confess the tyrant's power.
Here, as I take my solitary rounds,
Amid thy tangling walks and ruined grounds,
And, many a year elapsed, return to view
Where once the cottage stood, the hawthorn grew,
Remembrance wakes with all her busy train,
Swells at my breast, and turns the past to pain.
  In all my wanderings round this world of care,
In all my griefs, — and God has given my share, —
I still had hopes, my latest hours to crown,
Amid these humble bowers to lay me down;
To husband out life's taper at the close,
And keep the flame from wasting by repose:
I still had hopes, my long vexations past,
Here to return, — and die at home at last.
  O blest retirement! friend to life's decline,
Retreat from care, that never must be mine.
How blest is he who crowns, in shades like these,
A youth of labor with an age of ease:
Who quits a world where strong temptations try,
And, since 'tis hard to combat, learns to fly!
So on he moves to meet his latter end,
Angels around befriending virtue's friend;
Sinks to the grave with unperceived decay,
While resignation gently slopes the way;
And, all his prospects brightening to the last,
His heaven commences ere the world be past.

EVENING.

MILTON'S *"Paradise Lost."*

Now came still Evening on, and Twilight gray
Had in her sober livery all things clad.
Silence accompanied; for beast and bird,
They to their grassy couch, these to their nests,
Were slunk, all but the wakeful nightingale;
She all night long her amorous descant sung.
Silence was pleased.   Now glowed the firmament
With living sapphires: Hesperus, that led
The starry host, rode brightest; till the moon,
Rising in clouded majesty, at length
Apparent queen, unveiled her peerless light,
And o'er the dark her silver mantle threw.

THE DAFFODILS.

WORDSWORTH.

I WANDERED lonely as a cloud
   That floats on high o'er vales and hills,
When all at once I saw a crowd,
   A host of golden daffodils,
Beside the lake, beside the trees,
Fluttering and dancing in the breeze.

Continuous as the stars that shine
   And twinkle on the milky way,
They stretched in never-ending line
   Along the margin of a bay;
Ten thousand saw I at a glance,
Tossing their heads in sprightly dance.

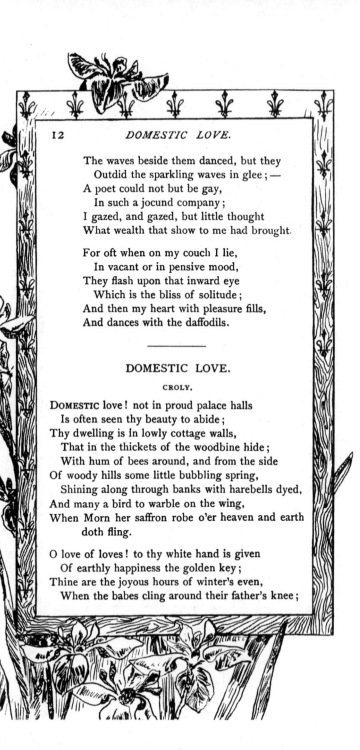

The waves beside them danced, but they
   Outdid the sparkling waves in glee ; —
A poet could not but be gay,
   In such a jocund company ;
I gazed, and gazed, but little thought
What wealth that show to me had brought.

For oft when on my couch I lie,
   In vacant or in pensive mood,
They flash upon that inward eye
   Which is the bliss of solitude ;
And then my heart with pleasure fills,
And dances with the daffodils.

DOMESTIC LOVE.

CROLY.

DOMESTIC love ! not in proud palace halls
   Is often seen thy beauty to abide ;
Thy dwelling is in lowly cottage walls,
   That in the thickets of the woodbine hide ;
   With hum of bees around, and from the side
Of woody hills some little bubbling spring,
   Shining along through banks with harebells dyed,
And many a bird to warble on the wing,
When Morn her saffron robe o'er heaven and earth
    doth fling.

O love of loves ! to thy white hand is given
   Of earthly happiness the golden key ;
Thine are the joyous hours of winter's even,
   When the babes cling around their father's knee ;

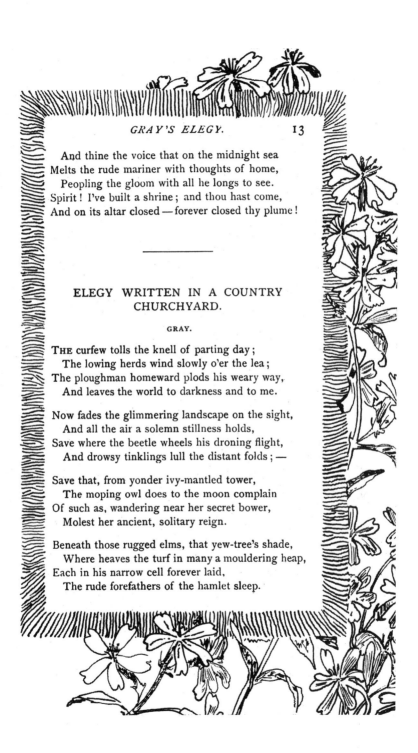

And thine the voice that on the midnight sea
Melts the rude mariner with thoughts of home,
 Peopling the gloom with all he longs to see.
Spirit! I've built a shrine; and thou hast come,
And on its altar closed — forever closed thy plume!

ELEGY WRITTEN IN A COUNTRY CHURCHYARD.

GRAY.

THE curfew tolls the knell of parting day;
 The lowing herds wind slowly o'er the lea;
The ploughman homeward plods his weary way,
 And leaves the world to darkness and to me.

Now fades the glimmering landscape on the sight,
 And all the air a solemn stillness holds,
Save where the beetle wheels his droning flight,
 And drowsy tinklings lull the distant folds; —

Save that, from yonder ivy-mantled tower,
 The moping owl does to the moon complain
Of such as, wandering near her secret bower,
 Molest her ancient, solitary reign.

Beneath those rugged elms, that yew-tree's shade,
 Where heaves the turf in many a mouldering heap,
Each in his narrow cell forever laid,
 The rude forefathers of the hamlet sleep.

The breezy call of incense-breathing morn,
   The swallow, twittering from the straw-built shed,
The cock's shrill clarion, or the echoing horn,
   No more shall rouse them from their lowly bed.

For them no more the blazing hearth shall burn,
   Or busy housewife ply her evening care;
Nor children run to lisp their sire's return,
   Or climb his knees the envied kiss to share.

Oft did the harvest to their sickle yield;
   Their furrow oft the stubborn glebe has broke;
How jocund did they drive their team a-field!
   How bowed the woods beneath their sturdy stroke!

Let not Ambition mock their useful toil,
   Their homely joy, and destiny obscure;
Nor Grandeur hear, with a disdainful smile,
   The short and simple annals of the poor.

The boast of heraldry, the pomp of power,
   And all that beauty, all that wealth e'er gave,
Await, alike, the inevitable hour; —
   The paths of glory lead but to the grave.

Nor you, ye proud, impute to these the fault,
   If memory o'er their tomb no trophies raise,
Where, through the long-drawn aisle and fretted vault,
   The pealing anthem swells the note of praise.

Can storied urn, or animated bust,
   Back to its mansion call the fleeting breath?
Can Honor's voice provoke the silent dust,
   Or Flattery soothe the dull, cold ear of death?

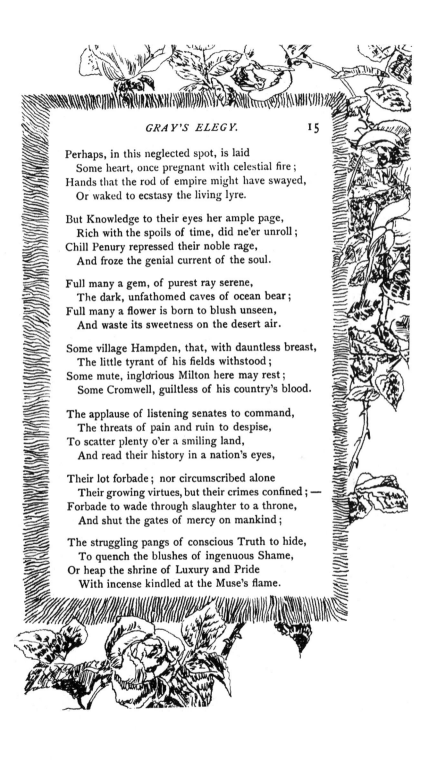

Perhaps, in this neglected spot, is laid
  Some heart, once pregnant with celestial fire ;
Hands that the rod of empire might have swayed,
  Or waked to ecstasy the living lyre.

But Knowledge to their eyes her ample page,
  Rich with the spoils of time, did ne'er unroll ;
Chill Penury repressed their noble rage,
  And froze the genial current of the soul.

Full many a gem, of purest ray serene,
  The dark, unfathomed caves of ocean bear ;
Full many a flower is born to blush unseen,
  And waste its sweetness on the desert air.

Some village Hampden, that, with dauntless breast,
  The little tyrant of his fields withstood ;
Some mute, inglorious Milton here may rest ;
  Some Cromwell, guiltless of his country's blood.

The applause of listening senates to command,
  The threats of pain and ruin to despise,
To scatter plenty o'er a smiling land,
  And read their history in a nation's eyes,

Their lot forbade ; nor circumscribed alone
  Their growing virtues, but their crimes confined ; —
Forbade to wade through slaughter to a throne,
  And shut the gates of mercy on mankind ;

The struggling pangs of conscious Truth to hide,
  To quench the blushes of ingenuous Shame,
Or heap the shrine of Luxury and Pride
  With incense kindled at the Muse's flame.

Far from the madding crowd's ignoble strife,
  Their sober wishes never learned to stray:
Along the cool, sequestered vale of life,
  They kept the noiseless tenor of their way.

Yet, e'en these bones from insult to protect,
  Some frail memorial, still erected nigh,
With uncouth rhymes and shapeless sculpture decked,
  Implores the passing tribute of a sigh.

Their name, their years, spelled by the unlettered Muse,
  The place of fame and elegy supply;
And many a holy text around she strews,
  That teach the rustic moralist to die.

For who, to dumb forgetfulness a prey,
  This pleasing, anxious being, e'er resigned, —
Left the warm precincts of the cheerful day, —
  Nor cast one longing, lingering look behind?

On some fond breast the parting soul relies;
  Some pious drops the closing eye requires:
E'en from the tomb the voice of Nature cries,
  E'en in our ashes live their wonted fires.

For thee, who, mindful of th' unhonored dead,
  Dost in these lines their artless tale relate,
If, chance, by lonely Contemplation led,
  Some kindred spirit shall inquire thy fate,

Haply, some hoary-headed swain may say,
  " Oft have we seen him, at the peep of dawn,
Brushing, with hasty steps, the dews away,
  To meet the sun upon the upland lawn.

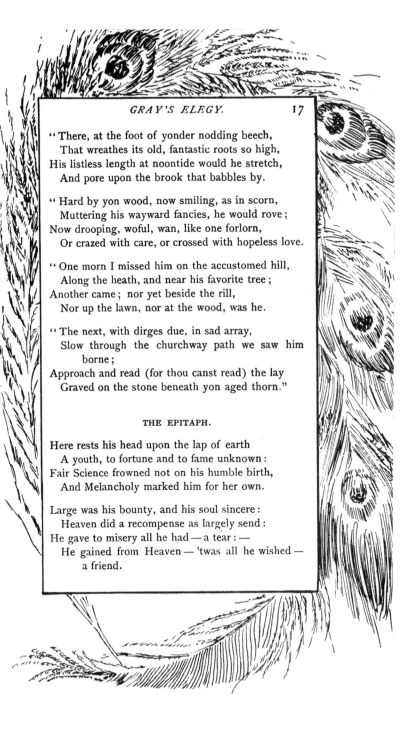

"There, at the foot of yonder nodding beech,
 That wreathes its old, fantastic roots so high,
His listless length at noontide would he stretch,
 And pore upon the brook that babbles by.

"Hard by yon wood, now smiling, as in scorn,
 Muttering his wayward fancies, he would rove;
Now drooping, woful, wan, like one forlorn,
 Or crazed with care, or crossed with hopeless love.

"One morn I missed him on the accustomed hill,
 Along the heath, and near his favorite tree;
Another came; nor yet beside the rill,
 Nor up the lawn, nor at the wood, was he.

"The next, with dirges due, in sad array,
 Slow through the churchway path we saw him
 borne;
Approach and read (for thou canst read) the lay
 Graved on the stone beneath yon aged thorn."

THE EPITAPH.

Here rests his head upon the lap of earth
 A youth, to fortune and to fame unknown:
Fair Science frowned not on his humble birth,
 And Melancholy marked him for her own.

Large was his bounty, and his soul sincere:
 Heaven did a recompense as largely send:
He gave to misery all he had — a tear: —
 He gained from Heaven — 'twas all he wished —
 a friend.

No farther seek his merits to disclose,
  Or draw his frailties from their dread abode,
(There they, alike, in trembling hope, repose),
  The bosom of his Father and his God.

THE BURIAL OF SIR JOHN MOORE.

WOLFE.

NOT a drum was heard, not a funeral note,
  As his corse to the ramparts we hurried;
Not a soldier discharged his farewell shot
  O'er the grave where our Hero we buried.

We buried him darkly; at dead of night;
  The sods with our bayonets turning,
By the struggling moonbeams' misty light,
  And the lantern dimly burning.

No useless coffin enclosed his breast,
  Nor in sheet nor in shroud we wound him;
But he lay like a warrior taking his rest,
  With his martial cloak around him.

Few and short were the prayers we said,
  And we spoke not a word of sorrow;
But we steadfastly gazed on the face of the dead,
  And we bitterly thought of the morrow.

We thought — as we hollowed his narrow bed,
　And smoothed down his lonely pillow —
How the foe and the stranger would tread o'er his
　　head
　And we far away on the billow!

Lightly they'll talk of the spirit that's gone,
　And o'er his cold ashes upbraid him;
But little he'll reck, if they let him sleep on
　In the grave where a Briton has laid him.

But half of our heavy task was done,
　When the clock tolled the hour for retiring,
And we heard the distant and random gun,
　That the foe was sullenly firing. —

Slowly and sadly we laid him down,
　From the field of his fame fresh and gory.
We carved not a line, we raised not a stone,
　But left him — alone with his glory!

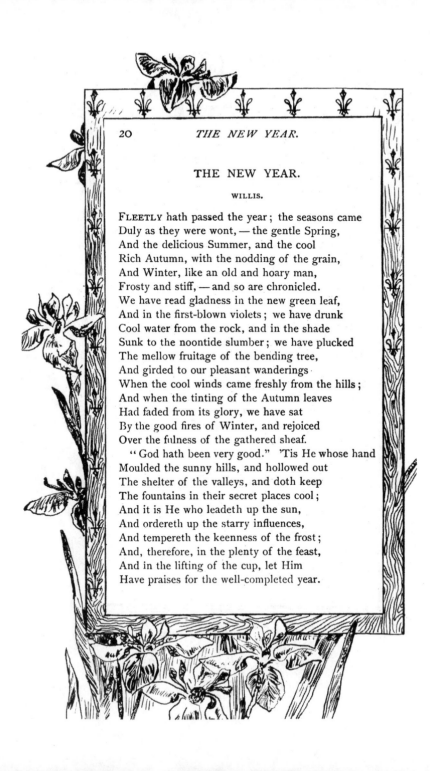

THE NEW YEAR.

WILLIS.

FLEETLY hath passed the year; the seasons came
Duly as they were wont, — the gentle Spring,
And the delicious Summer, and the cool
Rich Autumn, with the nodding of the grain,
And Winter, like an old and hoary man,
Frosty and stiff, — and so are chronicled.
We have read gladness in the new green leaf,
And in the first-blown violets; we have drunk
Cool water from the rock, and in the shade
Sunk to the noontide slumber; we have plucked
The mellow fruitage of the bending tree,
And girded to our pleasant wanderings
When the cool winds came freshly from the hills;
And when the tinting of the Autumn leaves
Had faded from its glory, we have sat
By the good fires of Winter, and rejoiced
Over the fulness of the gathered sheaf.
  " God hath been very good." 'Tis He whose hand
Moulded the sunny hills, and hollowed out
The shelter of the valleys, and doth keep
The fountains in their secret places cool;
And it is He who leadeth up the sun,
And ordereth up the starry influences,
And tempereth the keenness of the frost;
And, therefore, in the plenty of the feast,
And in the lifting of the cup, let Him
Have praises for the well-completed year.

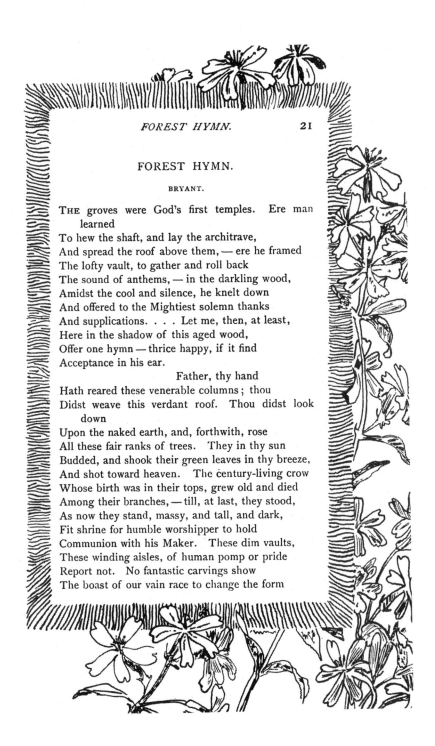

FOREST HYMN.

BRYANT.

THE groves were God's first temples. Ere man
    learned
To hew the shaft, and lay the architrave,
And spread the roof above them, — ere he framed
The lofty vault, to gather and roll back
The sound of anthems, — in the darkling wood,
Amidst the cool and silence, he knelt down
And offered to the Mightiest solemn thanks
And supplications. . . . Let me, then, at least,
Here in the shadow of this aged wood,
Offer one hymn — thrice happy, if it find
Acceptance in his ear.
                Father, thy hand
Hath reared these venerable columns; thou
Didst weave this verdant roof. Thou didst look
    down
Upon the naked earth, and, forthwith, rose
All these fair ranks of trees. They in thy sun
Budded, and shook their green leaves in thy breeze,
And shot toward heaven. The century-living crow
Whose birth was in their tops, grew old and died
Among their branches, — till, at last, they stood,
As now they stand, massy, and tall, and dark,
Fit shrine for humble worshipper to hold
Communion with his Maker. These dim vaults,
These winding aisles, of human pomp or pride
Report not. No fantastic carvings show
The boast of our vain race to change the form

Of thy fair works.   But thou art here; thou fill'st
The solitude; thou art in the soft winds
That run along the summit of these trees
In music; thou art in the cooler breath,
That, from the inmost darkness of the place,
Comes, scarcely felt; the barky trunks, the ground
The fresh, moist ground, are all instinct with thee.

LYCIDAS.

T. B. ALDRICH.

I WALKED with him one melancholy night
  Down by the sea, upon the moon-lit strands,
While in the silent heaven the Northern Light
  Beckoned with flaming hands!

Beckoned and vanished, like a woful ghost
  That fain would lure us to some dismal wood,
And tells us tales of ships that have been lost,
  Of violence and blood.

And where yon dædal rocks o'erhang the froth,
  We sat together, Lycidas and I,
Watching the great star-bear that in the North
  Guarded the midnight sky.

And while the moonlight wrought its miracles,
  Drenching the world with silent silver rain,
He spoke of life and its tumultuous ills;
  He told me of his pain. .

8

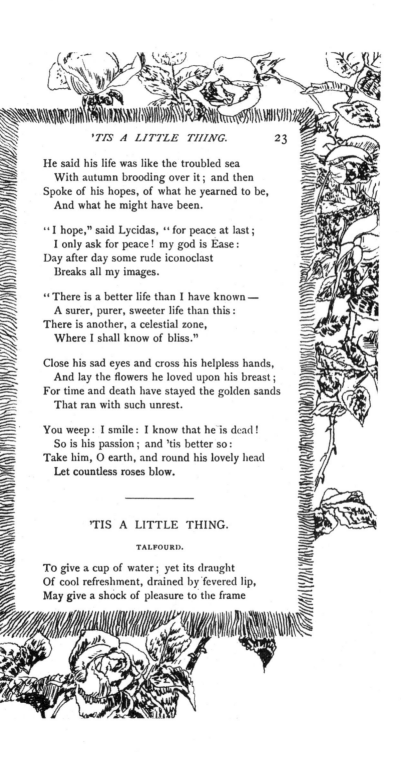

He said his life was like the troubled sea
  With autumn brooding over it; and then
Spoke of his hopes, of what he yearned to be,
  And what he might have been.

"I hope," said Lycidas, "for peace at last;
  I only ask for peace! my god is Ease:
Day after day some rude iconoclast
  Breaks all my images.

"There is a better life than I have known —
  A surer, purer, sweeter life than this:
There is another, a celestial zone,
  Where I shall know of bliss."

Close his sad eyes and cross his helpless hands,
  And lay the flowers he loved upon his breast;
For time and death have stayed the golden sands
  That ran with such unrest.

You weep: I smile: I know that he is dead!
  So is his passion; and 'tis better so:
Take him, O earth, and round his lovely head
  Let countless roses blow.

'TIS A LITTLE THING.

TALFOURD.

To give a cup of water; yet its draught
Of cool refreshment, drained by fevered lip,
May give a shock of pleasure to the frame

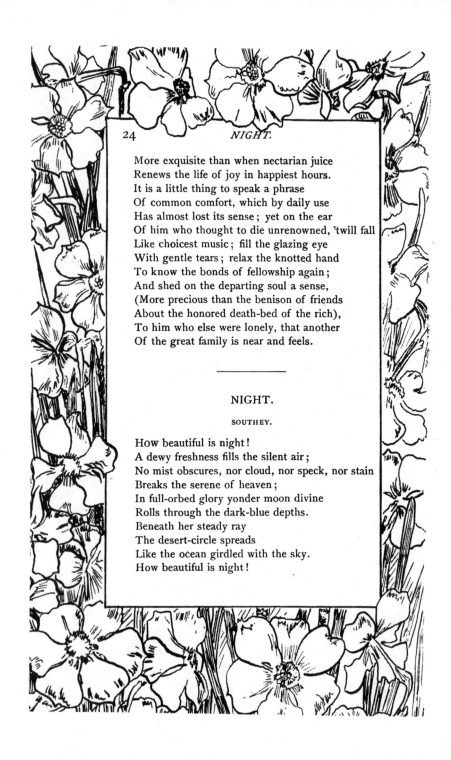

More exquisite than when nectarian juice
Renews the life of joy in happiest hours.
It is a little thing to speak a phrase
Of common comfort, which by daily use
Has almost lost its sense; yet on the ear
Of him who thought to die unrenowned, 'twill fall
Like choicest music; fill the glazing eye
With gentle tears; relax the knotted hand
To know the bonds of fellowship again;
And shed on the departing soul a sense,
(More precious than the benison of friends
About the honored death-bed of the rich),
To him who else were lonely, that another
Of the great family is near and feels.

NIGHT.

SOUTHEY.

How beautiful is night!
A dewy freshness fills the silent air;
No mist obscures, nor cloud, nor speck, nor stain
Breaks the serene of heaven;
In full-orbed glory yonder moon divine
Rolls through the dark-blue depths.
Beneath her steady ray
The desert-circle spreads
Like the ocean girdled with the sky.
How beautiful is night!

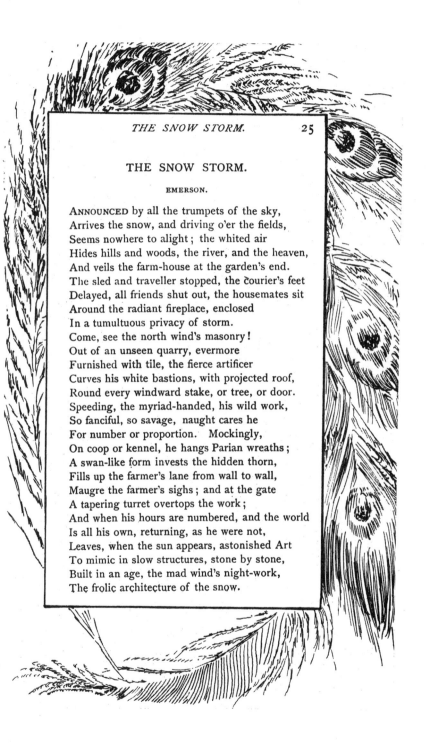

THE SNOW STORM.

EMERSON.

ANNOUNCED by all the trumpets of the sky,
Arrives the snow, and driving o'er the fields,
Seems nowhere to alight; the whited air
Hides hills and woods, the river, and the heaven,
And veils the farm-house at the garden's end.
The sled and traveller stopped, the courier's feet
Delayed, all friends shut out, the housemates sit
Around the radiant fireplace, enclosed
In a tumultuous privacy of storm.
Come, see the north wind's masonry!
Out of an unseen quarry, evermore
Furnished with tile, the fierce artificer
Curves his white bastions, with projected roof,
Round every windward stake, or tree, or door.
Speeding, the myriad-handed, his wild work,
So fanciful, so savage, naught cares he
For number or proportion. Mockingly,
On coop or kennel, he hangs Parian wreaths;
A swan-like form invests the hidden thorn,
Fills up the farmer's lane from wall to wall,
Maugre the farmer's sighs; and at the gate
A tapering turret overtops the work;
And when his hours are numbered, and the world
Is all his own, returning, as he were not,
Leaves, when the sun appears, astonished Art
To mimic in slow structures, stone by stone,
Built in an age, the mad wind's night-work,
The frolic architecture of the snow.

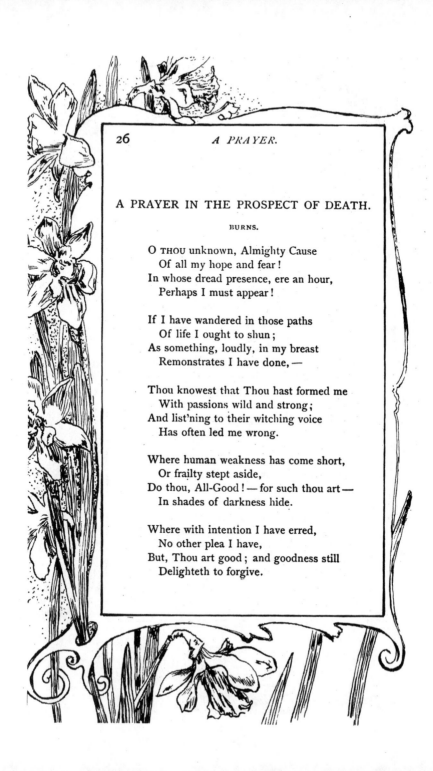

A PRAYER IN THE PROSPECT OF DEATH.

BURNS.

O THOU unknown, Almighty Cause
  Of all my hope and fear!
In whose dread presence, ere an hour,
  Perhaps I must appear!

If I have wandered in those paths
  Of life I ought to shun;
As something, loudly, in my breast
  Remonstrates I have done, —

Thou knowest that Thou hast formed me
  With passions wild and strong;
And list'ning to their witching voice
  Has often led me wrong.

Where human weakness has come short,
  Or frailty stept aside,
Do thou, All-Good! — for such thou art —
  In shades of darkness hide.

Where with intention I have erred,
  No other plea I have,
But, Thou art good; and goodness still
  Delighteth to forgive.

HALLOWEEN.

ROBERT BURNS.

Yes! let the Rich deride, the Proud disdain,
The simple pleasures of the lowly train;
To me more dear, congenial to my heart,
One native charm than all the gloss of art.
GOLDSMITH.

I.

UPON that night when fairies light,
  On Cassalis Downans dance,
Or owre the lays, in splendid blaze,
  On sprightly coursers prance;
Or for Colean the rout is taen,
  Beneath the moon's pale beams;
There, up the cove, to stray an' rove
  Amang the rocks an' streams,
      To sport that night.

II.

Amang the bonie, winding banks,
  Where Doon rins, wimplin, clear,
Where Bruce ance rul'd the martial ranks,
  And shook his Carrick spear,
Some merry, friendly, countra folks,
  Together did convene,
To burn their nits, an' pou their stocks,
  An' haud their Halloween,
      Fu' blythe that night.

III.

The lasses feat, an' cleanly neat,
  Mair braw than when they're fine;
Their faces blythe, fu' sweetly kythe,
  Hearts leal, an' warm, an' kin':
The lads sae trig, wi' wooer-babs,
  Weel knotted on their garten,
Some unco blate, and some wi' gabs,
  Gar lasses' hearts gang startin
      Whyles fast that night.

IV.

Then, first and foremost, thro' the kail
  Their stocks maun a' be sought ance;
They steek their een, an' graip an' wale,
  For muckle anes an' straught anes,
Poor hav'rel Will fell aff the drift,
  An' wander'd thro' the bow-kail,
An' pou't, for want o' better shift,
  A runt was like a sow-tail,
      Sae bow't that night.

V.

Then, straught or crooked, yird or nane,
  They roar an' cry a throu'ther;
The vera wee things, todlin, rin
  Wi' stocks out owre their shouther;
An' gif the custocks sweet or sour,
  Wi' joctelegs they taste them;
Syne coziely, aboon the door,
  Wi' cannie care they've plac'd them,
      To lie that night.

VI.

The lasses staw frae 'mang them a',
　To pou their stalks o' corn :
But Rab slips out, an' jinks about,
　Behint the muckle thorn :
He grippet Nelly hard an' fast,
　Loud skirled a' the lasses ;
But her tap-pickle maist was lost,
　When kiutlin in the fause-house,
　　Wi' him that night.

VII.

The auld guidwife's weel-hoordet nits
　Are round an' round divided,
An' monie lads' an' lasses' fates
　Are there that night decided :
Some kindle, couthie, side by side,
　An' burn thegither trimly ;
Some start awa wi' saucy pride,
　An' jump out owre the chimlie,
　　Fu' high that night.

VIII.

Jean slips in twa wi' tentie e'e ;
　Wha 'twas she wadna tell ;
But this is Jock, and this is me,
　She says in to hersel' :
He bleez'd owre her, an' she owre him,
　As they wad never mair part !
Till, fuff ! he started up the lum,
　An' Jean had e'en a sair heart,
　　To see't that night.

IX.

Poor Willie, wi' his bow-kail runt,
  Was brunt wi' primsie Mallie;
An' Mallie, nae doubt, took the drunt,
  To be compar'd to Willie;
Mall's nit lap out wi' pridefu' fling,
  An' her ain fit it brunt it;
While Willie lap, and swoor by jing,
  'Twas just the way he wanted
      To be that night.

X.

Nell had the fause-house in her min',
  She pits hersel' an' Rob in;
In loving bleeze they sweetly join,
  Till white in ase they're sobbin:
Nell's heart was dancin at the view,
  She whisper'd Rob to leuk for't:
Rob, stownlins, prie'd her bonie mou,
  Fu' cozie in the neuk for't,
      Unseen that night.

XI.

But Merran sat behint their backs,
  Her thoughts on Andrew Bell;
She lea'es them gashan at their cracks,
  An' slips out by hersel';
She thro' the yard the nearest taks,
  An' to the kiln she goes then,
An' darklins grapet for the bauks,
  And in the blue-clue throws then,
      Right fear't that night.

XII.

An' ay she wint, an' ay she swat,
 I wat she made nae jaukin;
Till something held within the pat,
 Guid L——d, but she was quaukin!
But whether 'twas the Deil himsel'
 Or whether 'twas a bauk-en',
Or whether it was Andrew Bell,
 She did nae wait on talkin
   To spier that night.

XIII.

Wee Jennie to her graunie says,
 " Will ye go wi' me, graunie?
I'll eat the apple at the glass,
 I gat frae uncle Johnnie : "
She fuf't her pipe wi' sic a lunt,
 In wrath she was sae vap'rin,
She notic't na, an aizle brunt
 Her braw new worset apron
   Out thro' that night.

XIV.

" Ye little skelpie-limmer's-face,
 How daur you try sic sportin,
As seek the foul thief onie place,
 For him to spae your fortune?
Nae doubt but ye may get a sight :
 Great cause ye have to fear it ;
For monie a ane has gotten a fright,
 An' liv'd an' died deleeret,
   On sic a night.

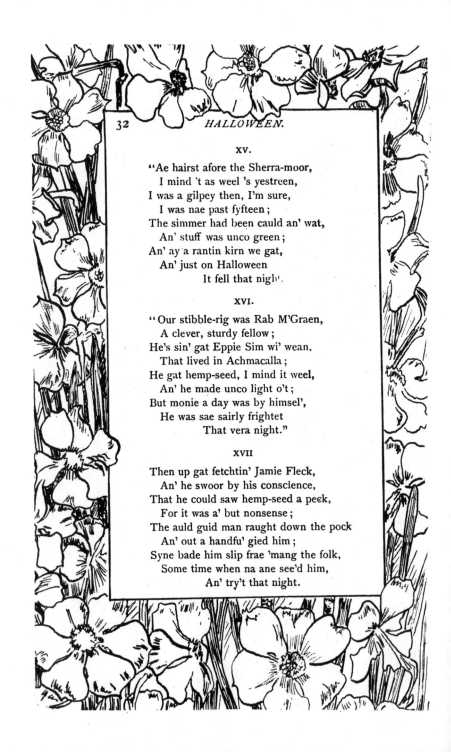

XV.

"Ae hairst afore the Sherra-moor,
  I mind 't as weel 's yestreen,
I was a gilpey then, I'm sure,
  I was nae past fyfteen;
The simmer had been cauld an' wat,
  An' stuff was unco green;
An' ay a rantin kirn we gat,
  An' just on Halloween
      It fell that night.

XVI.

"Our stibble-rig was Rab M'Graen,
  A clever, sturdy fellow;
He's sin' gat Eppie Sim wi' wean,
  That lived in Achmacalla;
He gat hemp-seed, I mind it weel,
  An' he made unco light o't;
But monie a day was by himsel',
  He was sae sairly frightet
      That vera night."

XVII

Then up gat fetchtin' Jamie Fleck,
  An' he swoor by his conscience,
That he could saw hemp-seed a peck,
  For it was a' but nonsense;
The auld guid man raught down the pock
  An' out a handfu' gied him;
Syne bade him slip frae 'mang the folk,
  Some time when na ane see'd him,
      An' try't that night.

XVIII.

He marches thro' amang the stacks,
 Tho' he was something sturtan;
The graip he for a harrow taks,
 An' haurls at his curpan;
An' ev'ry now an' then he says,
 "Hemp-seed, I saw thee,
An' her that is to be my lass,
 Come after me, an' draw thee
  As fast this night."

XIX.

He whistl'd up Lord Lenox march,
 To keep his courage cheery;
Although his hair began to arch,
 He was sae fley'd an' eerie;
Till presently he hears a squeak,
 An' then a grane an' gruntle:
He by his shouther gae a keek,
 An' tumbl'd wi' a wintle
  Out owre that night.

XX.

He roar'd a horrid murder-shout,
 In dreadfu' desperation!
An' young an' auld came rinnan out,
 To hear the sad narration;
He swoor 'twas hilchan Jean M'Craw,
 Or crouchie Merran Humphie,
Till stop! she trotted thro' them a',
 An' wha was it but Grumphie
  Asteer that night!

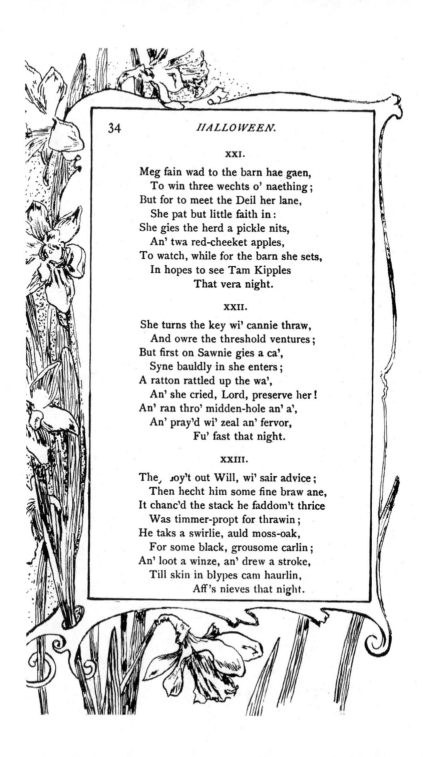

XXI.

Meg fain wad to the barn hae gaen,
  To win three wechts o' naething;
But for to meet the Deil her lane,
  She pat but little faith in:
She gies the herd a pickle nits,
  An' twa red-cheeket apples,
To watch, while for the barn she sets,
  In hopes to see Tam Kipples
      That vera night.

XXII.

She turns the key wi' cannie thraw,
  And owre the threshold ventures;
But first on Sawnie gies a ca',
  Syne bauldly in she enters;
A ratton rattled up the wa',
  An' she cried, Lord, preserve her!
An' ran thro' midden-hole an' a',
  An' pray'd wi' zeal an' fervor,
      Fu' fast that night.

XXIII.

The, joy't out Will, wi' sair advice;
  Then hecht him some fine braw ane,
It chanc'd the stack he faddom't thrice
  Was timmer-propt for thrawin;
He taks a swirlie, auld moss-oak,
  For some black, grousome carlin;
An' loot a winze, an' drew a stroke,
  Till skin in blypes cam haurlin,
      Aff's nieves that night.

XXIV.

A wanton widow Leezie was,
　　As canty as a kittlen;
But och! that night, amang the shaws,
　　She got a fearfu' settlin!
She thro' the whins, an' by the cairn,
　　An' owre the hill gaed scrievin,
Where three lairds' lands met at a burn,
　　To dip her left sark-sleeve in,
　　　　Was bent that night.

XXV.

Whyles o'er a linn the burnie plays,
　　As thro' the glen it wimpl't;
Whyles round a rocky scar it strays;
　　Whyles in a wiel it dimpl't;
Whyles glitter'd to the nightly rays,
　　Wi' bickering, dancin dazzle;
Whyles cocket underneath the braes,
　　Below the spreading hazel,
　　　　Unseen that night.

XXVI.

Amang the brackens, on the brae,
　　Between her an' the moon,
The Deil, or else an outler quey,
　　Gat up an' gae a croon!
Poor Leezie's heart maist lap the hool;
　　Near lav'rock-height she jumpet,
But mist a fit, an' in the pool,
　　Out owre the lugs she plumpet,
　　　　Wi' a plunge that night.

XXVII.

In order, on the clean hearth-stane,
  The luggies three are ranged,
An' ev'ry time great care is taen,
  To see them duly changed;
Auld uncle John, wha wedlock's joys,
  Sin' Mar's year did desire,
Because he gat the toom dish thrice,
  He heav'd them on the fire,
      In wrath that night.

XXVIII.

Wi' merry sangs, an' friendly cracks,
  I wat they did na weary;
An' unco tales, an funnie jokes,
  Their sports were cheap an' cheery,
Till butter'd so'ns, wi' fragrant lunt,
  Set a' their gabs a-steerin;
Syne, wi' a social glass o' strunt,
  They parted aff careerin,
      Fu' blythe that night.

WHEN I AM OLD.

CAROLINE A. BRIGGS.

WHEN I am old — (and O, how soon
Will life's sweet morning yield to noon,
And noon's broad, fervid, earnest light
Be shaded in the solemn night!

Till like a story well-nigh told
Will seem my life, when I am old.) —

When I am old, this breezy earth
Will lose for me its voice of mirth;
The streams will have an undertone
Of sadness not by right their own;
And spring's sweet power in vain unfold
In rosy charms — when I am old.

When I am old, I shall not care
To deck with flowers my faded hair;
'Twill be no vain desire of mine
In rich and costly dress to shine;
Bright jewels and the brightest gold
Will charm me naught — when I am old.

When I am old, my friends will be
Old and infirm and bowed, like me;
Or else, — (their bodies 'neath the sod,
Their spirits dwelling safe with God), —
The old church-bell will long have tolled
Above the rest — when I am old.

When I am old, I'd rather bend
Thus sadly o'er each buried friend,
Than see them lose the earnest truth
That marks the friendship of our youth;
'Twill be so sad to have them cold,
Or strange to me — when I am old!

.   .   .   .

When I am old — perhaps ere then
I shall be missed from haunts of men;

Perhaps my dwelling will be found
Beneath the green and quiet mound;
My name by stranger hands enrolled
Among the dead — *ere* I am old.

Ere I am old? — that time is now,
For youth sits lightly on my brow;
My limbs are firm, and strong, and free;
Life hath a thousand charms for me;
Charms that will long their influence hold
Within my heart — ere I am old.

Ere I am old, O, let me give
My life to learning *how to live!*
Then shall I meet with willing heart
An early summons to depart,
Or find my lengthened days consoled
By God's sweet peace — when I am old.

THE REVELLERS.

MRS. HEMANS.

RING, joyous chords! — ring out again!
A swifter still, and a wilder strain!
They are here — the fair face and the careless heart,
And stars shall wane ere the mirthful part.
But I met a dimly mournful glance,
In a sudden turn of the flying dance;
I heard the tone of a heavy sigh
In a pause of the thrilling melody!

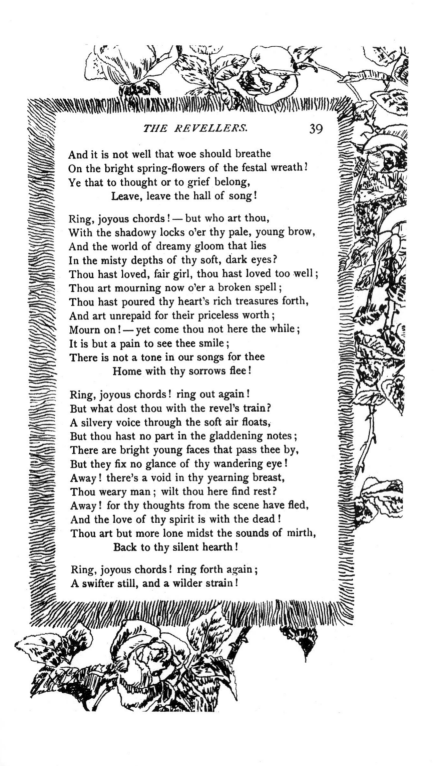

And it is not well that woe should breathe
On the bright spring-flowers of the festal wreath!
Ye that to thought or to grief belong,
    Leave, leave the hall of song!

Ring, joyous chords! — but who art thou,
With the shadowy locks o'er thy pale, young brow,
And the world of dreamy gloom that lies
In the misty depths of thy soft, dark eyes?
Thou hast loved, fair girl, thou hast loved too well;
Thou art mourning now o'er a broken spell;
Thou hast poured thy heart's rich treasures forth,
And art unrepaid for their priceless worth;
Mourn on! — yet come thou not here the while;
It is but a pain to see thee smile;
There is not a tone in our songs for thee
    Home with thy sorrows flee!

Ring, joyous chords! ring out again!
But what dost thou with the revel's train?
A silvery voice through the soft air floats,
But thou hast no part in the gladdening notes;
There are bright young faces that pass thee by,
But they fix no glance of thy wandering eye!
Away! there's a void in thy yearning breast,
Thou weary man; wilt thou here find rest?
Away! for thy thoughts from the scene have fled,
And the love of thy spirit is with the dead!
Thou art but more lone midst the sounds of mirth,
    Back to thy silent hearth!

Ring, joyous chords! ring forth again;
A swifter still, and a wilder strain!

But thou, though a reckless mien be thine,
And thy cup be crowned with the foaming wine,
By the fitful bursts of thy laughter loud,
By thine eye's quick flash through its troubled cloud,
I know thee! it is but the wakeful fear
Of a haunted bosom that brings thee here!
I know thee! thou fearest the solemn night,
With her piercing stars and her deep wind's might!
There's a tone in her voice which thou fain wouldst
    shun
For it asks what the secret soul hath done!
And thou, there's a dark weight on thine — away —
      Back to thy home and pray!

Ring, joyous chords! ring out again!
A swifter still, and a wilder strain!
And bring fresh wreaths! we will banish all
Save the free in heart from our festive hall.
On! through the maze of the fleet dance, on!
But where are the young and the lovely! gone?
Where are the brows with the Red Cross crowned,
And the floating forms with the bright zone bound?
And the waving locks and the flying feet,
That still should be where the mirthful meet?
They are gone, they are fled, they are parted all:
      Alas! the forsaken hall!

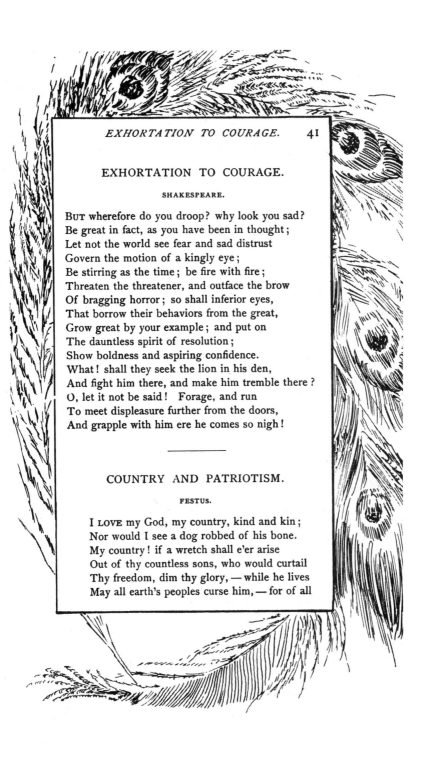

EXHORTATION TO COURAGE.

SHAKESPEARE.

BUT wherefore do you droop? why look you sad?
Be great in fact, as you have been in thought;
Let not the world see fear and sad distrust
Govern the motion of a kingly eye;
Be stirring as the time; be fire with fire;
Threaten the threatener, and outface the brow
Of bragging horror; so shall inferior eyes,
That borrow their behaviors from the great,
Grow great by your example; and put on
The dauntless spirit of resolution;
Show boldness and aspiring confidence.
What! shall they seek the lion in his den,
And fight him there, and make him tremble there?
O, let it not be said! Forage, and run
To meet displeasure further from the doors,
And grapple with him ere he comes so nigh!

COUNTRY AND PATRIOTISM.

FESTUS.

I LOVE my God, my country, kind and kin;
Nor would I see a dog robbed of his bone.
My country! if a wretch shall e'er arise
Out of thy countless sons, who would curtail
Thy freedom, dim thy glory, — while he lives
May all earth's peoples curse him, — for of all

THE OLD HOME.

Hast thou secured the blessing; and if one
Exists, who would not arm for liberty,
Be he, too, cursed while living, and when dead,
Let him be buried downwards, with his face
Looking to hell, and o'er his coward grave
The hare skulk in her form.

THE OLD HOME.

TENNYSON.

WE leave the well-belovéd place
   Where first we gazed upon the sky;
   The roofs that heard our earliest cry
Will shelter one of stranger race.

We go, but ere we go from home,
   As down the garden-walks I move,
   Two spirits of a diverse love
Contend for loving masterdom.

One whispers: — "Here thy boyhood sung
   Long since its matin song, and heard
   The low love-language of the bird,
In native hazels tassel-hung."

The other answers: — "Yea, but here
   Thy feet have strayed in after hours
   With thy lost friend among the bowers,
And this hath made them trebly dear."

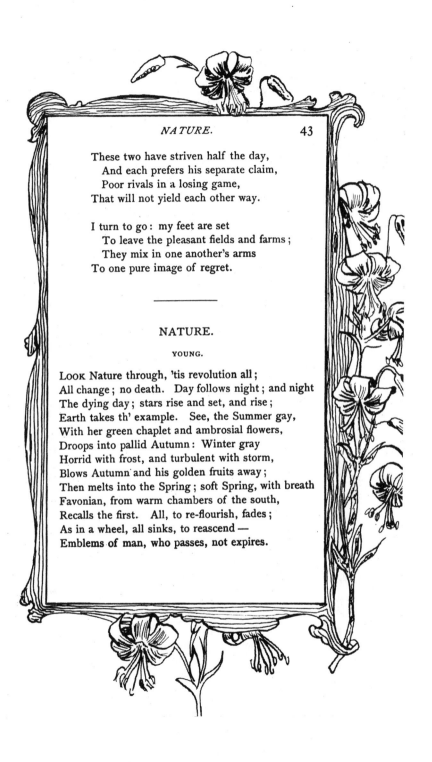

These two have striven half the day,
   And each prefers his separate claim,
   Poor rivals in a losing game,
That will not yield each other way.

I turn to go : my feet are set
   To leave the pleasant fields and farms ;
   They mix in one another's arms
To one pure image of regret.

NATURE.

YOUNG.

Look Nature through, 'tis revolution all ;
All change ; no death. Day follows night ; and night
The dying day ; stars rise and set, and rise ;
Earth takes th' example. See, the Summer gay,
With her green chaplet and ambrosial flowers,
Droops into pallid Autumn : Winter gray
Horrid with frost, and turbulent with storm,
Blows Autumn and his golden fruits away ;
Then melts into the Spring ; soft Spring, with breath
Favonian, from warm chambers of the south,
Recalls the first. All, to re-flourish, fades ;
As in a wheel, all sinks, to reascend —
Emblems of man, who passes, not expires.

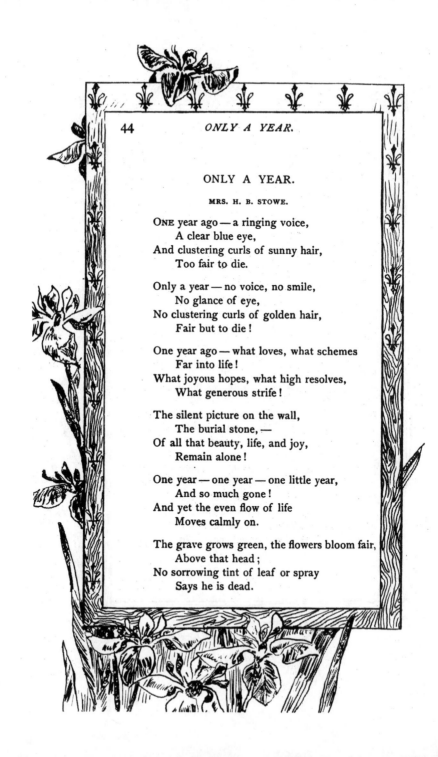

ONLY A YEAR.

MRS. H. B. STOWE.

ONE year ago — a ringing voice,
    A clear blue eye,
And clustering curls of sunny hair,
    Too fair to die.

Only a year — no voice, no smile,
    No glance of eye,
No clustering curls of golden hair,
    Fair but to die !

One year ago — what loves, what schemes
    Far into life !
What joyous hopes, what high resolves,
    What generous strife !

The silent picture on the wall,
    The burial stone, —
Of all that beauty, life, and joy,
    Remain alone !

One year — one year — one little year,
    And so much gone !
And yet the even flow of life
    Moves calmly on.

The grave grows green, the flowers bloom fair,
    Above that head ;
No sorrowing tint of leaf or spray
    Says he is dead.

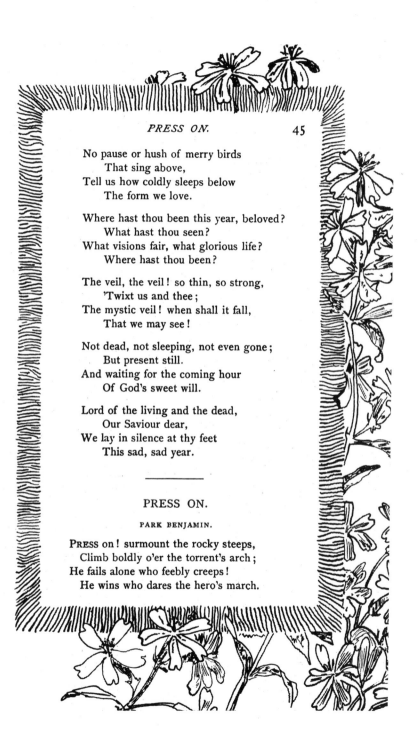

No pause or hush of merry birds
   That sing above,
Tell us how coldly sleeps below
   The form we love.

Where hast thou been this year, beloved?
   What hast thou seen?
What visions fair, what glorious life?
   Where hast thou been?

The veil, the veil! so thin, so strong,
   'Twixt us and thee;
The mystic veil! when shall it fall,
   That we may see!

Not dead, not sleeping, not even gone;
   But present still.
And waiting for the coming hour
   Of God's sweet will.

Lord of the living and the dead,
   Our Saviour dear,
We lay in silence at thy feet
   This sad, sad year.

PRESS ON.

PARK BENJAMIN.

PRESS on! surmount the rocky steeps,
   Climb boldly o'er the torrent's arch;
He fails alone who feebly creeps!
   He wins who dares the hero's march.

PRESS ON.

Be thou a hero! let thy might
   Tramp on eternal snows its way,
And, through the ebon walls of night,
   Hew down a passage unto day.

Press on! if once and twice thy feet
   Slip back and stumble, harder try;
From him who never dreads to meet
   Danger and death, they're sure to fly.
To coward ranks the bullet speeds,
   While on their breast who never quail,
Gleams, guardian of chivalric deeds,
   Bright courage, like a coat of mail.

Press on! if Fortune play thee false
   To-day, to-morrow she'll be true;
Whom now she sinks, she now exalts,
   Taking old gifts and granting new.
The wisdom of the present hour
   Makes up the follies past and gone;
To weakness, strength succeeds, and power
   From frailty springs! Press on, press on!

Therefore, press on, and reach the goal,
   And gain the prize, and wear the crown;
Faint not, for to the steadfast soul
   Come wealth, and honor, and renown.
To thine own self be true, and keep
   Thy mind from sloth, thy heart from soil,
Press on, and thou shalt surely reap
   A heavenly harvest for thy toil.

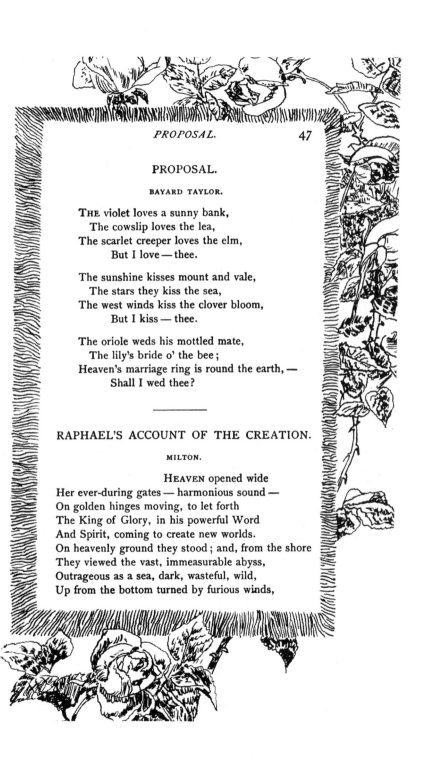

PROPOSAL.

BAYARD TAYLOR.

THE violet loves a sunny bank,
   The cowslip loves the lea,
The scarlet creeper loves the elm,
    But I love — thee.

The sunshine kisses mount and vale,
   The stars they kiss the sea,
The west winds kiss the clover bloom,
    But I kiss — thee.

The oriole weds his mottled mate,
   The lily's bride o' the bee ;
Heaven's marriage ring is round the earth, —
    Shall I wed thee?

RAPHAEL'S ACCOUNT OF THE CREATION.

MILTON.

           HEAVEN opened wide
Her ever-during gates — harmonious sound —
On golden hinges moving, to let forth
The King of Glory, in his powerful Word
And Spirit, coming to create new worlds.
On heavenly ground they stood ; and, from the shore
They viewed the vast, immeasurable abyss,
Outrageous as a sea, dark, wasteful, wild,
Up from the bottom turned by furious winds,

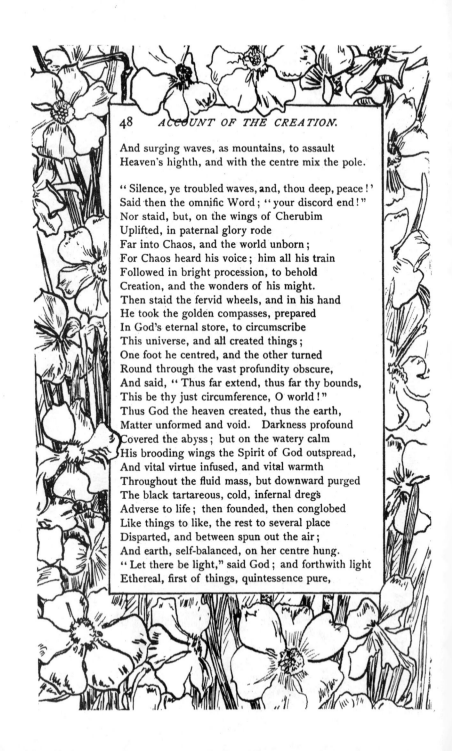

And surging waves, as mountains, to assault
Heaven's highth, and with the centre mix the pole.

" Silence, ye troubled waves, and, thou deep, peace ! '
Said then the omnific Word; " your discord end ! "
Nor staid, but, on the wings of Cherubim
Uplifted, in paternal glory rode
Far into Chaos, and the world unborn ;
For Chaos heard his voice; him all his train
Followed in bright procession, to behold
Creation, and the wonders of his might.
Then staid the fervid wheels, and in his hand
He took the golden compasses, prepared
In God's eternal store, to circumscribe
This universe, and all created things ;
One foot he centred, and the other turned
Round through the vast profundity obscure,
And said, " Thus far extend, thus far thy bounds,
This be thy just circumference, O world ! "
Thus God the heaven created, thus the earth,
Matter unformed and void.   Darkness profound
Covered the abyss ; but on the watery calm
His brooding wings the Spirit of God outspread,
And vital virtue infused, and vital warmth
Throughout the fluid mass, but downward purged
The black tartareous, cold, infernal dregs
Adverse to life ; then founded, then conglobed
Like things to like, the rest to several place
Disparted, and between spun out the air ;
And earth, self-balanced, on her centre hung.
" Let there be light," said God ; and forthwith light
Ethereal, first of things, quintessence pure,

Sprung from the deep, and from her native east,
To journey through the airy gloom began,
Sphered in a radiant cloud; for yet the sun
Was not; she in a cloudy tabernacle
Sojourned the while. God saw the light was good,
And light from darkness, by the hemisphere,
Divided: light the Day, and darkness Night,
He named; thus was the first day even and morn;
Nor passed uncelebrated, nor unsung
By the celestial choirs, when orient light
Exhaling first from darkness they beheld;
Birthday of heaven and earth: with joy and shout
The hollow universal orb they filled,
And touched their golden harps, and hymning praised
God and his works; Creator him they sung,
Both when first evening was, and when first morn.

DARKNESS.

BYRON.

I HAD a dream, which was not all a dream.
The bright sun was extinguished, and the stars
Did wander darkling in the eternal space,
Rayless and pathless, and the icy earth
Swung blind and blackening in the moonless air.
Morn came, and went, and came, and brought no day,
And men forgot their passions in the dread
Of this their desolation; and all hearts
Were chilled into a selfish prayer for light;

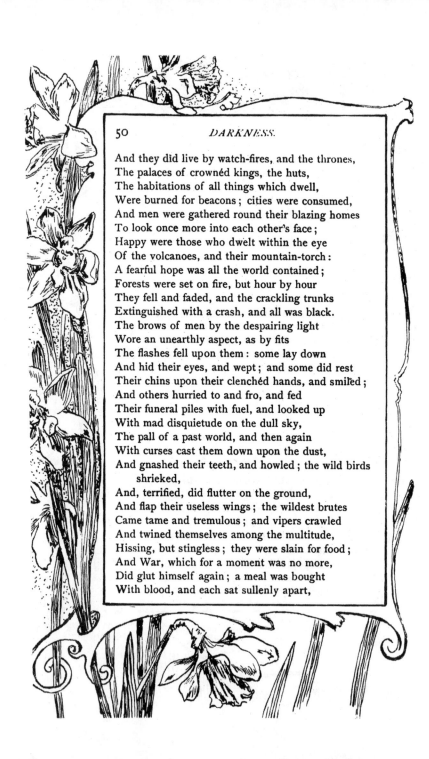

And they did live by watch-fires, and the thrones,
The palaces of crownéd kings, the huts,
The habitations of all things which dwell,
Were burned for beacons ; cities were consumed,
And men were gathered round their blazing homes
To look once more into each other's face ;
Happy were those who dwelt within the eye
Of the volcanoes, and their mountain-torch :
A fearful hope was all the world contained ;
Forests were set on fire, but hour by hour
They fell and faded, and the crackling trunks
Extinguished with a crash, and all was black.
The brows of men by the despairing light
Wore an unearthly aspect, as by fits
The flashes fell upon them : some lay down
And hid their eyes, and wept ; and some did rest
Their chins upon their clenchéd hands, and smiled ;
And others hurried to and fro, and fed
Their funeral piles with fuel, and looked up
With mad disquietude on the dull sky,
The pall of a past world, and then again
With curses cast them down upon the dust,
And gnashed their teeth, and howled ; the wild birds
    shrieked,
And, terrified, did flutter on the ground,
And flap their useless wings ; the wildest brutes
Came tame and tremulous ; and vipers crawled
And twined themselves among the multitude,
Hissing, but stingless ; they were slain for food ;
And War, which for a moment was no more,
Did glut himself again ; a meal was bought
With blood, and each sat sullenly apart,

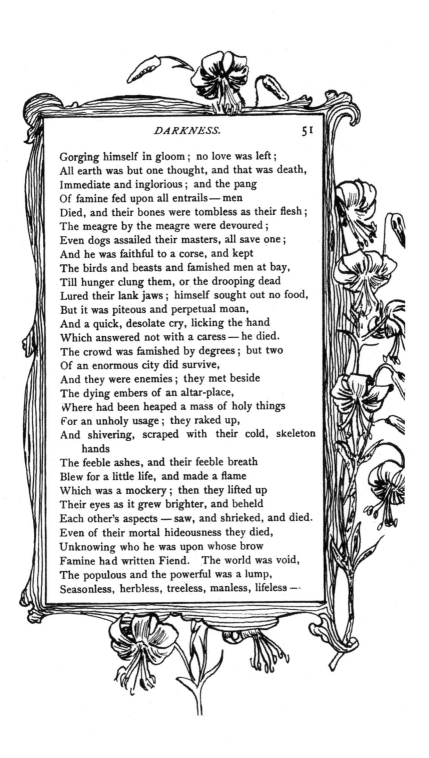

Gorging himself in gloom ; no love was left ;
All earth was but one thought, and that was death,
Immediate and inglorious ; and the pang
Of famine fed upon all entrails — men
Died, and their bones were tombless as their flesh ;
The meagre by the meagre were devoured ;
Even dogs assailed their masters, all save one ;
And he was faithful to a corse, and kept
The birds and beasts and famished men at bay,
Till hunger clung them, or the drooping dead
Lured their lank jaws ; himself sought out no food,
But it was piteous and perpetual moan,
And a quick, desolate cry, licking the hand
Which answered not with a caress — he died.
The crowd was famished by degrees ; but two
Of an enormous city did survive,
And they were enemies ; they met beside
The dying embers of an altar-place,
Where had been heaped a mass of holy things
For an unholy usage ; they raked up,
And shivering, scraped with their cold, skeleton
    hands
The feeble ashes, and their feeble breath
Blew for a little life, and made a flame
Which was a mockery ; then they lifted up
Their eyes as it grew brighter, and beheld
Each other's aspects — saw, and shrieked, and died.
Even of their mortal hideousness they died,
Unknowing who he was upon whose brow
Famine had written Fiend. The world was void,
The populous and the powerful was a lump,
Seasonless, herbless, treeless, manless, lifeless —·

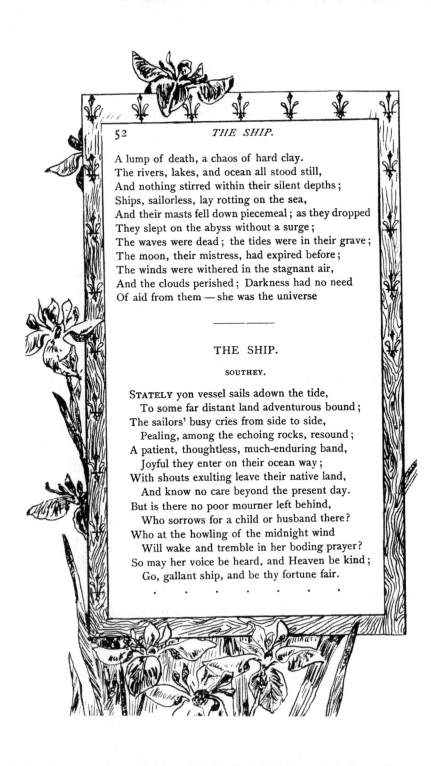

A lump of death, a chaos of hard clay.
The rivers, lakes, and ocean all stood still,
And nothing stirred within their silent depths;
Ships, sailorless, lay rotting on the sea,
And their masts fell down piecemeal; as they dropped
They slept on the abyss without a surge;
The waves were dead; the tides were in their grave;
The moon, their mistress, had expired before;
The winds were withered in the stagnant air,
And the clouds perished; Darkness had no need
Of aid from them — she was the universe

THE SHIP.

SOUTHEY.

STATELY yon vessel sails adown the tide,
   To some far distant land adventurous bound;
The sailors' busy cries from side to side,
   Pealing, among the echoing rocks, resound;
A patient, thoughtless, much-enduring band,
   Joyful they enter on their ocean way;
With shouts exulting leave their native land,
   And know no care beyond the present day.
But is there no poor mourner left behind,
   Who sorrows for a child or husband there?
Who at the howling of the midnight wind
   Will wake and tremble in her boding prayer?
So may her voice be heard, and Heaven be kind;
   Go, gallant ship, and be thy fortune fair.

O God, have mercy in this dreadful hour
  On the poor mariner; in comfort here,
  Safe sheltered as I am, I almost fear
The blast that rages with resistless power.
  What were it now to toss upon the waves,
The maddened waves, and know no succor near.
The howling of the storm alone to hear,
  And the wild sea that to the tempest raves;
To gaze amid the horrors of the night,
And only see the billows' gleaming light;
  Then, in the dread of death, to think of her
Who, as she listens, sleepless, to the gale,
Puts up a silent prayer, and waxes pale!
  O God, have mercy on the mariner.

        .   .   .   .   .

She comes majestic with her swelling sails,
  The gallant ship; along her watery way
Homeward she drives before the favoring gales;
  Now flirting at their length the streamers play,
And now they ripple with the ruffling breeze.
  Hark to the sailors' shouts! the rocks rebound,
  Thundering in echoes to the joyful sound.
Long have they voyaged o'er the distant seas;
  And what a heart-delight they feel at last,
  So many toils, so many dangers past,
To view the port desired, he only knows
  Who on the stormy deep for many a day
  Hath tossed, a-weary of his watery way,
And watched, all anxious, every wind that blows.

THE OLD MAN BY THE BROOK.

WORDSWORTH.

DOWN to the vale this water steers; how merrily it
    goes!
'Twill murmur on a thousand years, and flow as now
    it flows;
And here, on this delightful day, I cannot choose
    but think
How oft, a vigorous man, I lay beside this fountain's
    brink.
My eyes are filled with childish tears, my heart is
    idly stirred,
For the same sound is in my ears that in those days
    I heard.

MARMION.

SIR WALTER SCOTT.

NOT far advanced was morning day,
When Marmion did his troop array
   To Surrey's camp to ride;
He had safe conduct for his band,
Beneath the royal seal and hand,
   And Douglas gave a guide:
The ancient Earl, with stately grace,
Would Clara on her palfrey place,
And whisper'd in an under-tone,
  "Let the hawk stoop, his prey is flown."

The train from out the castle drew,
But Marmion stopped to bid adieu : —
   " Though something I might plain," he said,
" Of cold respect to stranger guest,
Sent hither by your King's behest,
   While in Tantallon's towers I staid ;
Part we in friendship from your land,
And, noble Earl, receive my hand." —
But Douglas round him drew his cloak,
Folded his arms, and thus he spoke : —
" My manors, halls, and bowers, shall still
Be open, at my Sovereign's will,
To each one whom he lists, howe'er
Unmeet to be the owner's peer.
My castles are my King's alone,
From turret to foundation-stone —
The hand of Douglas is his own ;
And never shall in friendly grasp
The hand of such as Marmion clasp." —

Burn'd Marmion's swarthy cheek like fire,
And shook his very frame for ire,
   And — " This to me ! " he said, —
" An 'twere not for thy hoary beard,
Such hand as Marmion's had not spared
   To cleave the Douglas' head !
And, first, I tell thee, haughty Peer,
He, who does England's message here,
Although the meanest in her state,
May well, proud Angus, be thy mate :
And, Douglas, more I tell thee here,
   Even in thy pitch of pride,

Here in thy hold, thy vassals near,
(Nay, never look upon your lord,
And lay your hands upon your sword,)
   I tell thee thou'rt defied!
And if thou saidst I am not peer
To any lord in Scotland here,
Lowland or Highland, far or near,
  Lord Angus, thou hast lied!"
On the Earl's cheek the flush of rage
O'ercame the ashen hue of age:
Fierce he broke forth, — " And darest thou, then,
To beard the lion in his den,
  The Douglas in his hall?
And hopest thou hence unscathed to go? —
No, by Saint Bride of Bothwell, no!
Up drawbridge, grooms — what, Warder, ho!
  Let the portcullis fall."
Lord Marmion turn'd, — well was his need,
And dash'd the rowels in his steed,
Like arrow through the archway sprung,
The ponderous grate behind him rung:
To pass there was such scanty room,
The bars, descending, razed his plume.

The steed along the drawbridge flies,
Just as it trembled on the rise;
Nor lighter does the swallow skim
Along the smooth lake's level brim:
And when Lord Marmion reach'd his band
He halts, and turns with clenchéd hand,
And shout of loud defiance pours,
And shook his gauntlet at the towers.

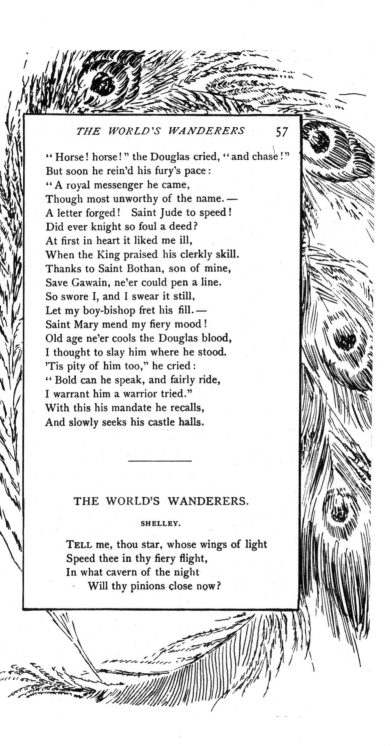

" Horse ! horse ! " the Douglas cried, " and chase ! "
But soon he rein'd his fury's pace :
" A royal messenger he came,
Though most unworthy of the name. —
A letter forged ! Saint Jude to speed !
Did ever knight so foul a deed ?
At first in heart it liked me ill,
When the King praised his clerkly skill.
Thanks to Saint Bothan, son of mine,
Save Gawain, ne'er could pen a line.
So swore I, and I swear it still,
Let my boy-bishop fret his fill. —
Saint Mary mend my fiery mood !
Old age ne'er cools the Douglas blood,
I thought to slay him where he stood.
'Tis pity of him too," he cried :
" Bold can he speak, and fairly ride,
I warrant him a warrior tried."
With this his mandate he recalls,
And slowly seeks his castle halls.

THE WORLD'S WANDERERS.

SHELLEY.

TELL me, thou star, whose wings of light
Speed thee in thy fiery flight,
In what cavern of the night
     Will thy pinions close now ?

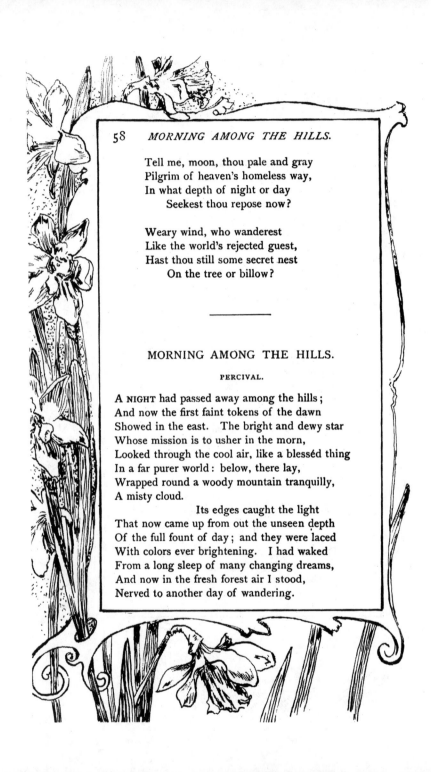

Tell me, moon, thou pale and gray
Pilgrim of heaven's homeless way,
In what depth of night or day
    Seekest thou repose now?

Weary wind, who wanderest
Like the world's rejected guest,
Hast thou still some secret nest
    On the tree or billow?

MORNING AMONG THE HILLS.

PERCIVAL.

A NIGHT had passed away among the hills;
And now the first faint tokens of the dawn
Showed in the east. The bright and dewy star
Whose mission is to usher in the morn,
Looked through the cool air, like a blessèd thing
In a far purer world: below, there lay,
Wrapped round a woody mountain tranquilly,
A misty cloud.
            Its edges caught the light
That now came up from out the unseen depth
Of the full fount of day; and they were laced
With colors ever brightening. I had waked
From a long sleep of many changing dreams,
And now in the fresh forest air I stood,
Nerved to another day of wandering.

Below, there lay a far-extended sea,
Rolling in feathery waves.   The wind blew o'er it
And tossed it round the high-ascending rocks,
And swept it through the half-hidden forest tops,
Till, like an ocean waking into storm,
It heaved and weltered.   Gloriously the light
Crested its billows ; and those craggy islands
Shone on it like to palaces of spar,
Built on a sea of pearl.
      The sky bent round
The awful dome of a most mighty temple,
Built by Omnipotent hands, for nothing less
Than infinite worship.   There I stood in silence ;
I had no words to tell the mingled thoughts
Of wonder and of joy which then came o'er me,
Even with a whirlwind's rush.
       So beautiful,
So bright, so glorious !   Such a majesty
In yon pure vault !   So many dazzling tints
In yonder waste of waves, — so like the ocean
With its unnumbered islands there encircled
By foaming surges : —
      Soon away the mist-cloud rolled,
Wave after wave.   They climbed the highest rocks,
Poured over them in surges, and then rushed
Down glens and valleys like a winter's torrent,
Dashed instant to the plain.   It seemed a moment,
And they were gone, as if the touch of fire
At once dissolved them !
      Then I found myself
Midway in air ; ridge after ridge below
Descended with their opulence of woods

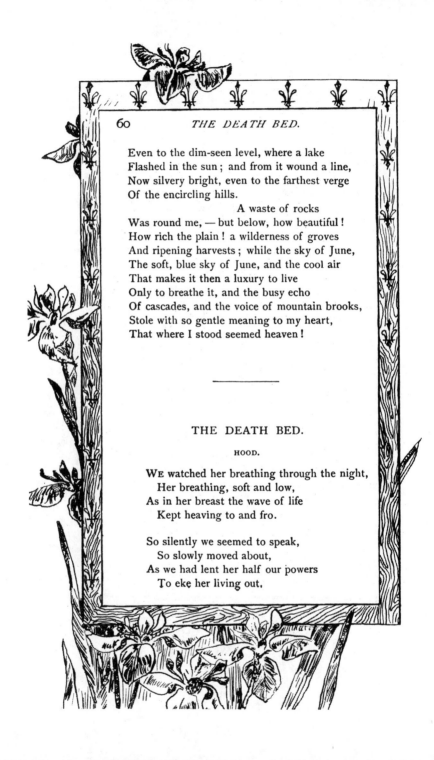

THE DEATH BED.

Even to the dim-seen level, where a lake
Flashed in the sun ; and from it wound a line,
Now silvery bright, even to the farthest verge
Of the encircling hills.

     A waste of rocks
Was round me, — but below, how beautiful !
How rich the plain ! a wilderness of groves
And ripening harvests ; while the sky of June,
The soft, blue sky of June, and the cool air
That makes it then a luxury to live
Only to breathe it, and the busy echo
Of cascades, and the voice of mountain brooks,
Stole with so gentle meaning to my heart,
That where I stood seemed heaven !

THE DEATH BED.

HOOD.

WE watched her breathing through the night,
 Her breathing, soft and low,
As in her breast the wave of life
 Kept heaving to and fro.

So silently we seemed to speak,
 So slowly moved about,
As we had lent her half our powers
 To eke her living out.

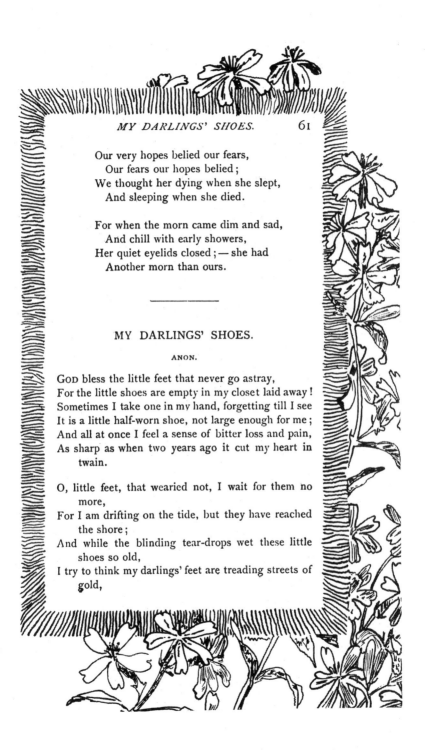

Our very hopes belied our fears,
  Our fears our hopes belied;
We thought her dying when she slept,
  And sleeping when she died.

For when the morn came dim and sad,
  And chill with early showers,
Her quiet eyelids closed; — she had
  Another morn than ours.

MY DARLINGS' SHOES.

ANON.

GOD bless the little feet that never go astray,
For the little shoes are empty in my closet laid away!
Sometimes I take one in my hand, forgetting till I see
It is a little half-worn shoe, not large enough for me;
And all at once I feel a sense of bitter loss and pain,
As sharp as when two years ago it cut my heart in
    twain.

O, little feet, that wearied not, I wait for them no
    more,
For I am drifting on the tide, but they have reached
    the shore;
And while the blinding tear-drops wet these little
    shoes so old,
I try to think my darlings' feet are treading streets of
    gold,

MY DARLINGS' SHOES.

And so I lay them down again, but always turn to
say —
God bless the little feet that now so surely cannot
stray.

And while I thus am standing, I almost seem to see
Two little forms beside me, just as they used to be;
Two little faces lifted with their sweet and tender
eyes!
Ah me! I might have known that look was born of
Paradise.
I reach my arms out fondly, but they clasp the
empty air!
There is nothing of my darlings but the shoes they
used to wear.

O, the bitterness of parting cannot be done away
Till I meet my darlings walking where their feet can
never stray;
When I no more am drifted upon the surging tide,
But with them safely landed upon the river side;
Be patient, heart, while waiting to see their shining
way,
For the little feet in the golden street can never go
astray.

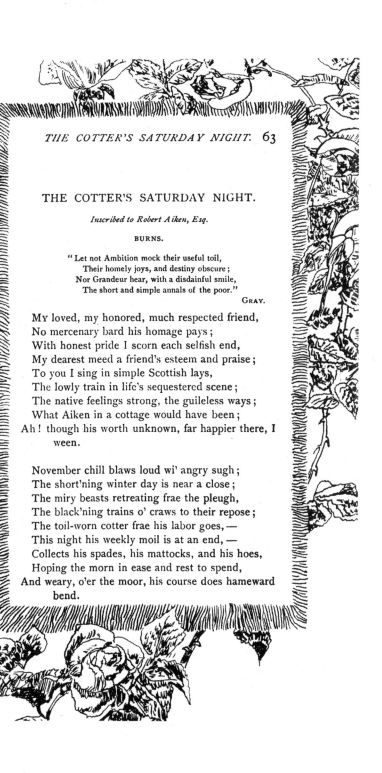

THE COTTER'S SATURDAY NIGHT.

Inscribed to Robert Aiken, Esq.

BURNS.

"Let not Ambition mock their useful toil,
  Their homely joys, and destiny obscure;
Nor Grandeur hear, with a disdainful smile,
  The short and simple annals of the poor."

GRAY.

MY loved, my honored, much respected friend,
No mercenary bard his homage pays;
With honest pride I scorn each selfish end,
My dearest meed a friend's esteem and praise;
To you I sing in simple Scottish lays,
The lowly train in life's sequestered scene;
The native feelings strong, the guileless ways;
What Aiken in a cottage would have been;
Ah! though his worth unknown, far happier there, I
    ween.

November chill blaws loud wi' angry sugh;
The short'ning winter day is near a close;
The miry beasts retreating frae the pleugh,
The black'ning trains o' craws to their repose;
The toil-worn cotter frae his labor goes, —
This night his weekly moil is at an end, —
Collects his spades, his mattocks, and his hoes,
Hoping the morn in ease and rest to spend,
And weary, o'er the moor, his course does hameward
    bend.

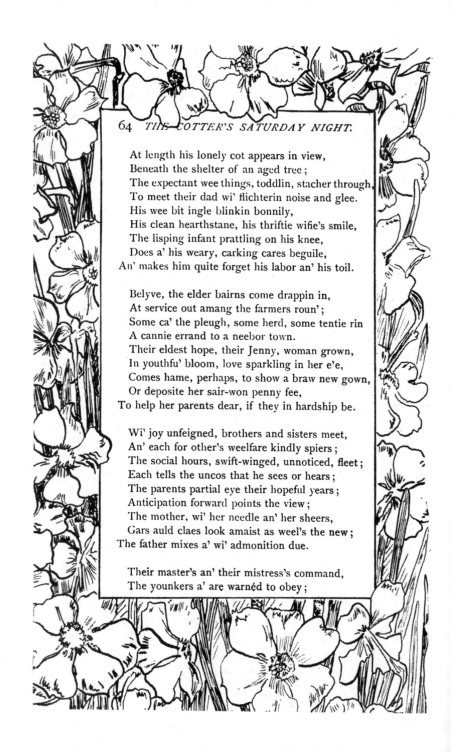

At length his lonely cot appears in view,
Beneath the shelter of an aged tree;
The expectant wee things, toddlin, stacher through,
To meet their dad wi' flichterin noise and glee.
His wee bit ingle blinkin bonnily,
His clean hearthstane, his thriftie wifie's smile,
The lisping infant prattling on his knee,
Does a' his weary, carking cares beguile,
An' makes him quite forget his labor an' his toil.

Belyve, the elder bairns come drappin in,
At service out amang the farmers roun';
Some ca' the pleugh, some herd, some tentie rin
A cannie errand to a neebor town.
Their eldest hope, their Jenny, woman grown,
In youthfu' bloom, love sparkling in her e'e,
Comes hame, perhaps, to show a braw new gown,
Or deposite her sair-won penny fee,
To help her parents dear, if they in hardship be.

Wi' joy unfeigned, brothers and sisters meet,
An' each for other's weelfare kindly spiers;
The social hours, swift-winged, unnoticed, fleet;
Each tells the uncos that he sees or hears;
The parents partial eye their hopeful years;
Anticipation forward points the view;
The mother, wi' her needle an' her sheers,
Gars auld claes look amaist as weel's the new;
The father mixes a' wi' admonition due.

Their master's an' their mistress's command,
The younkers a' are warnéd to obey;

An' mind their labors wi' an eydent hand,
An' ne'er though out o' sight to jauk or play;
" An' O, be sure to fear the Lord alway!
An' mind your duty, duly, morn an' night!
Lest in temptation's path ye gang astray,
Implore his counsel and assisting might;
They never sought in vain that sought the Lord
    aright ! "

But hark ! a rap comes gently to the door;
Jenny, wha kens the meaning o' the same,
Teils how a neebor lad came o'er the moor,
To do some errands, and convoy her hame.
The wily mother sees the conscious flame
Sparkle in Jenny's e'e, and flush her cheek;
Wi' heart-struck, anxious care inquires his name,
While Jenny hafflins is afraid to speak;
Weel pleased the mother hears it's nae wild, worthless
    rake.

Wi' kindly welcome Jenny brings him ben;
A strappan youth; he takes the mother's eye;
Blithe Jenny sees the visit's no ill ta'en;
The father cracks of horses, pleughs, and kye.
The youngster's artless heart o'erflows wi' joy,
But blate and laithfu', scarce can weel behave;
The mother wi' a woman's wiles, can spy
What makes the youth sae bashfu' an' sae grave;
Weel pleased to think her bairn's respected like the lave.

O happy love! where love like this is found!
O heartfelt raptures! bliss beyond compare!

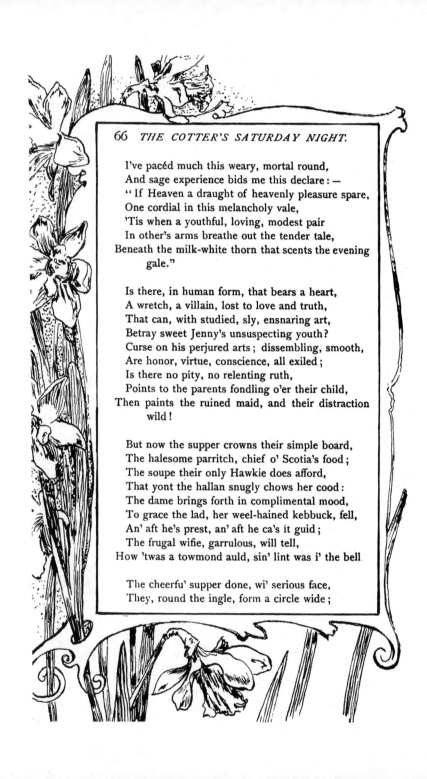

I've pacéd much this weary, mortal round,
And sage experience bids me this declare : —
" If Heaven a draught of heavenly pleasure spare,
One cordial in this melancholy vale,
'Tis when a youthful, loving, modest pair
In other's arms breathe out the tender tale,
Beneath the milk-white thorn that scents the evening
        gale."

Is there, in human form, that bears a heart,
A wretch, a villain, lost to love and truth,
That can, with studied, sly, ensnaring art,
Betray sweet Jenny's unsuspecting youth?
Curse on his perjured arts ; dissembling, smooth,
Are honor, virtue, conscience, all exiled ;
Is there no pity, no relenting ruth,
Points to the parents fondling o'er their child,
Then paints the ruined maid, and their distraction
        wild !

But now the supper crowns their simple board,
The halesome parritch, chief o' Scotia's food ;
The soupe their only Hawkie does afford,
That yont the hallan snugly chows her cood :
The dame brings forth in complimental mood,
To grace the lad, her weel-hained kebbuck, fell,
An' aft he's prest, an' aft he ca's it guid ;
The frugal wifie, garrulous, will tell,
How 'twas a towmond auld, sin' lint was i' the bell.

The cheerfu' supper done, wi' serious face,
They, round the ingle, form a circle wide ;

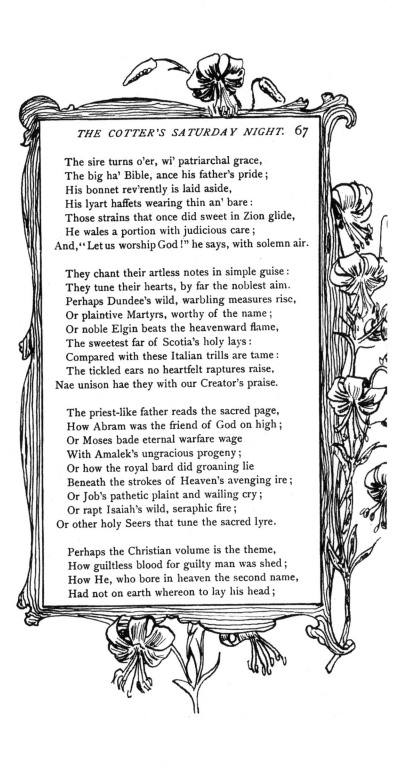

The sire turns o'er, wi' patriarchal grace,
The big ha' Bible, ance his father's pride;
His bonnet rev'rently is laid aside,
His lyart haffets wearing thin an' bare:
Those strains that once did sweet in Zion glide,
He wales a portion with judicious care;
And, "Let us worship God!" he says, with solemn air.

They chant their artless notes in simple guise:
They tune their hearts, by far the noblest aim.
Perhaps Dundee's wild, warbling measures rise,
Or plaintive Martyrs, worthy of the name;
Or noble Elgin beats the heavenward flame,
The sweetest far of Scotia's holy lays:
Compared with these Italian trills are tame:
The tickled ears no heartfelt raptures raise,
Nae unison hae they with our Creator's praise.

The priest-like father reads the sacred page,
How Abram was the friend of God on high;
Or Moses bade eternal warfare wage
With Amalek's ungracious progeny;
Or how the royal bard did groaning lie
Beneath the strokes of Heaven's avenging ire;
Or Job's pathetic plaint and wailing cry;
Or rapt Isaiah's wild, seraphic fire;
Or other holy Seers that tune the sacred lyre.

Perhaps the Christian volume is the theme,
How guiltless blood for guilty man was shed;
How He, who bore in heaven the second name,
Had not on earth whereon to lay his head;

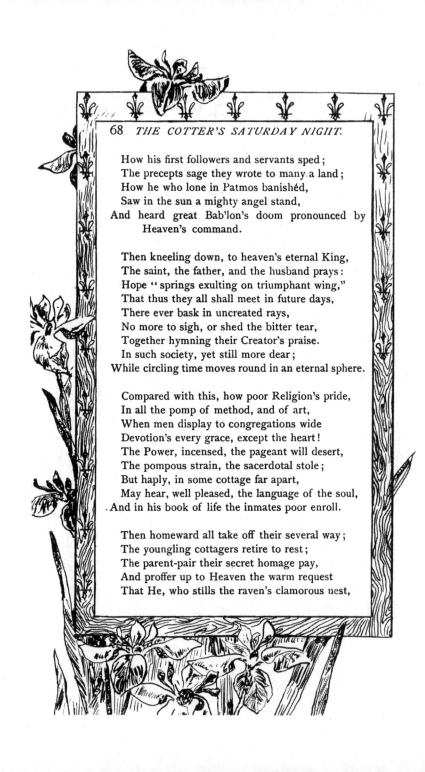

How his first followers and servants sped;
The precepts sage they wrote to many a land;
How he who lone in Patmos banishéd,
Saw in the sun a mighty angel stand,
And heard great Bab'lon's doom pronounced by
    Heaven's command.

Then kneeling down, to heaven's eternal King,
The saint, the father, and the husband prays:
Hope "springs exulting on triumphant wing,"
That thus they all shall meet in future days,
There ever bask in uncreated rays,
No more to sigh, or shed the bitter tear,
Together hymning their Creator's praise.
In such society, yet still more dear;
While circling time moves round in an eternal sphere.

Compared with this, how poor Religion's pride,
In all the pomp of method, and of art,
When men display to congregations wide
Devotion's every grace, except the heart!
The Power, incensed, the pageant will desert,
The pompous strain, the sacerdotal stole;
But haply, in some cottage far apart,
May hear, well pleased, the language of the soul,
And in his book of life the inmates poor enroll.

Then homeward all take off their several way;
The youngling cottagers retire to rest;
The parent-pair their secret homage pay,
And proffer up to Heaven the warm request
That He, who stills the raven's clamorous nest,

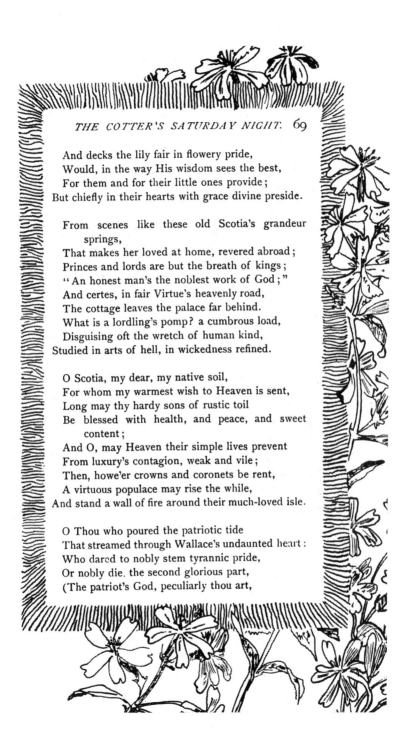

And decks the lily fair in flowery pride,
Would, in the way His wisdom sees the best,
For them and for their little ones provide ;
But chiefly in their hearts with grace divine preside.

From scenes like these old Scotia's grandeur
    springs,
That makes her loved at home, revered abroad ;
Princes and lords are but the breath of kings ;
" An honest man's the noblest work of God ; "
And certes, in fair Virtue's heavenly road,
The cottage leaves the palace far behind.
What is a lordling's pomp? a cumbrous load,
Disguising oft the wretch of human kind,
Studied in arts of hell, in wickedness refined.

O Scotia, my dear, my native soil,
For whom my warmest wish to Heaven is sent,
Long may thy hardy sons of rustic toil
Be blessed with health, and peace, and sweet
    content ;
And O, may Heaven their simple lives prevent
From luxury's contagion, weak and vile ;
Then, howe'er crowns and coronets be rent,
A virtuous populace may rise the while,
And stand a wall of fire around their much-loved isle.

O Thou who poured the patriotic tide
That streamed through Wallace's undaunted heart :
Who dared to nobly stem tyrannic pride,
Or nobly die. the second glorious part,
(The patriot's God, peculiarly thou art,

His friend, inspirer. guardian, and reward!)
O never, never, Scotia's realm desert:
But still the patriot, and the patriot bard,
In bright succession raise, her ornament and guard.

HAMLET'S SOLILOQUY.

SHAKESPEARE.

To be, or not to be, that is the question: —
Whether 'tis nobler in the mind to suffer
The slings and arrows of outrageous fortune,
Or to take arms against a sea of troubles,
And, by opposing, end them.   To die — to sleep;
No more; and, by a sleep, to say we end
The heart-ache, and the thousand natural shocks
That flesh is heir to, — 'tis a consummation
Devoutly to be wished.   To die — to sleep;
To sleep! perchance to dream: ay, there's the rub;
For in that sleep of death what dreams may come,
When we have shuffled off this mortal coil,
Must give us pause.   There's the respect,
That makes calamity of so long life;
For who would bear the whips and scorns of time,
The oppressor's wrong, the proud man's contumely;
The pangs of despised love. the law's delay,
The insolence of office, and the spurns
That patient merit of the unworthy takes,
When he himself might his quietus make
With a bare bodkin?   Who would fardels bear,

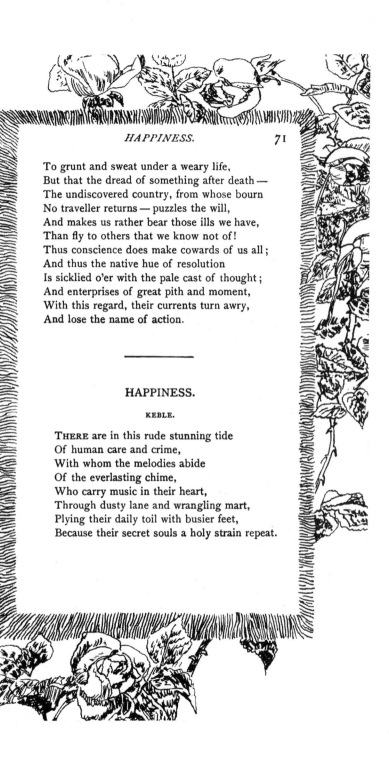

To grunt and sweat under a weary life,
But that the dread of something after death —
The undiscovered country, from whose bourn
No traveller returns — puzzles the will,
And makes us rather bear those ills we have,
Than fly to others that we know not of!
Thus conscience does make cowards of us all;
And thus the native hue of resolution
Is sicklied o'er with the pale cast of thought;
And enterprises of great pith and moment,
With this regard, their currents turn awry,
And lose the name of action.

HAPPINESS.

KEBLE.

THERE are in this rude stunning tide
Of human care and crime,
With whom the melodies abide
Of the everlasting chime,
Who carry music in their heart,
Through dusty lane and wrangling mart,
Plying their daily toil with busier feet,
Because their secret souls a holy strain repeat.

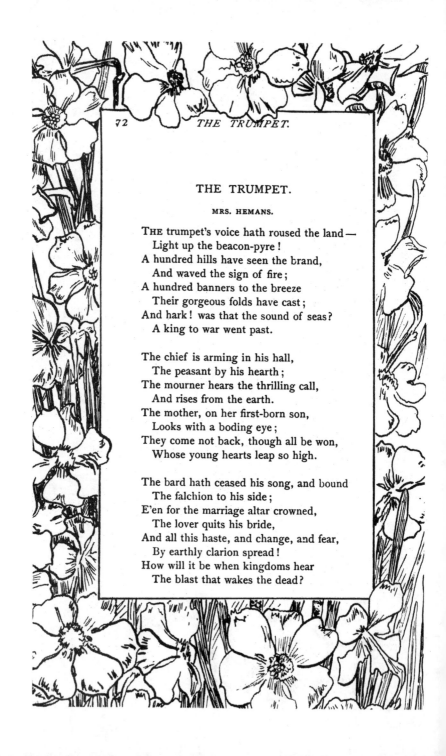

THE TRUMPET.

MRS. HEMANS.

THE trumpet's voice hath roused the land —
　Light up the beacon-pyre !
A hundred hills have seen the brand,
　And waved the sign of fire ;
A hundred banners to the breeze
　Their gorgeous folds have cast ;
And hark ! was that the sound of seas?
　A king to war went past.

The chief is arming in his hall,
　The peasant by his hearth ;
The mourner hears the thrilling call,
　And rises from the earth.
The mother, on her first-born son,
　Looks with a boding eye ;
They come not back, though all be won,
　Whose young hearts leap so high.

The bard hath ceased his song, and bound
　The falchion to his side ;
E'en for the marriage altar crowned,
　The lover quits his bride,
And all this haste, and change, and fear,
　By earthly clarion spread !
How will it be when kingdoms hear
　The blast that wakes the dead?

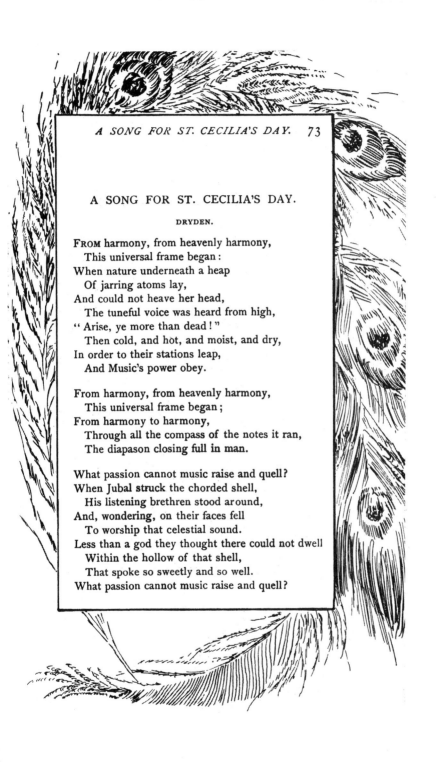

A SONG FOR ST. CECILIA'S DAY.

DRYDEN.

FROM harmony, from heavenly harmony,
  This universal frame began:
When nature underneath a heap
  Of jarring atoms lay,
And could not heave her head,
  The tuneful voice was heard from high,
" Arise, ye more than dead ! "
  Then cold, and hot, and moist, and dry,
In order to their stations leap,
  And Music's power obey.

From harmony, from heavenly harmony,
  This universal frame began;
From harmony to harmony,
  Through all the compass of the notes it ran,
  The diapason closing full in man.

What passion cannot music raise and quell?
When Jubal struck the chorded shell,
  His listening brethren stood around,
And, wondering, on their faces fell
  To worship that celestial sound.
Less than a god they thought there could not dwell
  Within the hollow of that shell,
  That spoke so sweetly and so well.
What passion cannot music raise and quell?

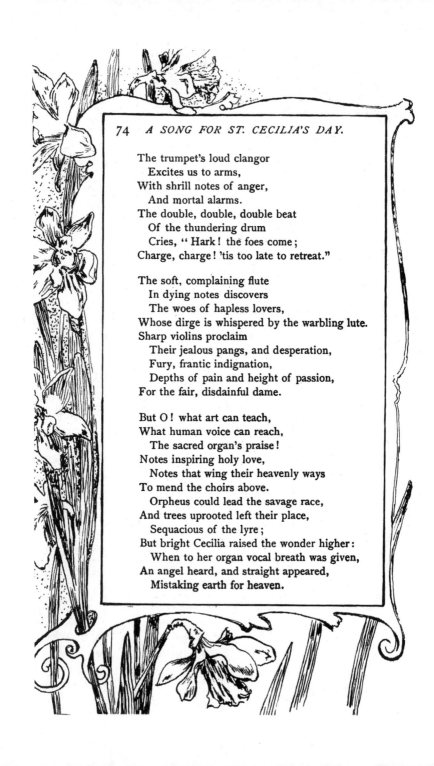

The trumpet's loud clangor
  Excites us to arms,
With shrill notes of anger,
  And mortal alarms.
The double, double, double beat
  Of the thundering drum
  Cries, " Hark! the foes come;
Charge, charge! 'tis too late to retreat."

The soft, complaining flute
  In dying notes discovers
  The woes of hapless lovers,
Whose dirge is whispered by the warbling lute.
Sharp violins proclaim
  Their jealous pangs, and desperation,
  Fury, frantic indignation,
  Depths of pain and height of passion,
For the fair, disdainful dame.

But O! what art can teach,
What human voice can reach,
  The sacred organ's praise!
Notes inspiring holy love,
  Notes that wing their heavenly ways
To mend the choirs above.
  Orpheus could lead the savage race,
And trees uprooted left their place,
  Sequacious of the lyre;
But bright Cecilia raised the wonder higher:
  When to her organ vocal breath was given,
An angel heard, and straight appeared,
  Mistaking earth for heaven.

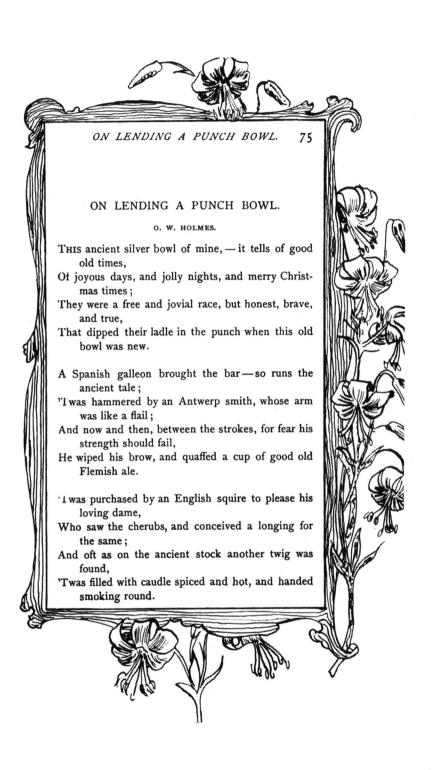

ON LENDING A PUNCH BOWL.

O. W. HOLMES.

THIS ancient silver bowl of mine, — it tells of good
old times,
Of joyous days, and jolly nights, and merry Christ-
mas times ;
They were a free and jovial race, but honest, brave,
and true,
That dipped their ladle in the punch when this old
bowl was new.

A Spanish galleon brought the bar — so runs the
ancient tale ;
'Twas hammered by an Antwerp smith, whose arm
was like a flail ;
And now and then, between the strokes, for fear his
strength should fail,
He wiped his brow, and quaffed a cup of good old
Flemish ale.

'Twas purchased by an English squire to please his
loving dame,
Who saw the cherubs, and conceived a longing for
the same ;
And oft as on the ancient stock another twig was
found,
'Twas filled with caudle spiced and hot, and handed
smoking round.

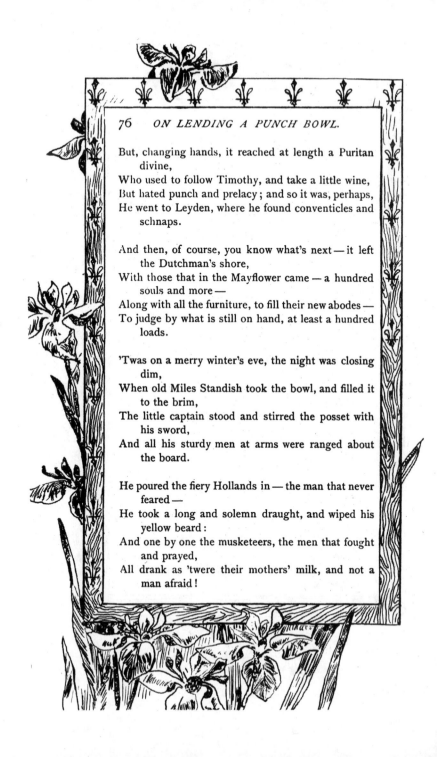

But, changing hands, it reached at length a Puritan
    divine,
Who used to follow Timothy, and take a little wine,
But hated punch and prelacy; and so it was, perhaps,
He went to Leyden, where he found conventicles and
    schnaps.

And then, of course, you know what's next — it left
    the Dutchman's shore,
With those that in the Mayflower came — a hundred
    souls and more —
Along with all the furniture, to fill their new abodes —
To judge by what is still on hand, at least a hundred
    loads.

'Twas on a merry winter's eve, the night was closing
    dim,
When old Miles Standish took the bowl, and filled it
    to the brim,
The little captain stood and stirred the posset with
    his sword,
And all his sturdy men at arms were ranged about
    the board.

He poured the fiery Hollands in — the man that never
    feared —
He took a long and solemn draught, and wiped his
    yellow beard:
And one by one the musketeers, the men that fought
    and prayed,
All drank as 'twere their mothers' milk, and not a
    man afraid!

That night, affrighted from his nest, the screaming
    eagle flew ;
He heard the Pequot's ringing whoop, the soldier's
    wild halloo ;
And there the sachem learned the rule he taught to
    kith and kin,
" Run from the white man when you find he smells
    of Hollands gin."

A hundred years, and fifty more, had spread their
    leaves and snows ;
A thousand rubs had flattened down each little
    cherub's nose ;
When once again the bowl was fixed, but not in
    mirth or joy ;
'Twas mingled by a mother's hand to cheer her
    parting boy.

" Drink, John," she said ; " 'twill do you good —
    poor child, you'll never bear
This working in the dismal trench, out in the mid-
    night air ;
And if — God bless me — you were hurt,' twould
    keep away the chill."
So John *did* drink — and well he wrought that night
    at Bunker's Hill !

I tell you, there was generous warmth in good old
    English cheer ;
I tell you, 'twas a pleasant thought to bring its sym-
    bol here ;

'Tis but the fool that loves excess — hast thou a
   drunken soul,
Thy bane is in thy shallow skull, not in my silver
   bowl!

I love the memory of the past — its pressed yet
   fragrant flowers!
The moss that clothes its broken walls — the ivy on
   its towers —
Nay, this poor bauble it bequeathed — my eyes grow
   moist and dim,
To think of all the vanished joys that danced around
   its brim.

Then fill a fair and honest cup, and bear it straight
   to me ;
The goblet hallows all it holds, whate'er the liquid be ;
And may the cherubs on its face protect me from
   the sin,
That dooms me to those dreadful words — " My dear,
   where *have* you been ? "

SONG.

T. B. ALDRICH.

THE chestnuts shine through the cloven rind,
   And the woodland is ves are red, my dear ;
The scarlet fuchsias burn in the wind —
   Funeral plumes for the year.

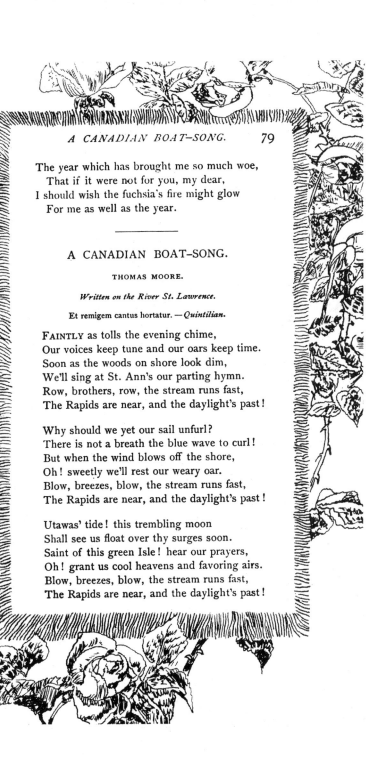

The year which has brought me so much woe,
  That if it were not for you, my dear,
I should wish the fuchsia's fire might glow
  For me as well as the year.

A CANADIAN BOAT-SONG.

THOMAS MOORE.

Written on the River St. Lawrence.

Et remigem cantus hortatur. — *Quintilian.*

FAINTLY as tolls the evening chime,
Our voices keep tune and our oars keep time.
Soon as the woods on shore look dim,
We'll sing at St. Ann's our parting hymn.
Row, brothers, row, the stream runs fast,
The Rapids are near, and the daylight's past!

Why should we yet our sail unfurl?
There is not a breath the blue wave to curl!
But when the wind blows off the shore,
Oh! sweetly we'll rest our weary oar.
Blow, breezes, blow, the stream runs fast,
The Rapids are near, and the daylight's past!

Utawas' tide! this trembling moon
Shall see us float over thy surges soon.
Saint of this green Isle! hear our prayers,
Oh! grant us cool heavens and favoring airs.
Blow, breezes, blow, the stream runs fast,
The Rapids are near, and the daylight's past!

THE OLD CLOCK ON THE STAIRS.

LONGFELLOW.

SOMEWHAT back from the village street,
Stands the old-fashioned country seat.
Across its antique portico
Tall poplar trees their shadows throw;
And from its station in the hall
An ancient time-piece says to all,
     " Forever — never!
     Never — forever! "

Half way up the stairs it stands,
And points and beckons with its hands,
From its case of massive oak,
Like a monk, who under his cloak
Crosses himself, and sighs, alas !
With sorrowful voice, to all who pass,
     " Forever — never!
     Never — forever! "

By day its voice is low and light,
But in the silent dead of night,
Distinct as a passing footstep's fall
It echoes along the vacant hall,
Along the ceiling, along the floor,
  nd seems to say at each chamber door,
     " Forever — never!
     Never — forever."

In that mansion used to be
Free-hearted hospitality;
His great fires by the chimney roared,
The stranger feasted at his board;
But like the skeleton at the feast,
The warning time-piece never ceased,
　"Forever — never!
　　Never — forever!"

There groups of merry children played,
There youths and maidens dreaming strayed;
O precious hours, O golden prime,
And affluence of love and time;
E'en as a miser counts his gold,
Those hours the ancient time-piece told,
　"Forever — never!
　　Never — forever."

From the chamber, clothed in white,
The bride came forth on her wedding-night;
There in that silent room below,
The dead lay in his shroud of snow;
And in the hush that followed the prayer,
We heard the old clock on the stair, —
　"Forever — never!
　　Never — forever!"

All are scattered now and fled:
Some are married, some are dead;
And when I ask, with throbs of pain,
"Ah, when shall they all meet again,

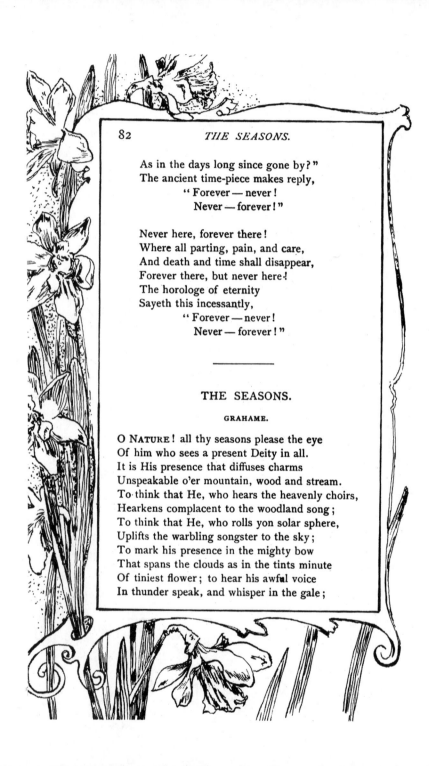

As in the days long since gone by?"
The ancient time-piece makes reply,
    " Forever — never !
      Never — forever !"

Never here, forever there !
Where all parting, pain, and care,
And death and time shall disappear,
Forever there, but never here !
The horologe of eternity
Sayeth this incessantly,
    " Forever — never !
      Never — forever !"

THE SEASONS.

GRAHAME.

O NATURE ! all thy seasons please the eye
Of him who sees a present Deity in all.
It is His presence that diffuses charms
Unspeakable o'er mountain, wood and stream.
To think that He, who hears the heavenly choirs,
Hearkens complacent to the woodland song ;
To think that He, who rolls yon solar sphere,
Uplifts the warbling songster to the sky ;
To mark his presence in the mighty bow
That spans the clouds as in the tints minute
Of tiniest flower ; to hear his awful voice
In thunder speak, and whisper in the gale ;

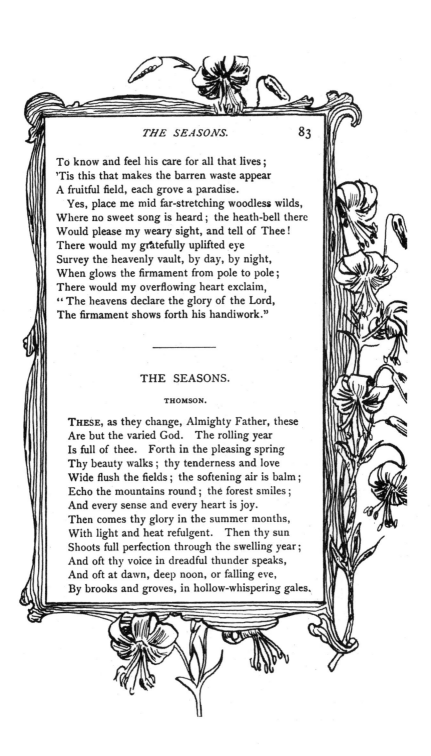

To know and feel his care for all that lives;
'Tis this that makes the barren waste appear
A fruitful field, each grove a paradise.
  Yes, place me mid far-stretching woodless wilds,
Where no sweet song is heard; the heath-bell there
Would please my weary sight, and tell of Thee!
There would my gratefully uplifted eye
Survey the heavenly vault, by day, by night,
When glows the firmament from pole to pole;
There would my overflowing heart exclaim,
"The heavens declare the glory of the Lord,
The firmament shows forth his handiwork."

THE SEASONS.

THOMSON.

THESE, as they change, Almighty Father, these
Are but the varied God.   The rolling year
Is full of thee.   Forth in the pleasing spring
Thy beauty walks; thy tenderness and love
Wide flush the fields; the softening air is balm;
Echo the mountains round; the forest smiles;
And every sense and every heart is joy.
Then comes thy glory in the summer months,
With light and heat refulgent.   Then thy sun
Shoots full perfection through the swelling year;
And oft thy voice in dreadful thunder speaks,
And oft at dawn, deep noon, or falling eve,
By brooks and groves, in hollow-whispering gales.

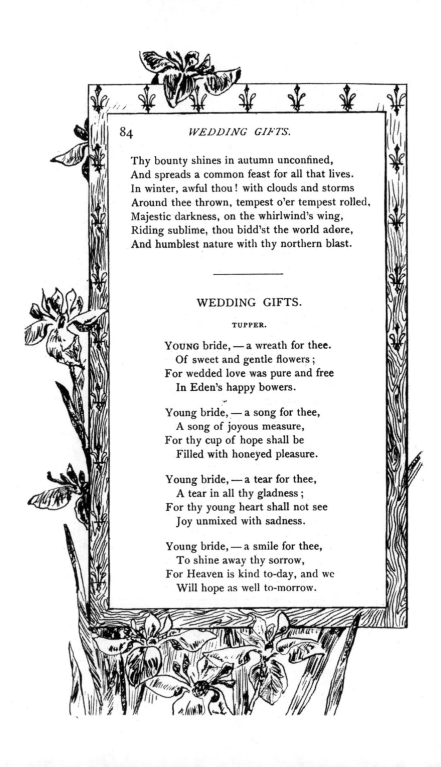

Thy bounty shines in autumn unconfined,
And spreads a common feast for all that lives.
In winter, awful thou! with clouds and storms
Around thee thrown, tempest o'er tempest rolled,
Majestic darkness, on the whirlwind's wing,
Riding sublime, thou bidd'st the world adore,
And humblest nature with thy northern blast.

WEDDING GIFTS.

TUPPER.

YOUNG bride, — a wreath for thee.
  Of sweet and gentle flowers;
For wedded love was pure and free
  In Eden's happy bowers.

Young bride, — a song for thee,
  A song of joyous measure,
For thy cup of hope shall be
  Filled with honeyed pleasure.

Young bride, — a tear for thee,
  A tear in all thy gladness;
For thy young heart shall not see
  Joy unmixed with sadness.

Young bride, — a smile for thee,
  To shine away thy sorrow,
For Heaven is kind to-day, and we
  Will hope as well to-morrow.

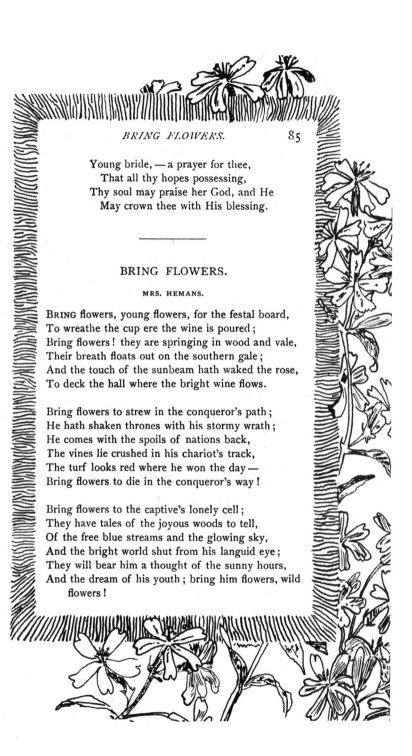

Young bride, — a prayer for thee,
That all thy hopes possessing,
Thy soul may praise her God, and He
May crown thee with His blessing.

BRING FLOWERS.

MRS. HEMANS.

BRING flowers, young flowers, for the festal board,
To wreathe the cup ere the wine is poured;
Bring flowers! they are springing in wood and vale,
Their breath floats out on the southern gale;
And the touch of the sunbeam hath waked the rose,
To deck the hall where the bright wine flows.

Bring flowers to strew in the conqueror's path;
He hath shaken thrones with his stormy wrath;
He comes with the spoils of nations back,
The vines lie crushed in his chariot's track,
The turf looks red where he won the day —
Bring flowers to die in the conqueror's way!

Bring flowers to the captive's lonely cell;
They have tales of the joyous woods to tell,
Of the free blue streams and the glowing sky,
And the bright world shut from his languid eye;
They will bear him a thought of the sunny hours,
And the dream of his youth; bring him flowers, wild
    flowers!

Bring flowers, fresh flowers, for the bride to wear;
They were born to blush in her shining hair.
She is leaving the home of her childhood's mirth,
She hath bid farewell to her father's hearth,
Her place is now by another's side —
Bring flowers for the locks of the fair young bride!

Bring flowers, pale flowers, o'er the bier to shed,
A crown for the brow of the early dead!
For this through its leaves hath the white rose burst,
For this in the woods was the violet nursed;
Though they smile in vain for what once was ours,
They are love's last gift; bring ye flowers, pale flowers!

Bring flowers to the shrine where we kneel in prayer ·
They are nature's offering, their place is there;
They speak of hope to the fainting heart,
With a voice of promise they come and part;
They sleep in dust through the wintry hours,
They break forth in glory; bring flowers, bright flowers!

SOLITUDE.

BYRON.

THERE is a pleasure in the pathless woods,
There is a rapture on the lonely shore,
There is society where none intrudes
By the deep sea, and music in its roar.
I love not man the less, but nature more,

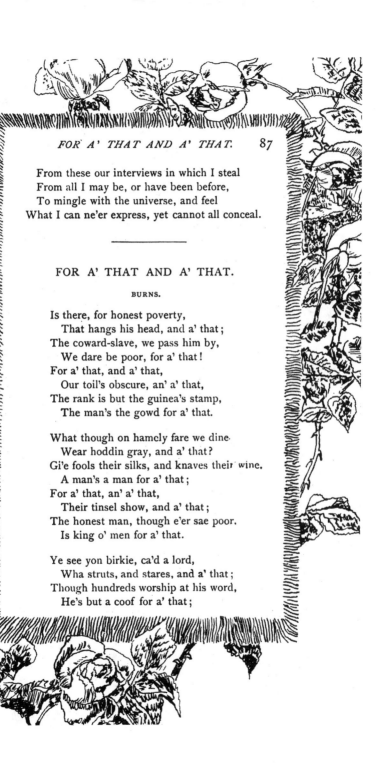

From these our interviews in which I steal
From all I may be, or have been before,
To mingle with the universe, and feel
What I can ne'er express, yet cannot all conceal.

FOR A' THAT AND A' THAT.

BURNS.

Is there, for honest poverty,
 That hangs his head, and a' that;
The coward-slave, we pass him by,
 We dare be poor, for a' that!
For a' that, and a' that,
 Our toil's obscure, an' a' that,
The rank is but the guinea's stamp,
 The man's the gowd for a' that.

What though on hamely fare we dine
 Wear hoddin gray, and a' that?
Gi'e fools their silks, and knaves their wine,
 A man's a man for a' that;
For a' that, an' a' that,
 Their tinsel show, and a' that;
The honest man, though e'er sae poor.
 Is king o' men for a' that.

Ye see yon birkie, ca'd a lord,
 Wha struts, and stares, and a' that;
Though hundreds worship at his word,
 He's but a coof for a' that;

For a' that, an' a' that,
  His ribbon, star, and a' that,
The man of independent mind,
  He looks an' laughs at a' that.

A prince can mak a belted knight,
  A marquis, duke, and a' that;
But an honest man's aboon his might,
  Guid faith he mauna fa' that.
For a' that, and a' that,
  Their dignities, an' a' that,
The pith o' sense and pride o' worth
  Are higher ranks than a' that.

Then let us pray that come it may,
  As come it will for a' that,
That sense and worth, o'er a' the earth,
  Should bear the gree, and a' that.
For a' that, an' a' that,
  It's coming yet, for a' that,
That man to man, the warld o'er,
  Shall brothers be for a' that.

———

KNOWLEDGE AND WISDOM.

COWPER.

KNOWLEDGE and wisdom, far from being one,
Have ofttimes no connection. Knowledge dwells
In heads replete with thoughts of other men;
Wisdom in minds attentive to their own.

Knowledge — a rude, unprofitable mass,
The mere materials with which Wisdom builds,
Till smoothed, and squared, and fitted to its place —
Does but encumber whom it seems to enrich.
Knowledge is proud that he has learned so much ;
Wisdom is humble that he knows no more.

NOVEMBER.

BRYANT.

LET one smile more, departing, distant sun,
  One mellow smile through the soft, vaporing air,
Ere o'er the frozen earth the loud winds run,
  Or snows are sifted o'er the meadows bare ;
One smile on the brown hills and naked trees ;
  And the dark rocks whose summer wreaths are cast,
And the blue gentian flower, that in the breeze
  Nods lonely, of her beauteous race the last.
Yet a few sunny days, in which the bee
  Shall murmur by the hedge that skirts the way,
The cricket chirp upon the russet lea,
  And man delight to linger in the ray.
Yet one rich smile, and we will try to bear
The piercing winter frost, and winds, and darkened
    air.

THE PRIMROSE OF THE ROCK.

WORDSWORTH.

A ROCK there is whose homely front
   The passing traveller slights ;
Yet there the glow-worms hang their lamps,
   Like stars, at various heights,
And one coy primrose to that rock
   The vernal breeze invites.

What hideous warfare hath been waged,
   What kingdoms overthrown,
Since first I spied that primrose tuft,
   And marked it for my own !
A lasting link in nature's chain,
   From highest heaven let down.

The flowers, still faithful to the stems,
   Their fellowship renew ;
The stems are faithful to the root,
   That worketh out of view ;
And to the rock the root adheres,
   In every fibre true.

Close clings to earth the living rock,
   Though threatening still to fall ;
The earth is constant to her sphere,
   And God upholds them all ;
So blooms this lonely plant, nor dreads
   Her annual funeral.

Here closed the meditative strain;
But air breathed soft that day,
The hoary mountain heights were cheered
The sunny vale looked gay;
And to the primrose of the rock
I gave this after-lay.

I sang, Let myriads of bright flowers,
Like thee, in field and grove
Revive unenvied; — mightier far
Than tremblings that reprove
Our vernal tendencies to hope
In God's redeeming love —

That love which changed, for wan disease,
For sorrow, that hath bent
O'er hopeless dust, for withered age,
Their moral element,
And turned the thistles of a curse
To types beneficent.

Sin-blighted though we are, we too,
The reasoning sons of men,
From one oblivious winter called,
Shall rise, and breathe again;
And in eternal summer lose
Our threescore years and ten.

To humbleness of heart descends
This prescience from on high,
The faith that elevates the just
Before and when they die,
And makes each soul a separate heaven,
A court for Deity.

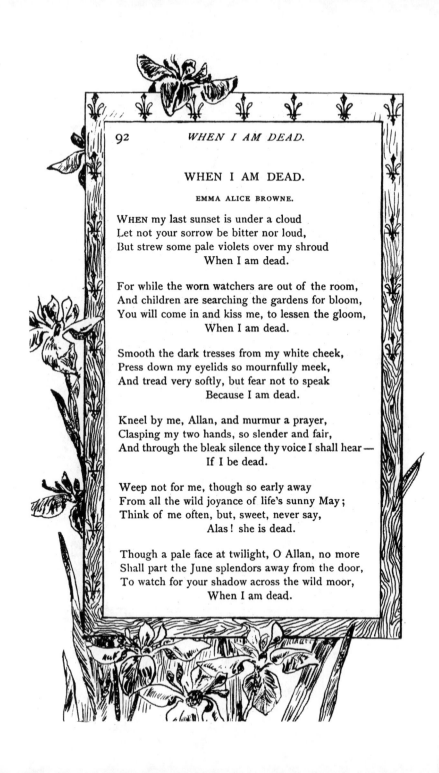

WHEN I AM DEAD.

EMMA ALICE BROWNE.

WHEN my last sunset is under a cloud
Let not your sorrow be bitter nor loud,
But strew some pale violets over my shroud
      When I am dead.

For while the worn watchers are out of the room,
And children are searching the gardens for bloom,
You will come in and kiss me, to lessen the gloom,
      When I am dead.

Smooth the dark tresses from my white cheek,
Press down my eyelids so mournfully meek,
And tread very softly, but fear not to speak
      Because I am dead.

Kneel by me, Allan, and murmur a prayer,
Clasping my two hands, so slender and fair,
And through the bleak silence thy voice I shall hear —
      If I be dead.

Weep not for me, though so early away
From all the wild joyance of life's sunny May;
Think of me often, but, sweet, never say,
      Alas! she is dead.

Though a pale face at twilight, O Allan, no more
Shall part the June splendors away from the door,
To watch for your shadow across the wild moor,
      When I am dead.

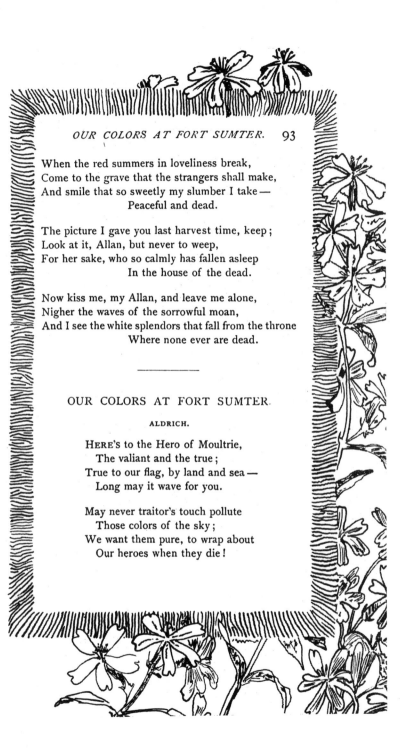

When the red summers in loveliness break,
Come to the grave that the strangers shall make,
And smile that so sweetly my slumber I take —
      Peaceful and dead.

The picture I gave you last harvest time, keep;
Look at it, Allan, but never to weep,
For her sake, who so calmly has fallen asleep
      In the house of the dead.

Now kiss me, my Allan, and leave me alone,
Nigher the waves of the sorrowful moan,
And I see the white splendors that fall from the throne
      Where none ever are dead.

OUR COLORS AT FORT SUMTER.

ALDRICH.

HERE's to the Hero of Moultrie,
    The valiant and the true;
True to our flag, by land and sea —
    Long may it wave for you.

May never traitor's touch pollute
    Those colors of the sky;
We want them pure, to wrap about
    Our heroes when they die!

TWO HUNDRED YEARS.

PIERPONT.

Two hundred years! — two hundred years!
  How much of human power and pride,
What glorious hopes, what gloomy fears,
  Have sunk beneath their noiseless tide!

The red man, at his horrid rite,
  Seen by the stars at night's cold noon,
His bark canoe its track of light
  Left on the wave beneath the moon, —

His dance, his yell, his council fire,
  The altar where his victim lay,
His death-song, and his funeral pyre,
  That still, strong tide hath borne away.

And that pale pilgrim band is gone,
  That on this shore with trembling trod,
Ready to faint, yet bearing on
  The ark of freedom and of God.

And war — that since o'er ocean came,
  And thundered loud from yonder hill,
And wrapped its foot in sheets of flame
  To blast that ark — its storm is still.

Chief, sachem, sage, bards, heroes, seers,
  That live in story and in song,
Time, for the last two hundred years,
  Has raised, and shown, and swept along.

'Tis like a dream when one awakes —
 This vision of the scenes of old;
'Tis like the moon, when morning breaks,
 'Tis like a tale round watch-fires told.

God of our fathers, — in whose sight
 The thousand years that swept away
Man, and the traces of his might,
 Are but the break and close of day, ·

Grant us that love of truth sublime,
 That love of goodness and of thee,
Which makes thy children, in all time,
 To share thine own eternity.

ONE HEART'S ENOUGH FOR ME.

AUGUSTE MIGNON.

ONE heart's enough for me —
 One heart to love, adore —
One heart's enough for me;
 O, who could wish for more?
The birds that soar above,
 And sing their songs on high,
Ask but for one to love,
 And therefore should not I?

One pair of eyes to gaze,
 One pair of sparkling blue,
In which sweet love betrays
 Her form of fairest hue;

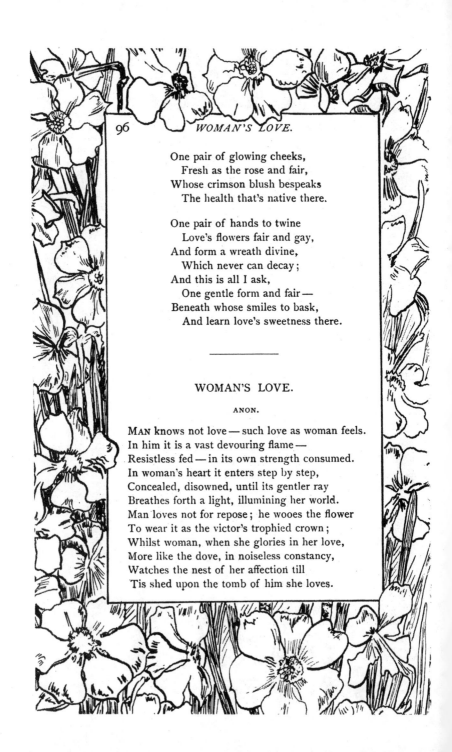

One pair of glowing cheeks,
  Fresh as the rose and fair,
Whose crimson blush bespeaks
  The health that's native there.

One pair of hands to twine
  Love's flowers fair and gay,
And form a wreath divine,
  Which never can decay;
And this is all I ask,
  One gentle form and fair—
Beneath whose smiles to bask,
  And learn love's sweetness there.

WOMAN'S LOVE.

ANON.

MAN knows not love—such love as woman feels.
In him it is a vast devouring flame—
Resistless fed—in its own strength consumed.
In woman's heart it enters step by step,
Concealed, disowned, until its gentler ray
Breathes forth a light, illumining her world.
Man loves not for repose; he wooes the flower
To wear it as the victor's trophied crown;
Whilst woman, when she glories in her love,
More like the dove, in noiseless constancy,
Watches the nest of her affection till
Tis shed upon the tomb of him she loves.

THE BRIDGE OF SIGHS.

HOOD.

ONE more unfortunate,
  Weary of breath,
Rashly importunate,
  Gone to her death!

Take her up tenderly,
  Lift her with care;
Fashioned so slenderly,
  Young, and so fair!

Look at her garments
Clinging like cerements;
  Whilst the wave constantly
Drips from her clothing;
  Take her up instantly,
Loving, not loathing. —

Touch her not scornfully!
Think of her mournfully,
  Gently and humanly,
Not of the stains of her;
All that remains of her
  Now is pure womanly.

Make no deep scrutiny
Into her mutiny,
  Rash and undutiful;

Past all dishonor,
  Death has left on her
Only the beautiful.

Still, for all slips of hers,
  One of Eve's family —
Wipe those poor lips of hers
  Oozing so clammily.

Loop up her tresses
  Escaped from the comb,
Her fair auburn tresses;
  Whilst wonderment guesses,
  Where was her home?

Who was her father?
  Who was her mother?
Had she a sister?
  Had she a brother?
Or was there a dearer one
Still, and a nearer one
  Yet than all other?

Alas! for the rarity
Of Christian charity
  Under the sun!
O! it was pitiful,
Near a whole city full,
  Home she had none.

Sisterly, brotherly,
Fatherly, motherly
  Feelings had changed;

Love, by harsh evidence,
Thrown from its eminence,
Even God's providence
   Seeming estranged.

Where the lamps quiver
So far in the river,
   With many a light
From window and casement,
From garret to basement,
She stood, with amazement,
   Houseless by night.

The bleak wind of March
   Made her tremble and shiver;
But not the dark arch,
   Or the black flowing river;
Mad from life's history,
Glad to death's mystery
   Swift to be hurled —
Anywhere, anywhere
   Out of the world!

In she plunged boldly,
No matter how coldly
   The rough river ran,
Over the brink of it;
Picture it — think of it,
   Dissolute man!
Lave in it, drink of it,
   Then, if you can.

Take her up tenderly,
  Lift her with care;
Fashioned so slenderly,
  Young, and so fair!

Ere her limbs frigidly
Stiffen too rigidly,
  Decently, kindly,
Smooth and compose them;
And her eyes, close them,
  Staring so blindly!

Dreadfully staring
  Through muddy impurity,
As when with the daring
Last look of despairing,
  Fixed on futurity.

Perishing gloomily,
Spurned by contumely,
  Burning insanity,
  Cold inhumanity,
Into her rest.
  Cross her hands humbly,
  As if praying dumbly,
Over her breast.

Owning her weakness,
  Her evil behavior,
And leaving, with meekness,
  Her sins to her Saviour.

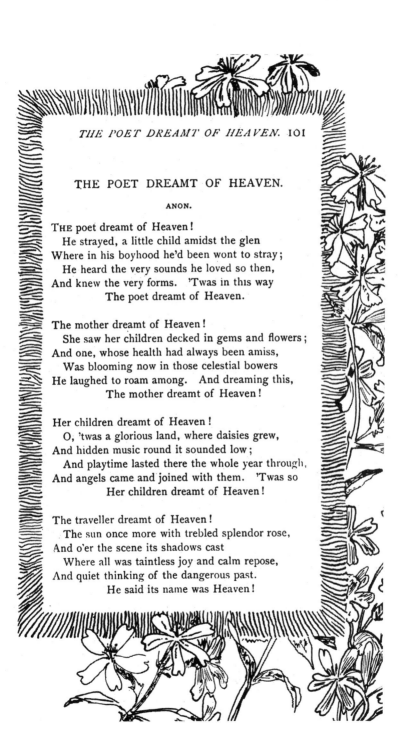

THE POET DREAMT OF HEAVEN.

ANON.

THE poet dreamt of Heaven!
　He strayed, a little child amidst the glen
Where in his boyhood he'd been wont to stray;
　He heard the very sounds he loved so then,
And knew the very forms. 'Twas in this way
　　　The poet dreamt of Heaven.

The mother dreamt of Heaven!
　She saw her children decked in gems and flowers;
And one, whose health had always been amiss,
　Was blooming now in those celestial bowers
He laughed to roam among. And dreaming this,
　　　The mother dreamt of Heaven!

Her children dreamt of Heaven!
　O, 'twas a glorious land, where daisies grew,
And hidden music round it sounded low;
　And playtime lasted there the whole year through,
And angels came and joined with them. 'Twas so
　　　Her children dreamt of Heaven!

The traveller dreamt of Heaven!
　The sun once more with trebled splendor rose,
And o'er the scene its shadows cast
　Where all was taintless joy and calm repose,
And quiet thinking of the dangerous past.
　　　He said its name was Heaven!

The mourner dreamt of Heaven!
  Before his eyes, so long with sorrow dim,
A glorious sheen, like lengthened lightning, blazed;
  And from the clouds one face looked down on him,
Whose beauty thrilled his veins.   And as he gazed
        He knew he gazed on Heaven!

And all dream on!
  Heaven's for the pure, the just, the undefiled;
And so our lives, by holy faith, are such;
  Our dreams may be erroneous, varying, wild;
But O, we cannot think and hope too much.
        So let them all dream on!

ON THE SEA.

BAYARD TAYLOR.

THE pathway of the sinking moon
  Fades from the silent bay;
The mountain isles loom large and faint,
  Folded in shadows gray,
And the lights of land are setting stars
  That soon will pass away.

O boatman, cease thy mellow song,
  O minstrel, drop thy lyre;
Let us hear the voice of the midnight sea,
  Let us speak as the waves inspire,
While the plashy dip of the languid oar
  Is a furrow of silver fire

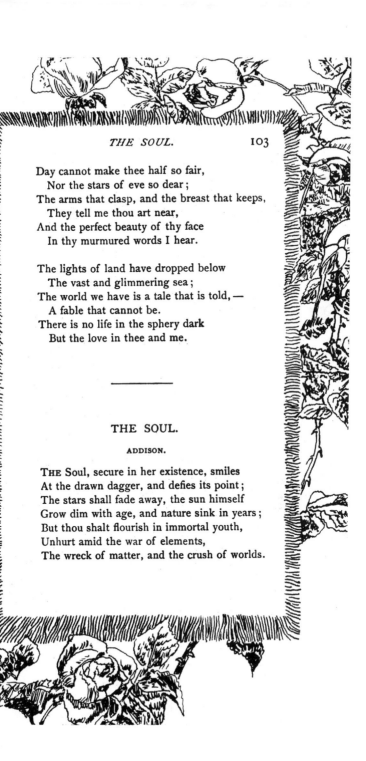

Day cannot make thee half so fair,
  Nor the stars of eve so dear;
The arms that clasp, and the breast that keeps,
  They tell me thou art near,
And the perfect beauty of thy face
  In thy murmured words I hear.

The lights of land have dropped below
  The vast and glimmering sea;
The world we have is a tale that is told, —
  A fable that cannot be.
There is no life in the sphery dark
  But the love in thee and me.

THE SOUL.

ADDISON.

THE Soul, secure in her existence, smiles
At the drawn dagger, and defies its point;
The stars shall fade away, the sun himself
Grow dim with age, and nature sink in years;
But thou shalt flourish in immortal youth,
Unhurt amid the war of elements,
The wreck of matter, and the crush of worlds.

THE PRAYER OF NATURE.

BYRON.

FATHER of Light! great God of Heaven,
  Hear'st thou the accents of despair?
Can guilt like man's be e'er forgiven?
  Can vice atone for crimes by prayer?

Father of Light, on thee I call;
  Thou seest my soul is dark within;
Thou, who canst mark the sparrow's fall,
  Avert from me the death of sin.

No shrine I seek to sects unknown;
  O, point to me the path of truth;
Thy dread omnipotence I own;
  Spare, yet amend the faults of youth.

Let bigots rear a gloomy fane,
  Let superstition hail the pile,
Let priests, to spread their sable reign,
  With tales of mystic rites beguile.

Shall man confine his Maker's sway
  To Gothic domes of mouldering stone?
Thy temple is the face of day;
  Earth, ocean, heaven thy boundless throne.

Shall man condemn his race to hell
  Unless they bend in pompous form;

Tell us that all, for one who fell,
    Must perish in the mingling storm?

Shall each pretend to reach the skies,
    Yet doom his brother to expire,
Whose soul a different hope supplies,
    Or doctrines less severe inspire?

Shall these, by creeds they can't expound,
    Prepare a fancied bliss or woe?
Shall reptiles, grovelling on the ground,
    Their great Creator's purpose know?

Shall those who live for self alone,
    Whose years float on in daily crime, —
Shall they by faith for guilt atone,
    And live beyond the bounds of time?

Father! no prophet's laws I seek;
    Thy laws in Nature's works appear; —
I own myself corrupt and weak;
    Yet will I pray, for thou wilt hear!

Thou, who canst guide the wandering star
    Through trackless realms of ether's space;
Who calm'st the elemental war,
    Whose hand from pole to pole I trace; —

Thou, who in wisdom placed me here,
    Who, when thou wilt, can take me hence,
Ah! while I tread this earthly sphere,
    Extend to me thy wide defence.

To thee, my God, to thee I call !
   Whatever weal or woe betide,
By thy command I rise or fall ;
   In thy protection I confide.

If, when this dust to dust's restored,
   My soul shall float on airy wing,
How shall thy glorious name adored
   Inspire her feeble voice to sing !

But, if this fleeting spirit share
   With clay the grave's eternal bed,
While life yet throbs I raise my prayer,
   Though doomed no more to quit the dead.

To thee I breathe my humble strain,
   Grateful for all thy mercies past,
And hope, my God, to thee again
   This erring life may fly at last.

IN REVERIE.

HARRIET M^cEWEN KIMBALL.

In the west, the weary Day
   Folds its amber wings and dies ;
Night, the long delaying Night,
   Walks abroad in starry guise.

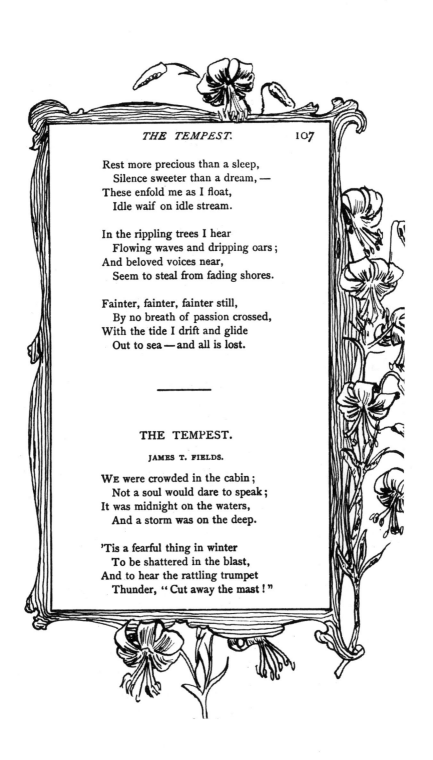

Rest more precious than a sleep,
  Silence sweeter than a dream, —
These enfold me as I float,
  Idle waif on idle stream.

In the rippling trees I hear
  Flowing waves and dripping oars;
And beloved voices near,
  Seem to steal from fading shores.

Fainter, fainter, fainter still,
  By no breath of passion crossed,
With the tide I drift and glide
  Out to sea — and all is lost.

THE TEMPEST.

JAMES T. FIELDS.

WE were crowded in the cabin;
  Not a soul would dare to speak;
It was midnight on the waters,
  And a storm was on the deep.

'Tis a fearful thing in winter
  To be shattered in the blast,
And to hear the rattling trumpet
  Thunder, "Cut away the mast!"

So we shuddered there in silence,
  For the stoutest held his breath
While the angry sea was roaring,
  And the breakers talked with Death.

And thus we sat in darkness,
  Each one busy in his prayers:
" We are lost ! " the captain shouted,
  As he staggered down the stairs.

But his little daughter whispered,
  As she took his icy hand,
" Is not God upon the ocean
  Just the same as on the land ? "

Then we kissed the little maiden,
  And we spoke in better cheer,
And we anchored safe in harbor
  When the morn was shining clear

FROM " THE PRINCESS."

TENNYSON.

TEARS, idle tears, I know not what they mean.
Tears from the depth of some divine despair
Rise in the heart and gather to the eyes,
In looking on the happy autumn fields,
And thinking of the days that are no more.

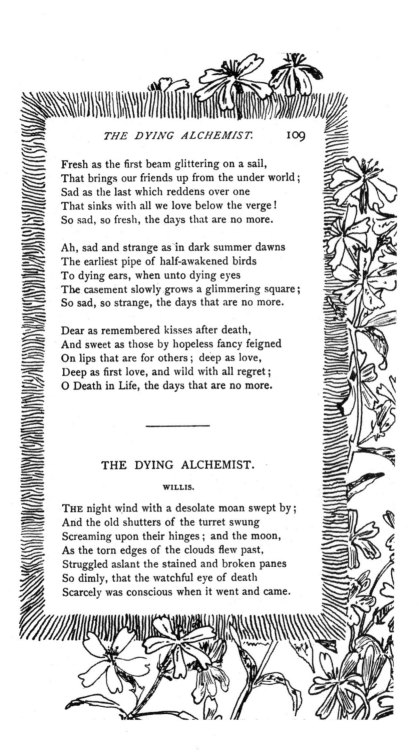

Fresh as the first beam glittering on a sail,
That brings our friends up from the under world;
Sad as the last which reddens over one
That sinks with all we love below the verge!
So sad, so fresh, the days that are no more.

Ah, sad and strange as in dark summer dawns
The earliest pipe of half-awakened birds
To dying ears, when unto dying eyes
The casement slowly grows a glimmering square;
So sad, so strange, the days that are no more.

Dear as remembered kisses after death,
And sweet as those by hopeless fancy feigned
On lips that are for others; deep as love,
Deep as first love, and wild with all regret;
O Death in Life, the days that are no more.

THE DYING ALCHEMIST.

WILLIS.

THE night wind with a desolate moan swept by;
And the old shutters of the turret swung
Screaming upon their hinges; and the moon,
As the torn edges of the clouds flew past,
Struggled aslant the stained and broken panes
So dimly, that the watchful eye of death
Scarcely was conscious when it went and came.

The fire beneath his crucible was low :
Yet still it burned ; and ever as his thoughts
Grew insupportable, he raised himself
Upon his wasted arm, and stirred the coals
With difficult energy ; and when the rod
Fell from his nerveless fingers, and his eye
Felt faint within its socket, he shrunk back
Upon his pallet, and with unclosed lips
Muttered a curse on death !   The silent room,
From its dim corners, mockingly gave back
His rattling breath ; the humming in the fire
Had the distinctness of a knell ; and when
Duly the antique horologe beat one,
He drew a phial from his breast,
And drank.   And instantly his lips compressed,
And, with a shudder in his skeleton frame,
He rose with supernatural strength, and sat
Upright, and communed with himself : —

    I did not think to die
Till I had finished what I had to do ;
I thought to pierce th' eternal secret through
    With this my mortal eye ;
I felt — O God ! it seemeth even now
This cannot be the death-dew on my brow.

    And yet it is — I feel
Of this dull sickness at my heart, afraid ;
And in my eyes the death-sparks flash and fade ;
    And something seems to steal
Over my bosom like a frozen hand,
Binding its pulses with an icy band.

And this is death! But why
Feel I this wild recoil? It cannot be
Th' immortal spirit shuddereth to be free!
    Would it not leap to fly,
Like a chained eaglet at its parent's call?
I fear — I fear — that this poor life is all.

    Yet thus to pass away!
To live but for a hope that mocks at last;
To agonize, to strive, to watch, to fast,
    To waste the light of day,
Night's better beauty, feeling, fancy, thought,
All that we have and are — for this — for naught.

    Grant me another year,
God of my spirit! but a day, to win
Something to satisfy this thirst within.
    I would *know* something here.
Break for me but one seal that is unbroken!
Speak for me but one word that is unspoken!

    Vain, vain! my brain is turning
With a swift dizziness, and my heart grows sick,
And these hot temple-throbs come fast and thick,
    And I am freezing, burning,
Dying. O God, if I might only live!
My phial — ha! it thrills me; I revive.

    Ay, were not man to die,
He were too mighty for this narrow sphere.
Had he but time to brood on knowledge here,
    Could he but train his eye,

Might he but wait the mystic word and hour,
Only his Maker would transcend his power.

     Earth has no mineral strange,
Th' illimitable air no hidden wings,
Water no quality in covert springs,
     And fire no power to change,
Seasons no mystery, and stars no spell,
Which the unwasting soul might not compel.

     O, but for time to track
The upper stars into the pathless sky,
To see th' invisible spirits eye to eye,
     To hurl the lightning back,
To tread unhurt the sea's dim-lighted halls,
To chase Day's chariot to the horizon walls —

     And more, much more; for now
The life-sealed fountains of my nature move,
To nurse and purify this human love;
     To clear the godlike brow
Of weakness and distrust, and bow it down,
Worthy and beautiful, to the much-loved one.

     This were indeed to feel
The soul-thirst slaken at the living stream;
To live — O God! that life is but a dream!
     And death — aha! I reel —
Dim — dim — I faint! darkness comes o'er my eye!
Cover me! save me. God of heaven! I die!

'Twas morning, and the old man lay alone.
No friend had closed his eyelids, and his lips,
Open and ashy pale, th' expression wore
Of his death struggle. His long, silvery hair
Lay on his hollow temples thin and wild ;
His frame was wasted, and his features wan
And haggard as with want, and in his palm
His nails were driven deep, as if the throe
Of the last agony had wrung him sore.
The storm was raging still. The shutters swung,
Screaming as harshly in the fitful wind,
And all without went on, as aye it will,
Sunshine or tempest, reckless that a heart
Is breaking, or has broken, in its change.

The fire beneath the crucible was out ;
The vessels of his mystic art lay round,
Useless and cold as the ambitious hand
That fashioned them, and the small rod,
Familiar to his touch for threescore years,
Lay on th' alembic's rim, as if it still
Might vex the elements at its master's will.

And thus had passed from its unequal frame
A soul of fire — a sun-bent eagle stricken
From his high soaring down — an instrument
Broken with its own compass. O, how poor
Seems the rich gift of genius, when it lies,
Like the adventurous bird that hath outflown
His strength upon the sea, ambition-wrecked —
A thing the thrush might pity, as she sits
Brooding in quiet on her lowly nest.

THE PLEASURES OF HOPE.

CAMPBELL.

'Tis summer eve, when heaven's ethereal bow
Spans with bright arch the glittering hills below.
Why to yon mountain turns the musing eye,
Whose sun-bright summit mingles with the sky?
Why do these cliffs of shadowy tint appear
More sweet than all the landscape smiling near?
'Tis distance lends enchantment to the view,
And robes the mountain in its azure hue.
Thus, with delight, we linger to survey:
The promised joy of life's unmeasured scene
More pleasing seems than all the past hath been;
And every form that Fancy can repair,
From dark oblivion, glows divinely there.

JUNE.

BRYANT.

There, through the long, long summer hours,
    The golden light should lie,
And thick young herbs and groups of flowers
    Stand in their beauty by.
The oriole should build and tell
His love-tale close beside my cell;
    The idle butterfly
Should rest him there, and there be heard
The housewife bee and humming-bird.

And what if cheerful shouts, at noon,
    Come from the village sent,
Or songs of maids, beneath the moon,
    With fairy laughter blent?
And what if, in the evening light,
Betrothéd lovers walk in sight
    Of my low monument?
I would the lovely scene around
Might know no sadder sight or sound.

I know, I know I should not see
    The season's glorious show,
Nor would its brightness shine for me,
    Nor its wild music flow;
But if, around my place of sleep,
The friends I love should come to weep,
    They might not haste to go.
Soft airs, and song, and light, and bloom
Should keep them lingering by my tomb.

These to their softened hearts should bear
    The thought of what has been,
And speak of one who cannot share
    The gladness of the scene;
Whose part in all the pomp that fills
The circuit of the summer hills,
    Is, that his grave is green;
And deeply would their hearts rejoice
To hear again his living voice.

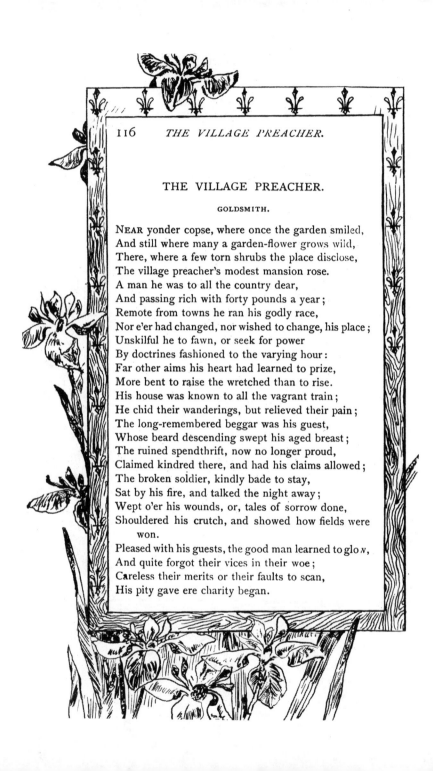

THE VILLAGE PREACHER.

GOLDSMITH.

NEAR yonder copse, where once the garden smiled,
And still where many a garden-flower grows wild,
There, where a few torn shrubs the place disclose,
The village preacher's modest mansion rose.
A man he was to all the country dear,
And passing rich with forty pounds a year;
Remote from towns he ran his godly race,
Nor e'er had changed, nor wished to change, his place;
Unskilful he to fawn, or seek for power
By doctrines fashioned to the varying hour:
Far other aims his heart had learned to prize,
More bent to raise the wretched than to rise.
His house was known to all the vagrant train;
He chid their wanderings, but relieved their pain;
The long-remembered beggar was his guest,
Whose beard descending swept his aged breast;
The ruined spendthrift, now no longer proud,
Claimed kindred there, and had his claims allowed;
The broken soldier, kindly bade to stay,
Sat by his fire, and talked the night away;
Wept o'er his wounds, or, tales of sorrow done,
Shouldered his crutch, and showed how fields were
    won.
Pleased with his guests, the good man learned to glow,
And quite forgot their vices in their woe;
Careless their merits or their faults to scan,
His pity gave ere charity began.

Thus to relieve the wretched was his pride,
And e'en his failings leaned to virtue's side;
But, in his duty prompt at every call,
He watched and wept, he prayed and felt for all;
And, as a bird each fond endearment tries
To tempt its new-fledged offspring to the skies,
He tried each art, reproved each dull delay,
Allured to brighter worlds, and led the way.
Beside the bed where parting life was laid,
And sorrow, guilt, and pain, by turns dismayed,
The reverend champion stood. At his control,
Despair and anguish fled the struggling soul;
Comfort came down the trembling wretch to raise,
And his last, faltering accents whispered praise.
At church, with meek and unaffected grace,
His looks adorned the venerable place;
Truth from his lips prevailed with double sway,
And fools, who came to scoff, remained to pray.
The service past, around the pious man,
With ready zeal, each honest rustic ran;
E'en children followed with endearing wile,
And plucked his gown, to share the good man's smile;
His ready smile a parent's warmth expressed;
Their welfare pleased him, and their cares distressed;
To them his heart, his love, his griefs were given,
But all his serious thought had rest in heaven.
As some tall cliff that lifts its awful form,
Swells from the vale, and midway leaves the storm,
Though round its breast the rolling clouds are spread,
Eternal sunshine settles on its head.

HE LIVES LONG WHO LIVES WELL.

RANDOLPH.

WOULDST thou live long? The only means are
    these —
'Bove Galen's diet, or Hippocrates':
Strive to live well; tread in the upright ways,
And rather count thy actions than thy days:
Then thou hast lived enough amongst us here,
For every day well spent I count a year.
Live well, and then, how soon soe'er thou die,
Thou art of age to claim eternity.
But he that outlives Nestor, and appears
To have passed the date of gray Methuselah's years,
If he his life to sloth and sin doth give,
I say he only WAS — he did not LIVE.

FAIR INES.

HOOD.

O SAW ye not fair Ines?
    She's gone into the west,
To dazzle when the sun is down
    And rob the world of rest;
She took our daylight with her,
    The smiles that we love best,
With morning blushes on her cheek,
    And pearls upon her breast.

O, turn again, fair Ines,
  Before the fall of night,
For fear the moon should shine alone,
  And stars unrivalled bright;
And blessed will the lover be
  That walks beneath their light,
And breathes the love against thy cheek
  I dare not even write.

Would I had been, fair Ines,
  That gallant cavalier
Who rode so gayly by thy side,
  And whispered thee so near!—
Were there no bonny dames at home,
  Or no true lovers here,
That he should cross the seas to win
  The dearest of the dear?

I saw thee, lovely Ines,
  Descend along the shore,
With bands of noble gentlemen,
  And banners waved before;
And gentle youth and maidens gay,
  And snowy plumes they wore;
It would have been a beauteous dream,
  If it had been no more!

Alas, alas, fair Ines,
  She went away with song,
With Music waiting on her steps,
  And shoutings of the throng;

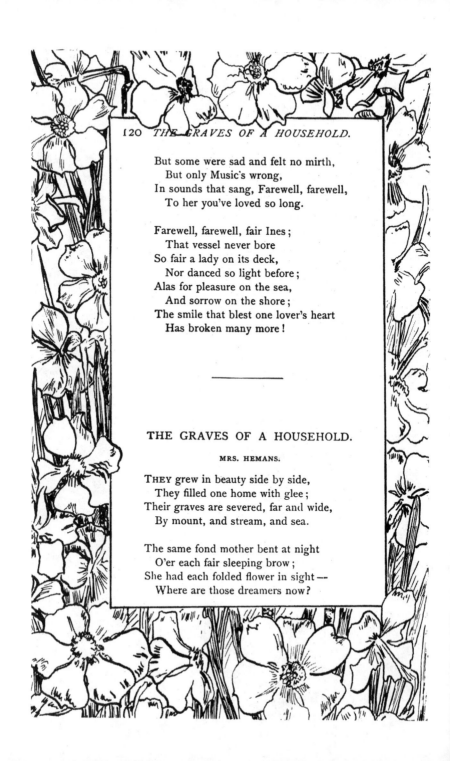

But some were sad and felt no mirth,
  But only Music's wrong,
In sounds that sang, Farewell, farewell,
  To her you've loved so long.

Farewell, farewell, fair Ines ;
  That vessel never bore
So fair a lady on its deck,
  Nor danced so light before ;
Alas for pleasure on the sea,
  And sorrow on the shore ;
The smile that blest one lover's heart
  Has broken many more !

THE GRAVES OF A HOUSEHOLD.

MRS. HEMANS.

THEY grew in beauty side by side,
  They filled one home with glee ;
Their graves are severed, far and wide,
  By mount, and stream, and sea.

The same fond mother bent at night
  O'er each fair sleeping brow ;
She had each folded flower in sight —
  Where are those dreamers now?

One, midst the forest of the west,
   By a dark stream is laid —
The Indian knows his place of rest,
   Far in the cedar shade.

The sea, the blue lone sea, hath one —
   He lies where pearls lie deep ;
He was the loved of all, yet none
   O'er his low bed may weep.

One sleeps where southern vines are drest
   Above the noble slain ;
He wrapt his colors round his breast
   On a blood-red field of Spain.

And one — o'er *her* the myrtle showers
   Its leaves, by soft winds fanned ;
She faded midst Italian flowers,
   The last of that bright band.

And parted thus they rest, who played
   Beneath the same green tree ;
Whose voices mingled as they prayed
   Around one parent knee.

They that with smiles lit up the hall,
   And cheered with song the hearth —
Alas ! for love, if thou wert all,
   And naught beyond, O earth !

THE BEAUTIFUL.

BURRINGTON.

WALK with the Beautiful and with the Grand;
 Let nothing on the earth thy feet deter;
Sorrow may lead thee weeping by the hand,
 But give not all thy bosom thoughts to her:
  Walk with the Beautiful.

I hear thee say, " The Beautiful! What is it?"
 O, thou art darkly ignorant! Be sure
'Tis no long, weary road its form to visit;
 For thou canst make it smile beside thy door: —
  Then love the Beautiful.

Ay, love it; 'tis a sister that will bless,
 And teach thee patience when the heart is lonely;
The angels love it, for they wear its dress;
 And thou art made a little lower only; —
  Then love the Beautiful.

Sigh for it, — clasp it when 'tis in thy way!
 Be its idolater, as of a maiden!
Thy parents bent to it, and more than they; —
 Be thou its worshipper. Another Eden
  Comes with the Beautiful.

Some boast its presence in a Grecian face;
 Some, on a favorite warbler of the skies;
But be not foiled; where'er thine eyes might trace,
 Seeking the Beautiful, it will arise; —
  Then seek it every where.

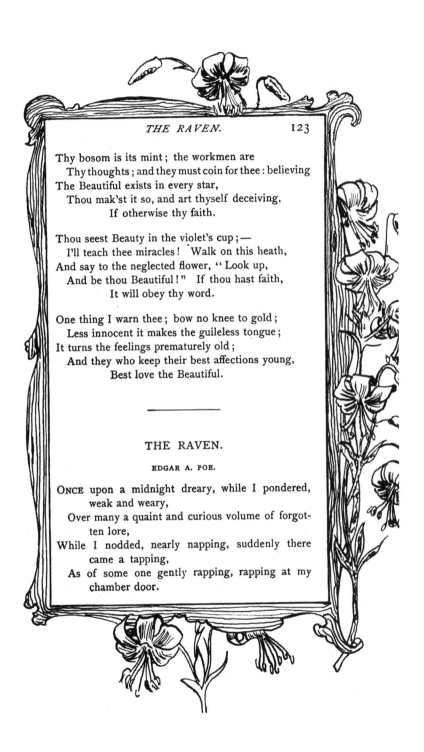

Thy bosom is its mint; the workmen are
  Thy thoughts; and they must coin for thee: believing
The Beautiful exists in every star,
  Thou mak'st it so, and art thyself deceiving,
    If otherwise thy faith.

Thou seest Beauty in the violet's cup; —
  I'll teach thee miracles! Walk on this heath,
And say to the neglected flower, "Look up,
  And be thou Beautiful!" If thou hast faith,
    It will obey thy word.

One thing I warn thee; bow no knee to gold;
  Less innocent it makes the guileless tongue;
It turns the feelings prematurely old;
  And they who keep their best affections young,
    Best love the Beautiful.

THE RAVEN.

EDGAR A. POE.

ONCE upon a midnight dreary, while I pondered,
    weak and weary,
  Over many a quaint and curious volume of forgot-
    ten lore,
While I nodded, nearly napping, suddenly there
    came a tapping,
  As of some one gently rapping, rapping at my
    chamber door.

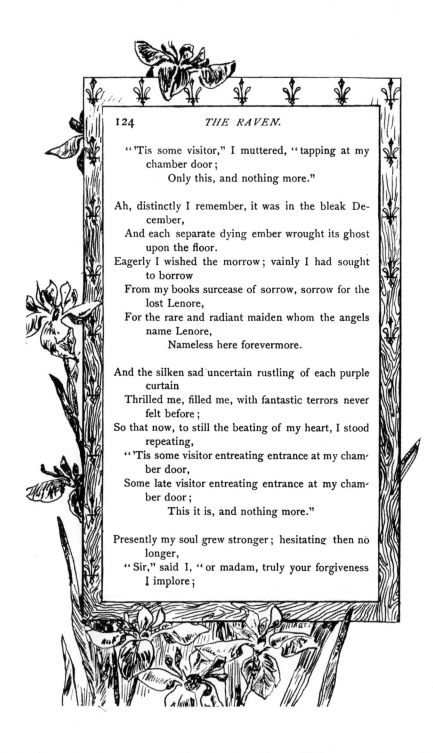

" 'Tis some visitor," I muttered, "tapping at my
  chamber door ;
      Only this, and nothing more."

Ah, distinctly I remember, it was in the bleak De-
  cember,
  And each separate dying ember wrought its ghost
    upon the floor.
Eagerly I wished the morrow ; vainly I had sought
  to borrow
  From my books surcease of sorrow, sorrow for the
    lost Lenore,
  For the rare and radiant maiden whom the angels
    name Lenore,
      Nameless here forevermore.

And the silken sad uncertain rustling of each purple
  curtain
  Thrilled me, filled me, with fantastic terrors never
    felt before ;
So that now, to still the beating of my heart, I stood
  repeating,
  " 'Tis some visitor entreating entrance at my cham-
    ber door,
  Some late visitor entreating entrance at my cham-
    ber door ;
      This it is, and nothing more."

Presently my soul grew stronger ; hesitating then no
  longer,
  " Sir," said I, " or madam, truly your forgiveness
    I implore ;

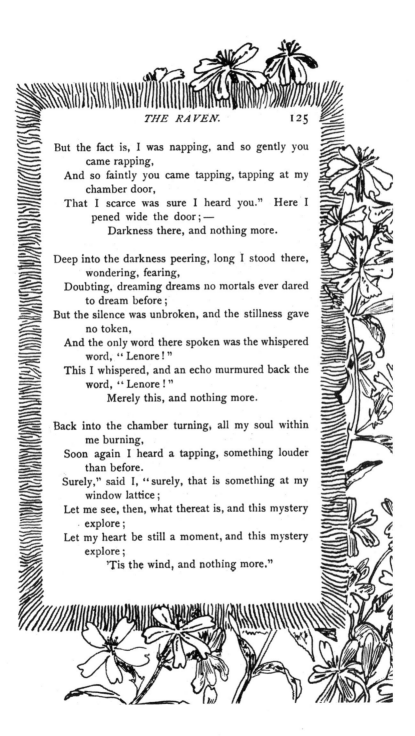

But the fact is, I was napping, and so gently you
    came rapping,
And so faintly you came tapping, tapping at my
    chamber door,
That I scarce was sure I heard you." Here I
    pened wide the door ; —
        Darkness there, and nothing more.

Deep into the darkness peering, long I stood there,
    wondering, fearing,
Doubting, dreaming dreams no mortals ever dared
    to dream before ;
But the silence was unbroken, and the stillness gave
    no token,
And the only word there spoken was the whispered
    word, " Lenore ! "
This I whispered, and an echo murmured back the
    word, " Lenore ! "
        Merely this, and nothing more.

Back into the chamber turning, all my soul within
    me burning,
Soon again I heard a tapping, something louder
    than before.
Surely," said I, "surely, that is something at my
    window lattice ;
Let me see, then, what thereat is, and this mystery
    explore ;
Let my heart be still a moment, and this mystery
    explore ;
        'Tis the wind, and nothing more."

Open here I flung the shutter, when, with many a flirt
    and flutter,
    In there stepped a stately raven, of the saintly
        days of yore.
Not the least obeisance made he; not a minute
        stopped or staid he;
    But with mien of lord or lady, perched above my
        chamber door,
    Perched upon a bust of Pallas, just above my
        chamber door;
            Perched, and sat, and nothing more.

Then this ebon bird beguiling my sad fancy into
        smiling,
    By the grave and stern decorum of the countenance
        it wore,
" Though thy crest be shorn and shaven, thou," I
        said, " art sure no craven,
    Ghastly, grim, and ancient raven, wandering from
        the Nightly shore.
    Tell me what thy lordly name is on the Night's
        Plutonian shore."
            Quoth the raven, " Nevermore."

Much I marvelled this ungainly fowl to hear discourse
        so plainly,
    Though its answer little meaning, little relevancy
        bore;
For we cannot help agreeing that no living human
        being
    Ever yet was blessed with seeing bird above his
        chamber door,

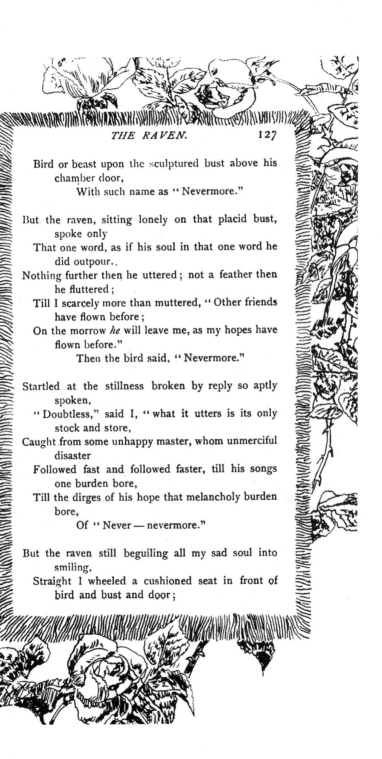

Bird or beast upon the sculptured bust above his
chamber door,
With such name as " Nevermore."

But the raven, sitting lonely on that placid bust,
spoke only
That one word, as if his soul in that one word he
did outpour..
Nothing further then he uttered; not a feather then
he fluttered;
Till I scarcely more than muttered, " Other friends
have flown before;
On the morrow *he* will leave me, as my hopes have
flown before."
Then the bird said, " Nevermore."

Startled at the stillness broken by reply so aptly
spoken,
" Doubtless," said I, " what it utters is its only
stock and store,
Caught from some unhappy master, whom unmerciful
disaster
Followed fast and followed faster, till his songs
one burden bore,
Till the dirges of his hope that melancholy burden
bore,
Of " Never — nevermore."

But the raven still beguiling all my sad soul into
smiling,
Straight I wheeled a cushioned seat in front of
bird and bust and door;

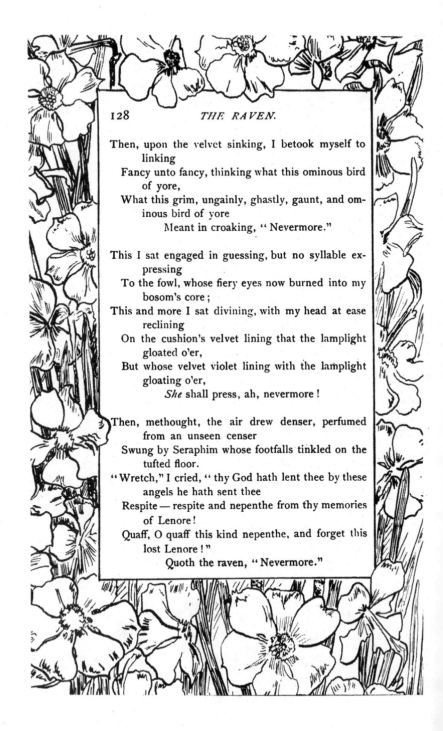

Then, upon the velvet sinking, I betook myself to
  linking
  Fancy unto fancy, thinking what this ominous bird
    of yore,
  What this grim, ungainly, ghastly, gaunt, and om-
    inous bird of yore
        Meant in croaking, "Nevermore."

This I sat engaged in guessing, but no syllable ex-
  pressing
  To the fowl, whose fiery eyes now burned into my
    bosom's core;
  This and more I sat divining, with my head at ease
    reclining
  On the cushion's velvet lining that the lamplight
    gloated o'er,
  But whose velvet violet lining with the lamplight
    gloating o'er,
        She shall press, ah, nevermore!

Then, methought, the air drew denser, perfumed
    from an unseen censer
  Swung by Seraphim whose footfalls tinkled on the
    tufted floor.
"Wretch," I cried, " thy God hath lent thee by these
    angels he hath sent thee
  Respite — respite and nepenthe from thy memories
    of Lenore!
  Quaff, O quaff this kind nepenthe, and forget this
    lost Lenore!"
        Quoth the raven, "Nevermore."

"Prophet!" said I, "thing of evil!—prophet still,
   if bird or devil!
Whether tempter sent, or whether tempest tossed
   thee here ashore,
Desolate, yet all undaunted, on this desert land en-
   chanted,—
On this home by horror haunted—tell me truly, I
   implore—
Is there—*is* there balm in Gilead?—tell me—tell
   me, I implore!"
      Quoth the raven, "Nevermore."

"Prophet!" said I, "thing of evil—prophet still, if
   bird or devil!
By that heaven that bends above us—by that God
   we both adore—
Tell this soul with sorrow laden, if, within the distant
   Aidenn,
It shall clasp a sainted maiden, whom the angels
   name Lenore—
Clasp a rare and radiant maiden, whom the angels
   name Lenore?"
      Quoth the raven, "Nevermore."

"Be that word our sign of parting, bird or fiend!" I
   shrieked, upstarting—
"Get thee back into the tempest and the night's
   Plutonian shore!
Leave no black plume as a token of that lie thy soul
   hath spoken!
Leave my loneliness unbroken!—quit the bust
   above my door!

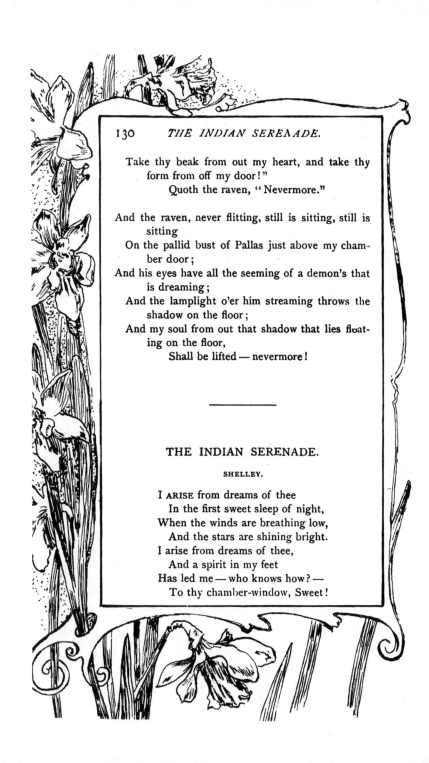

Take thy beak from out my heart, and take thy
form from off my door!"
    Quoth the raven, "Nevermore."

And the raven, never flitting, still is sitting, still is
sitting
On the pallid bust of Pallas just above my cham-
ber door;
And his eyes have all the seeming of a demon's that
is dreaming;
And the lamplight o'er him streaming throws the
shadow on the floor;
And my soul from out that shadow that lies float-
ing on the floor,
    Shall be lifted — nevermore!

———

THE INDIAN SERENADE.

SHELLEY.

I ARISE from dreams of thee
    In the first sweet sleep of night,
When the winds are breathing low,
    And the stars are shining bright.
I arise from dreams of thee,
    And a spirit in my feet
Has led me — who knows how? —
    To thy chamber-window, Sweet!

The wandering airs, they faint
  On the dark, the silent stream —
The champak odors fail
  Like sweet thoughts in a dream :
The nightingale's complaint,
  It dies upon her heart,
As I must die on thine,
  O, belovéd as thou art !

O, lift me from the grass !
  I die, I faint, I fail !
Let thy love in kisses rain
  On my lips and eyelids pale.
My cheek is cold and white, alas !
  My heart beats loud and fast :
O, press it close to thine again,
  Where it will break at last !

ANGEL OF THE RAIN.

HARRIET MCEWEN KIMBALL.

AWAKE thy cloud-harp, angel of the rain !
Sweep thy dark fingers o'er the waiting strings ;
And pour thy melodies in silvery showers
In the great heart of earth !

I love thy notes when in the hush of night
They fall with tranquil gladness on the roof,
Liquid and faint as laughter heard in dreams.

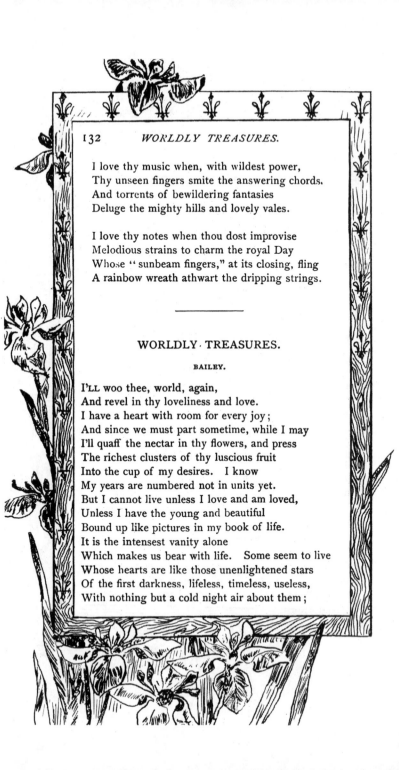

I love thy music when, with wildest power,
Thy unseen fingers smite the answering chords.
And torrents of bewildering fantasies
Deluge the mighty hills and lovely vales.

I love thy notes when thou dost improvise
Melodious strains to charm the royal Day
Whose "sunbeam fingers," at its closing, fling
A rainbow wreath athwart the dripping strings.

WORLDLY · TREASURES.

BAILEY.

I'LL woo thee, world, again,
And revel in thy loveliness and love.
I have a heart with room for every joy;
And since we must part sometime, while I may
I'll quaff the nectar in thy flowers, and press
The richest clusters of thy luscious fruit
Into the cup of my desires. I know
My years are numbered not in units yet.
But I cannot live unless I love and am loved,
Unless I have the young and beautiful
Bound up like pictures in my book of life.
It is the intensest vanity alone
Which makes us bear with life. Some seem to live
Whose hearts are like those unenlightened stars
Of the first darkness, lifeless, timeless, useless,
With nothing but a cold night air about them;

Not suns, not planets; darkness organized;
Orbs of a desert darkness; with no soul
To light its watch-fires in the wilderness,
And civilize the solitude one moment.
There are such seemingly; but how or why
They live, I know not. This to me is life;
That if life be a burden, I will join
To make it but the burden of a song;
I hate the world's coarse thought. And this is life;
To watch young beauty's bud-like feelings burst
And load the soul with love; as that pale flower,
Which opes at eve, spreads sudden on the dark
Its yellow bloom, and sinks the air down with its sweets.
Let heaven take all that's good, hell all that's foul;
Leave us the lovely, and we will ask no more.

THE DEATH OF THE FLOWERS

BRYANT.

THE melancholy days are come, the saddest of the year,
Of wailing winds, and naked woods, and meadows
    brown and sere.
Heaped in the hollows of the grove, the withered
    leaves lie dead;   .
They rustle to the eddying gust, and to the rabbit's
    tread.
The robin and the wren are flown, and from the
    shrub the jay,
And from the wood-top calls the crow, through all
    the gloomy day.

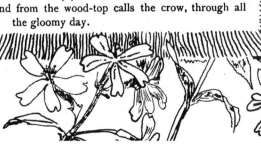

Where are the flowers, the fair young flowers, that
    lately sprung and stood
In brighter light and softer airs, a beauteous sister-
    hood?
Alas! they all are in their graves; the gentle race of
    flowers
Are lying in their lowly beds with the fair and good
    of ours.
The rain is falling where they lie; but the cold No-
    vember rain
Calls not, from out the gloomy earth, the lovely ones
    again.

The wind-flower and the violet, they perished long ago,
And the wild rose and the orchis died amid the sum-
    mer glow;
But on the hill the golden-rod, and the aster in the
    wood,
And the yellow sun-flower by the brook in autumn
    beauty stood,
Till fell the frost from the clear cold heaven, as falls
    the plague on men,
And the brightness of their smile was gone from
    upland, glade, and glen.

And now, when comes the calm mild day, as still
    such days will come,
To call the squirrel and the bee from out their winter
    home,
When the sound of dropping nuts is heard, though
    all the trees are still,
And twinkle in the smoky light the waters of the rill,

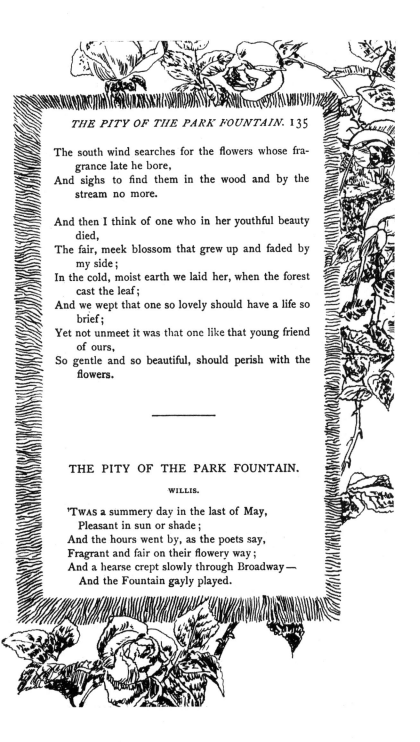

The south wind searches for the flowers whose fragrance late he bore,
And sighs to find them in the wood and by the stream no more.

And then I think of one who in her youthful beauty died,
The fair, meek blossom that grew up and faded by my side;
In the cold, moist earth we laid her, when the forest cast the leaf;
And we wept that one so lovely should have a life so brief;
Yet not unmeet it was that one like that young friend of ours,
So gentle and so beautiful, should perish with the flowers.

THE PITY OF THE PARK FOUNTAIN.

WILLIS.

'TWAS a summery day in the last of May,
    Pleasant in sun or shade;
And the hours went by, as the poets say,
Fragrant and fair on their flowery way;
And a hearse crept slowly through Broadway —
    And the Fountain gayly played.

The Fountain played right merrily,
　　And the world looked bright and gay;
And a youth went by, with a restless eye,
Whose heart was sick and whose brain was dry;
And he prayed to God that he might die —
　　And the Fountain played away.

Uprose the spray like a diamond throne,
　　And the drops like music rang —
And of those who marvelled how it shone
Was a proud man left in his shame alone:
And he shut his teeth with a smothered groan —
　　And the Fountain sweetly sang.

And a rainbow spanned it changefully,
　　Like a bright ring broke in twain;
And the pale, fair girl, who stopped to see,
Was sick with the pangs of poverty —
And from hunger to guilt she chose to flee,
　　As the rainbow smiled again.

With as fair a ray, on another day,
　　The morning will have shone;
And as little marked, in bright Broadway,
A hearse will glide amid busy and gay,
And the bard who sings will have passed away —
　　And the Fountain will play on!

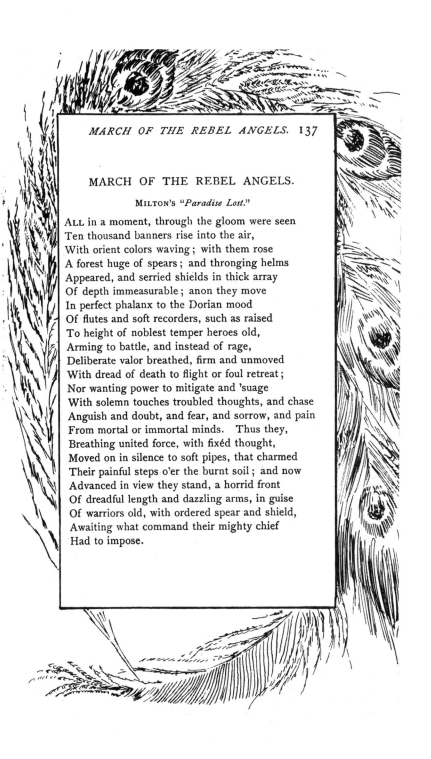

MARCH OF THE REBEL ANGELS.

MILTON'S *"Paradise Lost."*

ALL in a moment, through the gloom were seen
Ten thousand banners rise into the air,
With orient colors waving ; with them rose
A forest huge of spears ; and thronging helms
Appeared, and serried shields in thick array
Of depth immeasurable ; anon they move
In perfect phalanx to the Dorian mood
Of flutes and soft recorders, such as raised
To height of noblest temper heroes old,
Arming to battle, and instead of rage,
Deliberate valor breathed, firm and unmoved
With dread of death to flight or foul retreat ;
Nor wanting power to mitigate and 'suage
With solemn touches troubled thoughts, and chase
Anguish and doubt, and fear, and sorrow, and pain
From mortal or immortal minds.   Thus they,
Breathing united force, with fixéd thought,
Moved on in silence to soft pipes, that charmed
Their painful steps o'er the burnt soil ; and now
Advanced in view they stand, a horrid front
Of dreadful length and dazzling arms, in guise
Of warriors old, with ordered spear and shield,
Awaiting what command their mighty chief
Had to impose.

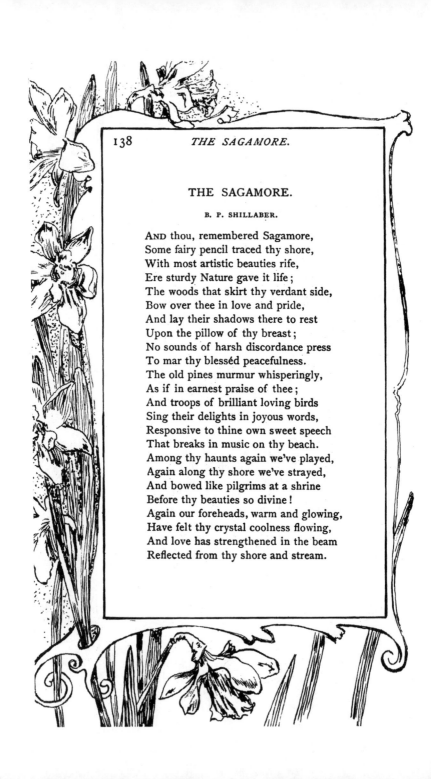

THE SAGAMORE.

B. P. SHILLABER.

AND thou, remembered Sagamore,
Some fairy pencil traced thy shore,
With most artistic beauties rife,
Ere sturdy Nature gave it life;
The woods that skirt thy verdant side,
Bow over thee in love and pride,
And lay their shadows there to rest
Upon the pillow of thy breast;
No sounds of harsh discordance press
To mar thy blesséd peacefulness.
The old pines murmur whisperingly,
As if in earnest praise of thee;
And troops of brilliant loving birds
Sing their delights in joyous words,
Responsive to thine own sweet speech
That breaks in music on thy beach.
Among thy haunts again we've played,
Again along thy shore we've strayed,
And bowed like pilgrims at a shrine
Before thy beauties so divine!
Again our foreheads, warm and glowing,
Have felt thy crystal coolness flowing,
And love has strengthened in the beam
Reflected from thy shore and stream.

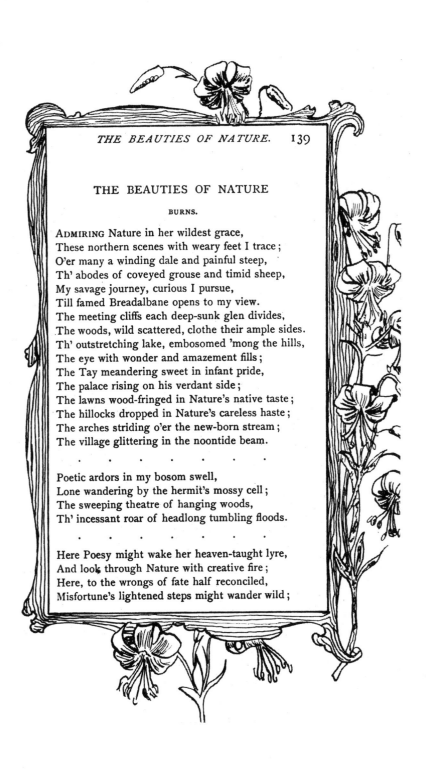

THE BEAUTIES OF NATURE

BURNS.

ADMIRING Nature in her wildest grace,
These northern scenes with weary feet I trace;
O'er many a winding dale and painful steep,
Th' abodes of coveyed grouse and timid sheep,
My savage journey, curious I pursue,
Till famed Breadalbane opens to my view.
The meeting cliffs each deep-sunk glen divides,
The woods, wild scattered, clothe their ample sides.
Th' outstretching lake, embosomed 'mong the hills,
The eye with wonder and amazement fills;
The Tay meandering sweet in infant pride,
The palace rising on his verdant side;
The lawns wood-fringed in Nature's native taste;
The hillocks dropped in Nature's careless haste;
The arches striding o'er the new-born stream;
The village glittering in the noontide beam.

.   .   .   .   .   .

Poetic ardors in my bosom swell,
Lone wandering by the hermit's mossy cell;
The sweeping theatre of hanging woods,
Th' incessant roar of headlong tumbling floods.

.   .   .   .   .   .

Here Poesy might wake her heaven-taught lyre,
And look through Nature with creative fire;
Here, to the wrongs of fate half reconciled,
Misfortune's lightened steps might wander wild;

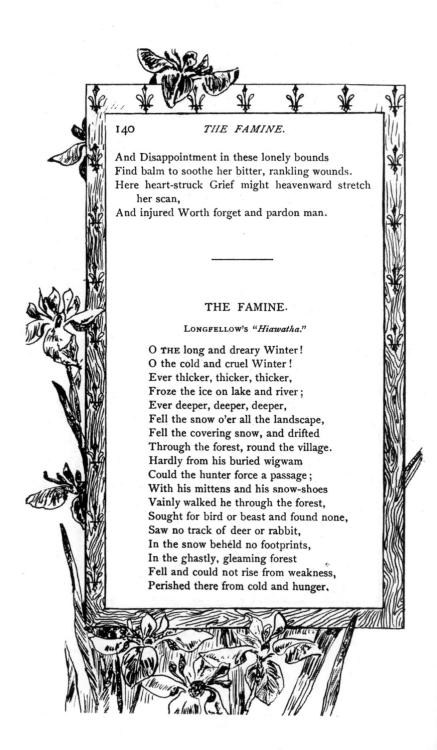

And Disappointment in these lonely bounds
Find balm to soothe her bitter, rankling wounds.
Here heart-struck Grief might heavenward stretch
   her scan,
And injured Worth forget and pardon man.

THE FAMINE.

LONGFELLOW'S *"Hiawatha."*

O THE long and dreary Winter!
O the cold and cruel Winter!
Ever thicker, thicker, thicker,
Froze the ice on lake and river;
Ever deeper, deeper, deeper,
Fell the snow o'er all the landscape,
Fell the covering snow, and drifted
Through the forest, round the village.
Hardly from his buried wigwam
Could the hunter force a passage;
With his mittens and his snow-shoes
Vainly walked he through the forest,
Sought for bird or beast and found none,
Saw no track of deer or rabbit,
In the snow beheld no footprints,
In the ghastly, gleaming forest
Fell and could not rise from weakness,
Perished there from cold and hunger.

O the famine and the fever!
O the wasting of the famine!
O the blasting of the fever!
O the wailing of the children!
O the anguish of the women!

All the earth was sick and famished;
Hungry was the air around them,
Hungry was the sky above them,
And the hungry stars in heaven
Like the eyes of wolves glared at them!

Into Hiawatha's wigwam
Came two other guests, as silent
As the ghosts were, and as gloomy,
Waited not to be invited,
Did not parley at the doorway,
Sat there without word of welcome
In the seat of Laughing Water;
Looked with haggard eyes and hollow
At the face of Laughing Water.
And the foremost said, "Behold me!
I am Famine, Bukadawin!"
And the other said, "Behold me!
I am Fever, Ahkosewin!"

And the lovely Minnehaha
Shuddered as they looked upon her,
Shuddered at the words they uttered.
Lay down on her bed in silence,
Hid her face, but made no answer;
Lay there trembling, freezing, burning

At the looks they cast upon her;
At the fearful words they uttered.

Forth into the empty forest
Rushed the maddened Hiawatha;
In his heart was deadly sorrow,
In his face a stony firmness;
On his brow the sweat of anguish
Started, but it froze, and fell not.

Wrapt in furs and armed for hunting,
With his mighty bow of ash-tree,
With his quiver full of arrows,
With his mittens, Minjekahwun,
Into the vast and vacant forest
On his snow-shoes strode he forward.

"Gitche Manito, the Mighty!"
Cried he with his face uplifted
In that bitter hour of anguish,
"Give your children food, O father!
Give us food, or we must perish,
Give me food for Minnehaha,
For my dying Minnehaha!"

Through the far-resounding forest,
Through the forest vast and vacant,
Rang that cry of desolation;
But there came no other answer
Than the echo of his crying,
Than the echo of the woodlands,
"Minnehaha! Minnehaha!"

All day long roved Hiawatha
In that melancholy forest,
Through the shadow of whose thickets,
In the pleasant days of summer,
Of that ne'er forgotten summer,
He had brought his young bride homeward
From the land of the Dacotahs;
When the birds sang in the thickets,
And the air was full of fragrance,
And the lovely Laughing Water
Said with voice that did not tremble,
" I will follow you, my husband!"

In the wigwam with Nokomis,
With those gloomy guests that watched her,
With the Famine and the Fever,
She was lying, the Beloved,
She, the dying Minnehaha.

" Hark!" she said; " I hear a rushing,
Hear a roaring and a rushing,
Hear the Falls of Minnehaha
Calling to me from a distance!"
" No, my child," said old Nokomis,
" 'Tis the night-wind in the pine-trees!"
" Look!" she said; " I see my father
Standing lonely at his doorway,
Beckoning to me from his wigwam
In the land of the Dacotahs!"
" No, my child!" said old Nokomis,
" 'Tis the smoke, that waves and beckons!"
"Ah!" she said, " the eyes of Pauguk

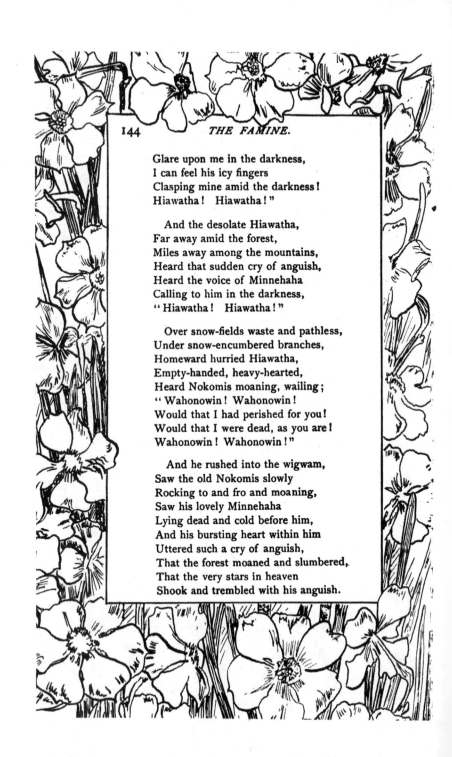

Glare upon me in the darkness,
I can feel his icy fingers
Clasping mine amid the darkness!
Hiawatha!   Hiawatha!"

And the desolate Hiawatha,
Far away amid the forest,
Miles away among the mountains,
Heard that sudden cry of anguish,
Heard the voice of Minnehaha
Calling to him in the darkness,
"Hiawatha!   Hiawatha!"

Over snow-fields waste and pathless,
Under snow-encumbered branches,
Homeward hurried Hiawatha,
Empty-handed, heavy-hearted,
Heard Nokomis moaning, wailing;
"Wahonowin! Wahonowin!
Would that I had perished for you!
Would that I were dead, as you are!
Wahonowin! Wahonowin!"

And he rushed into the wigwam,
Saw the old Nokomis slowly
Rocking to and fro and moaning,
Saw his lovely Minnehaha
Lying dead and cold before him,
And his bursting heart within him
Uttered such a cry of anguish,
That the forest moaned and slumbered,
That the very stars in heaven
Shook and trembled with his anguish.

Then he sat down, still and speechless,
On the bed of Minnehaha,
At the feet of Laughing Water,
At those willing feet, that never
More would lightly run to meet him;
Never more would lightly follow.

With both hands his face he covered,
Seven long days and nights he sat there,
As if in a swoon he sat there,
Speechless, motionless, unconscious
Of the daylight or the darkness.

Then they buried Minnehaha;
In the snow a grave they made her,
In the forest, deep and darksome,
Underneath the moaning hemlocks;
Clothed her in her richest garments,
Wrapped her in her robes of ermine, —
Covered her with snow, like ermine;
Thus they buried Minnehaha.

And at night a fire was lighted,
On her grave four times was kindled,
For her soul upon its journey
To the Island of the Blesséd.
From his doorway Hiawatha
Saw it burning in the forest,
Lighting up the gloomy hemlocks;
From his sleepless bed uprising,
From the bed of Minnehaha,
Stood and watched it at the doorway,

That it might not be extinguished,
Might not leave her in the darkness.

"Farewell," said he, "Minnehaha!
Farewell, O my Laughing Water!
All my heart is buried with you,
All my thoughts go onward with you;
Come not back again to labor,
Come not back again to suffer,
Where the famine and the fever
Wear the heart and waste the body.
Soon my task will be completed,
Soon your footsteps I shall follow
To the Island of the Blesséd,
To the Kingdom of Ponemah,
To the Land of the Hereafter."

MIGNON ASPIRING TO HEAVEN.

GOETHE.

SUCH let me seem till such I be;
  Take not my snow-white robe away;
Soon from the dreary earth I flee,
  Up to the glittering realms of day.

There first a little space I'll rest,
  Then ope my eyes with joyful mind,
In robes of lawn no longer dressed,
  Girdle and garland left behind.

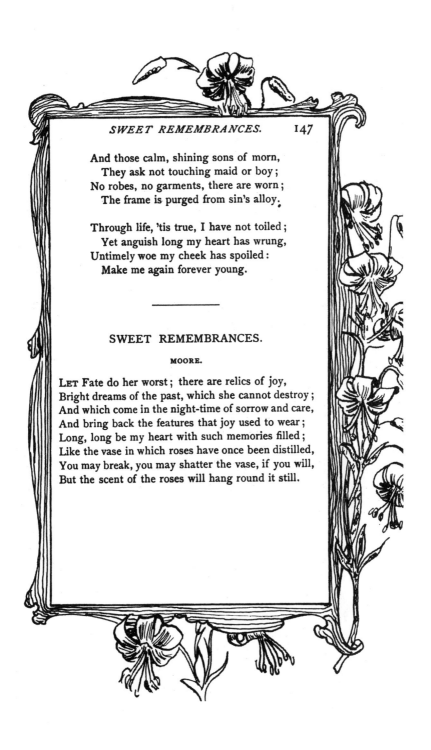

And those calm, shining sons of morn,
    They ask not touching maid or boy;
No robes, no garments, there are worn;
    The frame is purged from sin's alloy.

Through life, 'tis true, I have not toiled;
    Yet anguish long my heart has wrung,
Untimely woe my cheek has spoiled:
    Make me again forever young.

SWEET REMEMBRANCES.

MOORE.

LET Fate do her worst; there are relics of joy,
Bright dreams of the past, which she cannot destroy;
And which come in the night-time of sorrow and care,
And bring back the features that joy used to wear;
Long, long be my heart with such memories filled;
Like the vase in which roses have once been distilled,
You may break, you may shatter the vase, if you will,
But the scent of the roses will hang round it still.

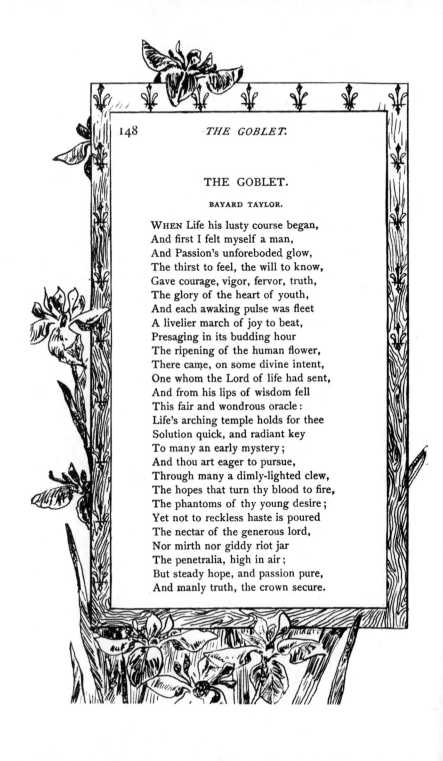

THE GOBLET.

BAYARD TAYLOR.

WHEN Life his lusty course began,
And first I felt myself a man,
And Passion's unforeboded glow,
The thirst to feel, the will to know,
Gave courage, vigor, fervor, truth,
The glory of the heart of youth,
And each awaking pulse was fleet
A livelier march of joy to beat,
Presaging in its budding hour
The ripening of the human flower,
There came, on some divine intent,
One whom the Lord of life had sent,
And from his lips of wisdom fell
This fair and wondrous oracle:
Life's arching temple holds for thee
Solution quick, and radiant key
To many an early mystery;
And thou art eager to pursue,
Through many a dimly-lighted clew,
The hopes that turn thy blood to fire,
The phantoms of thy young desire;
Yet not to reckless haste is poured
The nectar of the generous lord,
Nor mirth nor giddy riot jar
The penetralia, high in air;
But steady hope, and passion pure,
And manly truth, the crown secure.

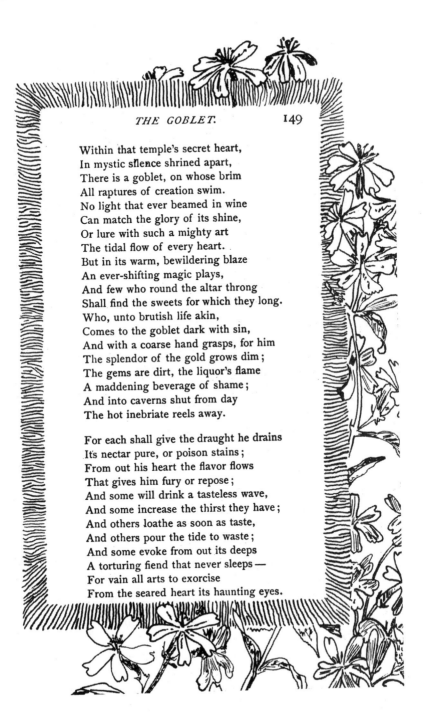

Within that temple's secret heart,
In mystic silence shrined apart,
There is a goblet, on whose brim
All raptures of creation swim.
No light that ever beamed in wine
Can match the glory of its shine,
Or lure with such a mighty art
The tidal flow of every heart.
But in its warm, bewildering blaze
An ever-shifting magic plays,
And few who round the altar throng
Shall find the sweets for which they long.
Who, unto brutish life akin,
Comes to the goblet dark with sin,
And with a coarse hand grasps, for him
The splendor of the gold grows dim;
The gems are dirt, the liquor's flame
A maddening beverage of shame;
And into caverns shut from day
The hot inebriate reels away.

For each shall give the draught he drains
Its nectar pure, or poison stains;
From out his heart the flavor flows
That gives him fury or repose;
And some will drink a tasteless wave,
And some increase the thirst they have;
And others loathe as soon as taste,
And others pour the tide to waste;
And some evoke from out its deeps
A torturing fiend that never sleeps —
For vain all arts to exorcise
From the seared heart its haunting eyes.

But he who burns with pure desire,
With chastened love and sacred fire,
With soul and being all a-glow
Life's holiest mystery to know,
Shall see the goblet flash and gleam
As in the glory of a dream ;
And from its starry lip shall drink
A bliss to lift him on the brink
Of mighty rapture, joy intense,
That far outlives its subsidence.
The draught shall strike Life's narrow goal,
And make an outlet for his soul,
That down the ages, broad and far,
Shall brighten like a rising star.
In other forms his pulse shall beat,
His spirit walk in other feet,
And every generous hope and aim
That spurred him on to honest fame,
To other hearts give warmth and grace,
And keep on earth his honored place,
Become immortal in his race.

THE DAY IS DONE.

LONGFELLOW.

THE day is done, and the darkness
 Falls from the wings of night,
As a feather is wafted downward
 From an eagle in his flight.

I see the lights of the village
  Gleam through the rain and the mist,
And a feeling of sadness comes o'er me,
  That my soul cannot resist —

A feeling of sadness and longing,
  That is not akin to pain,
And resembles sorrow only
  As the mist resembles rain.

Come read to me some poem,
  Some simple and heartfelt lay,
That shall soothe this restless feeling
  And banish the thoughts of day.

Not from the grand old masters,
  Not from the bards sublime,
Whose distant footsteps echo
  Through the corridors of time ; —

For, like strains of martial music,
  Their mighty thoughts suggest
Life's endless toil and endeavor,
  And to-night I long for rest.

Read from some humbler poet,
  Whose songs gushed from his heart,
As showers from the clouds of summer,
  Or tears from the eyelids start ; —

Who through long days of labor,
  And nights devoid of ease,

Still hear in soul the music
   Of wonderful melodies.

Such songs have power to quiet
   The restless pulse of care,
And come like the benediction
   That follows after prayer.

Then read from the treasured volume
   The poem of thy choice,
And lend to the rhyme of the poet
   The beauty of thy voice.

And the night shall be filled with music,
   And the cares, that infest the day,
Shall fold their tents, like the Arabs,
   And as silently steal away.

THOUGHTS.

BAILEY.

WE do not make our thoughts; they grow in us,
Like grain in wood; the growth is of the skies,
Which are of nature; nature is of God.
The world is full of glorious likenesses.

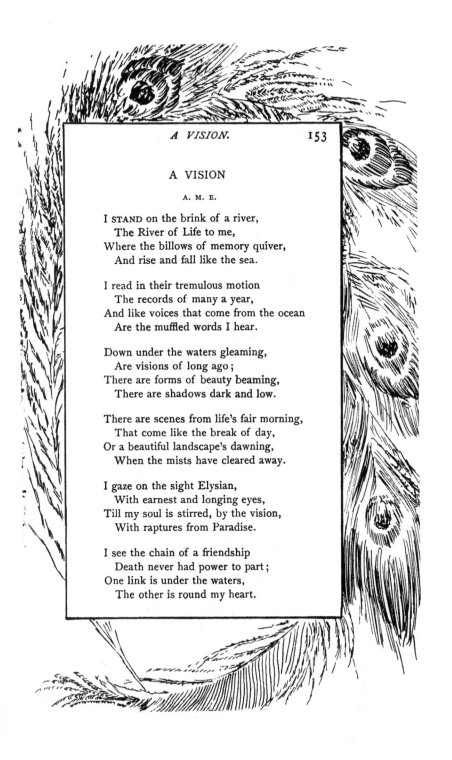

A VISION

A. M. E.

I STAND on the brink of a river,
  The River of Life to me,
Where the billows of memory quiver,
  And rise and fall like the sea.

I read in their tremulous motion
  The records of many a year,
And like voices that come from the ocean
  Are the muffled words I hear.

Down under the waters gleaming,
  Are visions of long ago;
There are forms of beauty beaming,
  There are shadows dark and low.

There are scenes from life's fair morning,
  That come like the break of day,
Or a beautiful landscape's dawning,
  When the mists have cleared away.

I gaze on the sight Elysian,
  With earnest and longing eyes,
Till my soul is stirred, by the vision,
  With raptures from Paradise.

I see the chain of a friendship
  Death never had power to part;
One link is under the waters,
  The other is round my heart.

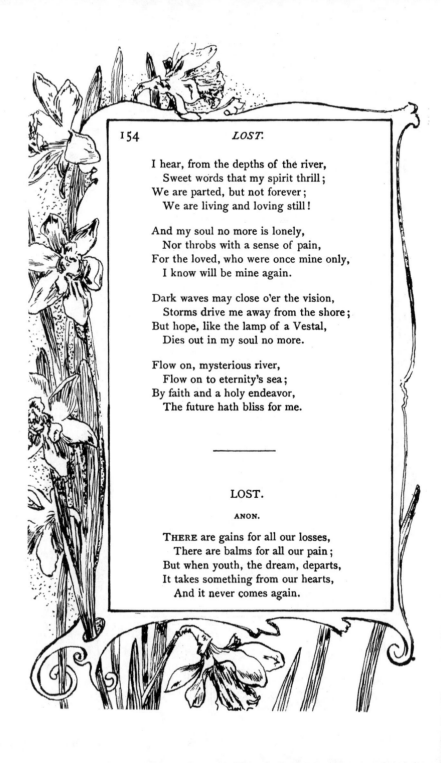

LOST.

I hear, from the depths of the river,
  Sweet words that my spirit thrill;
We are parted, but not forever;
  We are living and loving still!

And my soul no more is lonely,
  Nor throbs with a sense of pain,
For the loved, who were once mine only,
  I know will be mine again.

Dark waves may close o'er the vision,
  Storms drive me away from the shore;
But hope, like the lamp of a Vestal,
  Dies out in my soul no more.

Flow on, mysterious river,
  Flow on to eternity's sea;
By faith and a holy endeavor,
  The future hath bliss for me.

LOST.

ANON.

THERE are gains for all our losses,
  There are balms for all our pain;
But when youth, the dream, departs,
It takes something from our hearts,
  And it never comes again.

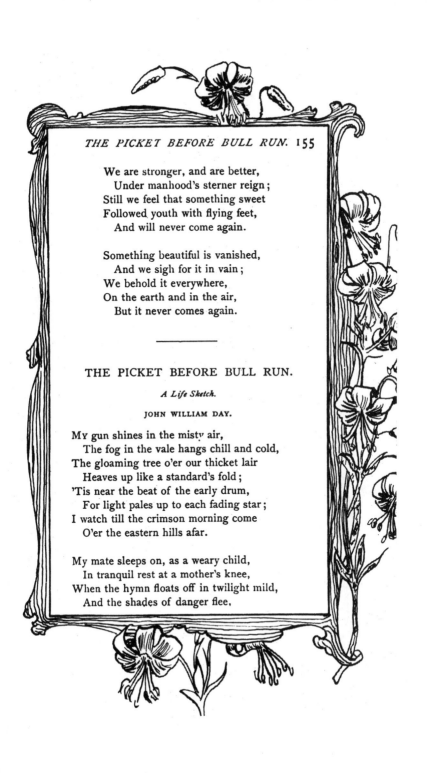

We are stronger, and are better,
  Under manhood's sterner reign;
Still we feel that something sweet
Followed youth with flying feet,
  And will never come again.

Something beautiful is vanished,
  And we sigh for it in vain;
We behold it everywhere,
On the earth and in the air,
  But it never comes again.

THE PICKET BEFORE BULL RUN.

A Life Sketch.

JOHN WILLIAM DAY.

My gun shines in the misty air,
  The fog in the vale hangs chill and cold,
The gloaming tree o'er our thicket lair
  Heaves up like a standard's fold;
'Tis near the beat of the early drum,
  For light pales up to each fading star;
I watch till the crimson morning come
  O'er the eastern hills afar.

My mate sleeps on, as a weary child,
  In tranquil rest at a mother's knee,
When the hymn floats off in twilight mild,
  And the shades of danger flee.

For him the prayers of a household band
   This night o'er the cloudy stair have striven,
Where the great archangels flaming stand,
   At the golden doors of Heaven.

'Tis still; my heart, in the early morn,
   Yearns fondly back to the closing past;
The joys of youth, in their glory born,
   As pearls from the genii cast;
The love that burned as a vestal fire,
   Though lit on a shrine of crumbling mould —
The chant of fame in a far-off choir,
   That down through the years hath rolled.

A stealthy tread in yon thicket's brow —
   'Tis the foeman stirs each weary limb;
Perchance his thought is a pilgrim now;
   Through the gates of memory dim,
He hears the plash of Edisto's wave,
   He sees the star of the morning shine
On Yarvo's breast, or evening lave
   In the tide of swift Saline.

    .   .   .   .

A shot! aha! 'tis their parting word;
   A smothered groan at my side I hear.
O, down the hill, like a prairie herd,
   They burst, with a rolling cheer;
And our captain points with waving blade,
   " Fall back, boys! back to your farm-house wall
On, on through the woodland's tangled shade! "
   Up, boy; 'tis our bugle call.

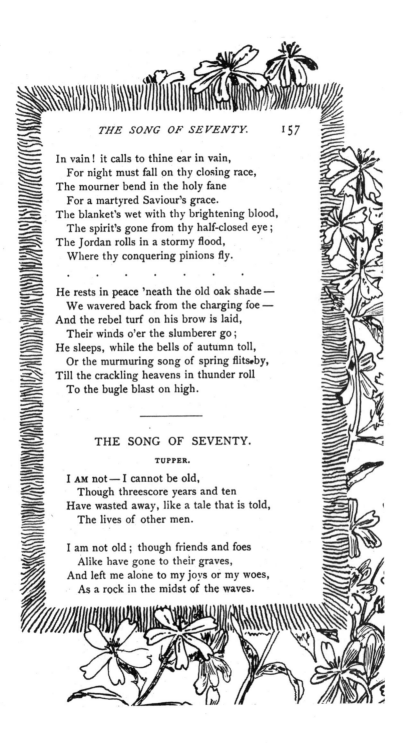

In vain ! it calls to thine ear in vain,
  For night must fall on thy closing race,
The mourner bend in the holy fane
  For a martyred Saviour's grace.
The blanket's wet with thy brightening blood,
  The spirit's gone from thy half-closed eye ;
The Jordan rolls in a stormy flood,
  Where thy conquering pinions fly.

. . . .

He rests in peace 'neath the old oak shade —
  We wavered back from the charging foe —
And the rebel turf on his brow is laid,
  Their winds o'er the slumberer go ;
He sleeps, while the bells of autumn toll,
  Or the murmuring song of spring flits by,
Till the crackling heavens in thunder roll
  To the bugle blast on high.

THE SONG OF SEVENTY.

TUPPER.

I AM not — I cannot be old,
  Though threescore years and ten
Have wasted away, like a tale that is told,
  The lives of other men.

I am not old ; though friends and foes
  Alike have gone to their graves,
And left me alone to my joys or my woes,
  As a rock in the midst of the waves.

I am not old—I cannot be old,
  Though tottering, wrinkled, and gray;
Though my eyes are dim, and my marrow is cold,
  Call me not old to-day.

For early memories round me throng,—
  Old times, and manners, and men,—
As I look behind on my journey so long,
  Of threescore miles and ten.

I look behind, and am once more young,
  Buoyant, and brave, and bold,
And my heart can sing, as of yore it sung,
  Before they called me old.

I do not see her—the old wife there—
  Shrivelled, and haggard, and gray,
But I look on her blooming, and soft, and fair
  As she was on her wedding-day!

I do not see you, daughters and sons,
  In the likeness of women and men,
But I kiss you now as I kissed you once,
  My fond little children then!

And as my grandson rides on my knee,
  Or plays with his hoop or kite,
I can well recollect I was merry as he—
  The bright-eyed little wight!

'Tis not long since—it cannot be long,
  My years so soon were spent—

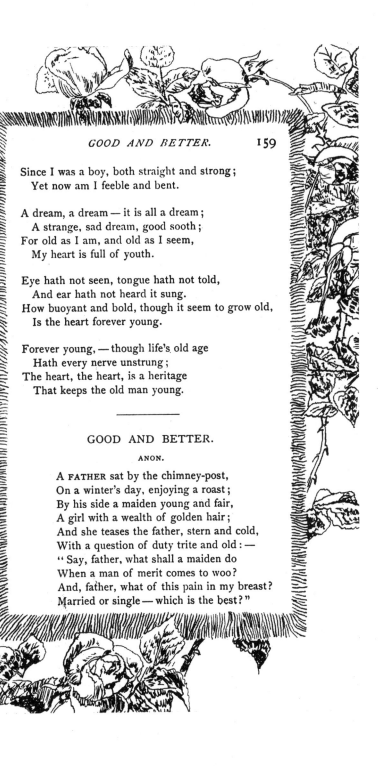

Since I was a boy, both straight and strong;
   Yet now am I feeble and bent.

A dream, a dream — it is all a dream;
   A strange, sad dream, good sooth;
For old as I am, and old as I seem,
   My heart is full of youth.

Eye hath not seen, tongue hath not told,
   And ear hath not heard it sung.
How buoyant and bold, though it seem to grow old,
   Is the heart forever young.

Forever young, — though life's old age
   Hath every nerve unstrung;
The heart, the heart, is a heritage
   That keeps the old man young.

GOOD AND BETTER.

ANON.

A FATHER sat by the chimney-post,
On a winter's day, enjoying a roast;
By his side a maiden young and fair,
A girl with a wealth of golden hair;
And she teases the father, stern and cold,
With a question of duty trite and old : —
" Say, father, what shall a maiden do
When a man of merit comes to woo?
And, father, what of this pain in my breast?
Married or single — which is the best?"

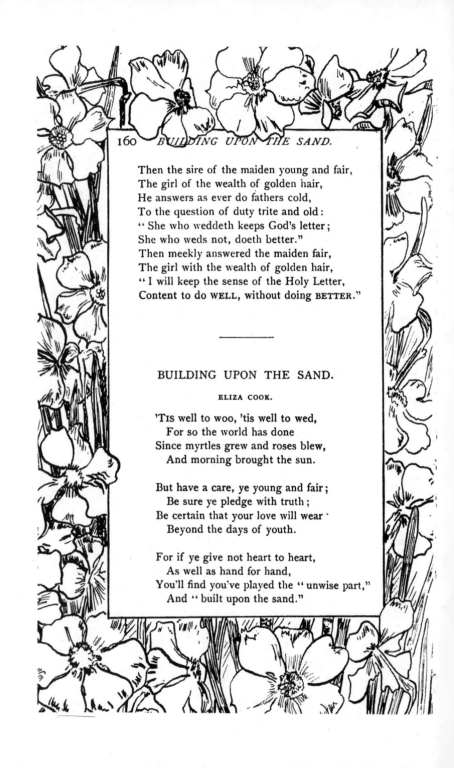

Then the sire of the maiden young and fair,
The girl of the wealth of golden hair,
He answers as ever do fathers cold,
To the question of duty trite and old:
" She who weddeth keeps God's letter;
She who weds not, doeth better."
Then meekly answered the maiden fair,
The girl with the wealth of golden hair,
" I will keep the sense of the Holy Letter,
Content to do WELL, without doing BETTER."

BUILDING UPON THE SAND.

ELIZA COOK.

'Tis well to woo, 'tis well to wed,
  For so the world has done
Since myrtles grew and roses blew,
  And morning brought the sun.

But have a care, ye young and fair;
  Be sure ye pledge with truth;
Be certain that your love will wear
  Beyond the days of youth.

For if ye give not heart to heart,
  As well as hand for hand,
You'll find you've played the " unwise part,"
  And " built upon the sand."

'Tis well to save, 'tis well to have
  A goodly store of gold,
And hold enough of sterling stuff,
  For charity is cold.

But place not all your hopes and trust
  In what the deep mine brings;
We cannot live on yellow dust,
  Unmixed with purer things.

And he who piles up wealth alone
  Will often have to stand
Behind his coffer-chest, and own
  'Tis " built upon the sand."

'Tis good to speak in kindly guise,
  And soothe whate'er we can;
For speech should bind the human mind,
  And love link man to man.

But stay not at the gentle words;
  Let deeds with language dwell;
The one who pities starving birds
  Should scatter crumbs as well.

The mercy that is warm and true
  Must lend a helping hand;
For those who talk, yet fail to do,
  But " build upon the sand."

THE ANGELS IN THE HOUSE.

ANON.

THREE pairs of dimpled arms, as white as snow,
  Held me in soft embrace ;
Three little cheeks, like velvet peaches soft,
  Were placed against my face.

Three pairs of tiny eyes, so clear, so deep,
  Looked up in mine this even ;
Three pairs of lips kissed me a sweet " Good-night,"
  Three little forms from Heaven.

Ah, it is well that " little ones " should love us ;
  It lights our faith when dim,
To know that once our blesséd Saviour bade them
  Bring " little ones " to him.

And said he not, " Of such is Heaven," and blessed
    them,
  And held them to his breast?
Is it not sweet to know that, when they leave us,
  'Tis then they go to rest?

And yet, ye tiny angels of my house,
  Three hearts encased in mine,
How 'twould be shattered if the Lord should say,
  " Those angels are not thine ! "

WOMAN'S FOUR SEASONS.

BAILEY.

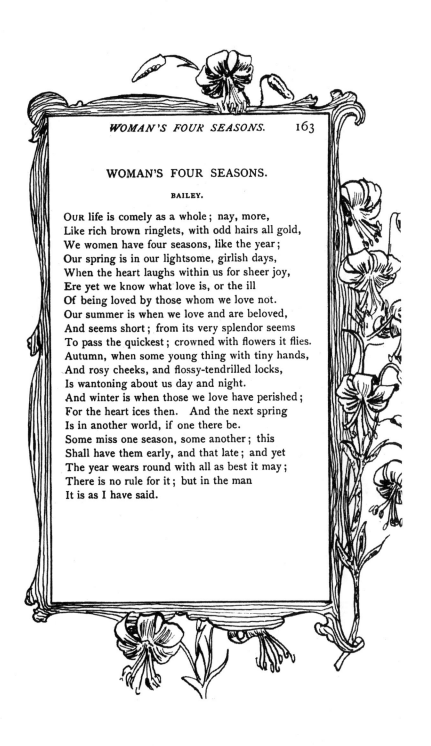

OUR life is comely as a whole; nay, more,
Like rich brown ringlets, with odd hairs all gold,
We women have four seasons, like the year;
Our spring is in our lightsome, girlish days,
When the heart laughs within us for sheer joy,
Ere yet we know what love is, or the ill
Of being loved by those whom we love not.
Our summer is when we love and are beloved,
And seems short; from its very splendor seems
To pass the quickest; crowned with flowers it flies.
Autumn, when some young thing with tiny hands,
And rosy cheeks, and flossy-tendrilled locks,
Is wantoning about us day and night.
And winter is when those we love have perished;
For the heart ices then. And the next spring
Is in another world, if one there be.
Some miss one season, some another; this
Shall have them early, and that late; and yet
The year wears round with all as best it may;
There is no rule for it; but in the man
It is as I have said.

MAUD MULLER.

WHITTIER.

MAUD MULLER, on a summer's day,
Raked the meadows sweet with hay.

Beneath her torn hat glowed the wealth
Of simple beauty and rustic health.

Singing, she wrought, and her merry glee
The mock-bird echoed from his tree.

But when she glanced to the far-off town,
White from its hill-slope looking down,

The sweet song died and a vague unrest
And a nameless longing filled her breast —

A wish, that she had hardly dared to own,
For something better than she had known.

The Judge rode slowly down the lane,
Smoothing his horse's chestnut mane.

He drew his bridle in the shade
Of the apple-trees, to greet the maid,

And ask a draught from the spring that flowed
Through the meadow across the road.

She stooped where the cool spring bubbled up,
And filled for him her small tin cup,

And blushed as she gave it, looking down
On her feet so bare, and her tattered gown.

Then said the Judge, "A sweeter draught
From a fairer hand was never quaffed."

He spoke of the grass and flowers and trees,
Of the singing birds and the humming bees;

Then talked of the haying, and wondered whether
The cloud in the west would bring foul weather.

And Maud forgot her brier-torn gown,
And her graceful ankles, bare and brown,

And listened, while a pleased surprise
Looked from her long-lashed hazel eyes.

At last, like one who for delay
Seeks a vain excuse, he rode away.

Maud Muller looked, and sighed: "Ah me!
That I the Judge's bride might be!

"He would dress me up in silks so fine,
And praise and toast me at his wine.

"My father should wear a broadcloth coat;
My brother should sail a painted boat;

"I'd dress my mother so grand and gay,
And the baby should have a new toy each day,

"And I'd feed the hungry and clothe the poor,
And all should bless me who left our door."

The Judge looked back as he climbed the hill,
And saw Maud Muller standing still.

"A form more fair, a face more sweet,
Ne'er hath it been my lot to meet;

"And her modest and graceful air
Shows her wise and good as she is fair.

"Would she were mine, and I to-day,
Like her, a harvester of hay;

"No doubtful balance of rights and wrongs,
Nor weary lawyers with endless tongues,

"But low of cattle and song of birds,
And health and quiet and loving words."

But he thought of his sisters, proud and cold,
And his mother, vain of her rank and gold.

So, closing his heart, the Judge rode on,
And Maud was left in the field alone.

But the lawyers smiled that afternoon,
When he hummed in court an old love-tune;

And the young girl mused beside the well,
Till the rain on the unraked clover fell.

He wedded a wife of richest dower,
Who lived for fashion, as he for power.

Yet oft, in his marble hearth's bright glow,
He watched a picture come and go;

And sweet Maud Muller's hazel eyes
Looked out in their innocent surprise.

Oft when the wine in his glass was red,
He longed for the wayside rill instead,

And closed his eyes on his garnished rooms,
To dream of meadows and clover-blooms.

And the proud man sighed with a secret pain,
"Ah, that I was free again!

" Free as when I rode that day
Where the barefoot maiden raked her hay."

She wedded a man unlearned and poor,
And many children played round her door;

But care and sorrow and childbirth pain
Left their traces on heart and brain.

And oft, when the summer sun shone hot
On the new-mown hay in the meadow lot,

And she heard the little spring-brook fall
Over the roadside, through the wall,

In the shade of the apple-tree again
She saw a rider draw his rein,

And, gazing down with tender grace,
She felt his pleased eyes read her face.

Sometimes her narrow kitchen walls
Stretched away into stately halls;

The weary wheel to a spinet turned,
The tallow candle an astral burned.

And for him who sat by the chimney log,
Dozing and grumbling o'er pipe and mug,

A manly form at her side she saw,
And joy was duty, and love was law.

Then she took up her burden of life again,
Saying only, " It might have been."

Alas for maiden, alas for Judge,
For rich repiner and household drudge!

God pity them both! and pity us all,
Who vainly the dreams of youth recall.

For of all sad words of tongue or pen,
The saddest are these: " It might have been!"

Ah, well! for us all some sweet hope lies
Deeply buried from human eyes;

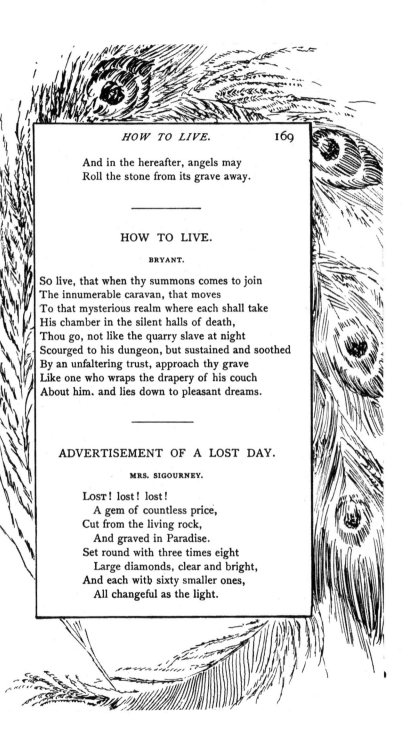

And in the hereafter, angels may
Roll the stone from its grave away.

HOW TO LIVE.

BRYANT.

So live, that when thy summons comes to join
The innumerable caravan, that moves
To that mysterious realm where each shall take
His chamber in the silent halls of death,
Thou go, not like the quarry slave at night
Scourged to his dungeon, but sustained and soothed
By an unfaltering trust, approach thy grave
Like one who wraps the drapery of his couch
About him. and lies down to pleasant dreams.

ADVERTISEMENT OF A LOST DAY.

MRS. SIGOURNEY.

LOST! lost! lost!
    A gem of countless price,
Cut from the living rock,
    And graved in Paradise.
Set round with three times eight
    Large diamonds, clear and bright,
And each with sixty smaller ones,
    All changeful as the light.

Lost — where the thoughtless throng
   In fashion's mazes wind,
Where trilleth folly's song,
   Leaving a sting behind;
Yet to my hand 'twas given
   A golden harp to buy,
Such as the white-robed choir attune
   To deathless minstrelsy.

Lost! lost! lost!
   I feel all search is vain;
That gem of countless cost
   Can ne'er be mine again.
I offer no reward,
   For till these heart-strings sever,
I know that Heaven-intrusted gift
   Is reft away forever.

But when the sea and land
   Like burning scroll have fled,
I'll see it in His hand
   Who judgeth quick and dead;
And when of scath and loss
   That man can ne'er repair,
The dread inquiry meets my soul,
   What shall it answer there?

THE WRECK.

MRS. HEMANS.

ALL night the booming minute gun
   Had pealed along the deep,
And mournfully the rising sun
   Looked o'er the tide-worn steep.
A bark from India's coral strand,
   Before the raging blast,
Had vailed her topsails to the sand,
   And bowed her noble mast.

The queenly ship! brave hearts had striven,
   And true ones died with her!
We saw her mighty cable riven
   Like floating gossamer.
We saw her proud flag struck that morn,
   A star once o'er the seas —
Her anchor gone, her deck uptorn —
   And sadder things than these!

We saw her treasures cast away;
   The rocks with pearls were sown,
And, strangely sad, the ruby's ray
   Flashed out o'er fretted stone.
And gold was strewn the wet sands o'er,
   Like ashes by a breeze;
And gorgeous robes — but O, that shore
   Had sadder things than these.

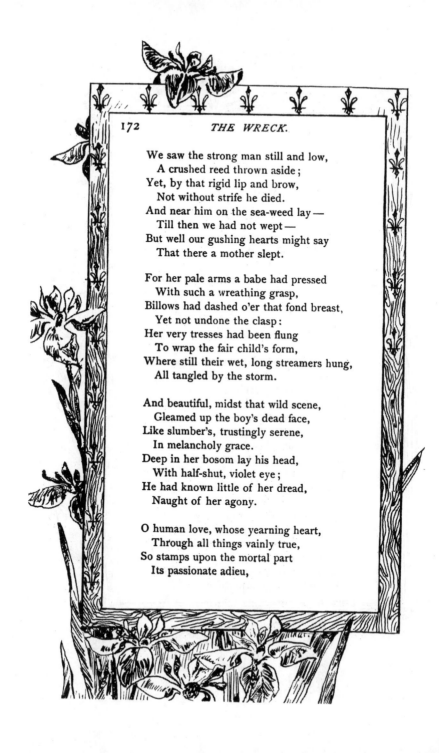

We saw the strong man still and low,
  A crushed reed thrown aside;
Yet, by that rigid lip and brow,
  Not without strife he died.
And near him on the sea-weed lay —
  Till then we had not wept —
But well our gushing hearts might say
  That there a mother slept.

For her pale arms a babe had pressed
  With such a wreathing grasp,
Billows had dashed o'er that fond breast,
  Yet not undone the clasp:
Her very tresses had been flung
  To wrap the fair child's form,
Where still their wet, long streamers hung,
  All tangled by the storm.

And beautiful, midst that wild scene,
  Gleamed up the boy's dead face,
Like slumber's, trustingly serene,
  In melancholy grace.
Deep in her bosom lay his head,
  With half-shut, violet eye;
He had known little of her dread,
  Naught of her agony.

O human love, whose yearning heart,
  Through all things vainly true,
So stamps upon the mortal part
  Its passionate adieu,

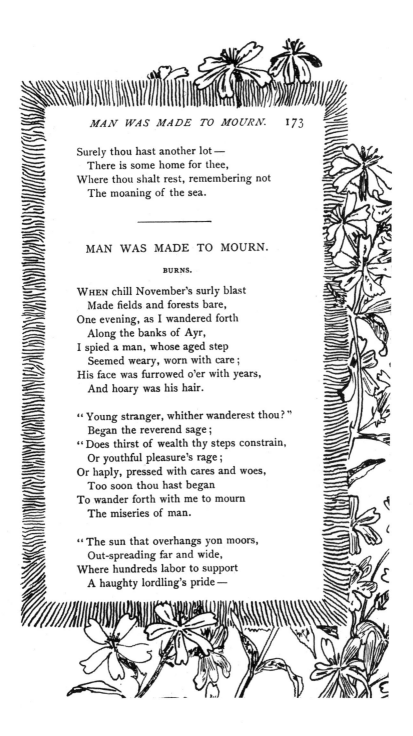

Surely thou hast another lot —
  There is some home for thee,
Where thou shalt rest, remembering not
  The moaning of the sea.

MAN WAS MADE TO MOURN.

BURNS.

WHEN chill November's surly blast
  Made fields and forests bare,
One evening, as I wandered forth
  Along the banks of Ayr,
I spied a man, whose aged step
  Seemed weary, worn with care;
His face was furrowed o'er with years,
  And hoary was his hair.

"Young stranger, whither wanderest thou?"
  Began the reverend sage;
"Does thirst of wealth thy steps constrain,
  Or youthful pleasure's rage;
Or haply, pressed with cares and woes,
  Too soon thou hast began
To wander forth with me to mourn
  The miseries of man.

"The sun that overhangs yon moors,
  Out-spreading far and wide,
Where hundreds labor to support
  A haughty lordling's pride —

I've seen yon weary winter's sun
    Twice forty times return;
And every time has added proofs
    That man was made to mourn.

" O man! while in thy early years
    How prodigal of time!
Mis-spending all thy precious hours,
    Thy glorious youthful prime;
Alternate follies take the sway,
    Licentious passions burn;
Which tenfold force gives nature's law,
    That man was made to mourn.

" Look not alone on youthful prime,
    Or manhood's active might;
Man then is useful to his kind,
    Supported in his right;
But see him on the edge of life,
    With cares and sorrows worn;
Then age and want — O, ill-matched pair —
    Show man was made to mourn.

" A few seem favorites of Fate,
    In Pleasure's lap carest;
Yet think not all the rich and great
    Are likewise truly blest.
But O, what crowds in every land
    Are wretched and forlorn!
Through weary life this lesson learn,
    That man was made to mourn.

" Many and sharp the numerous ills
   Inwoven with our frame!
More pointed still we make ourselves,
   Regret, remorse, and shame!
And man, whose heaven-erected face
   The smiles of love adorn,
Man's inhumanity to man
   Makes countless thousands mourn.

" See yonder poor, o'erlabored wight,
   So abject, mean, and vile,
Who begs a brother of the earth
   To give him leave to toil;
And see his lordly fellow-worm
   The poor petition spurn,
Unmindful, though a weeping wife
   And helpless offspring mourn.

" If I'm designed yon lordling's slave, —
   By nature's law designed, —
Why was an independent wish
   E'er planted in my mind?
If not, why am I subject to
   His cruelty or scorn?
Or why has man the will and power
   To make his fellow mourn?

" Yet, let not this too much, my son,
   Disturb thy youthful breast;
This partial view of human kind
   Is surely not the best!

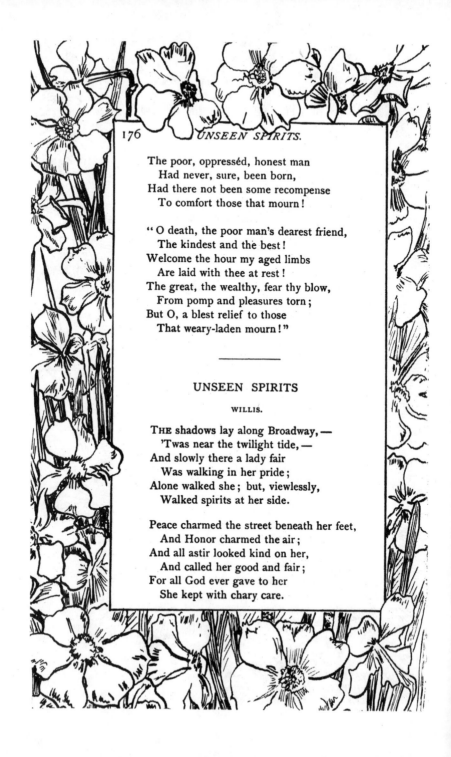

The poor, oppresséd, honest man
  Had never, sure, been born,
Had there not been some recompense
  To comfort those that mourn!

" O death, the poor man's dearest friend,
  The kindest and the best!
Welcome the hour my aged limbs
  Are laid with thee at rest!
The great, the wealthy, fear thy blow,
  From pomp and pleasures torn;
But O, a blest relief to those
  That weary-laden mourn!"

UNSEEN SPIRITS

WILLIS.

THE shadows lay along Broadway, —
  'Twas near the twilight tide, —
And slowly there a lady fair
  Was walking in her pride;
Alone walked she; but, viewlessly,
  Walked spirits at her side.

Peace charmed the street beneath her feet,
  And Honor charmed the air;
And all astir looked kind on her,
  And called her good and fair;
For all God ever gave to her
  She kept with chary care.

She kept with care her beauties rare
 From lovers warm and true;
For her heart was cold to all but gold,
 And the rich came not to woo:
But honored well are charms to sell,
 If priests the selling do.

Now walking there was one more fair, —
 A slight girl, lily pale;
And she had unseen company
 To make the spirit quail:
'Twixt Want and Scorn she walked forlorn,
 And nothing could avail.

No mercy now can clear her brow
 For this world's peace to pray;
For, as love's wild prayer dissolved in air,
 Her woman's heart gave way;
But the sin forgiven by Christ in heaven,
 By man is cursed alway.

THE TRUE MEASURE OF LIFE.

P. J. BAILEY.

WE live in deeds, not years; in thoughts, not breath;
In feelings, not in figures on the dial.
We should count time by heart-throbs when they beat
For God, for man, for duty. He most lives,
Who thinks most, feels noblest, acts the best.
Life is but a means unto an end — that end,
Beginning, mean, and end to all things, God.

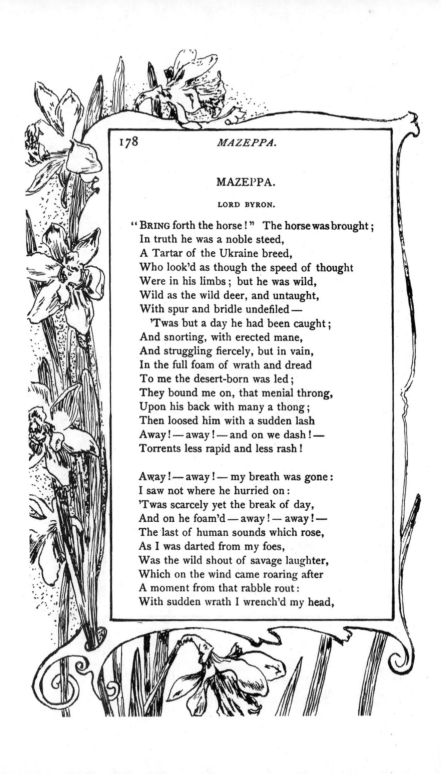

MAZEPPA.

LORD BYRON.

" Bring forth the horse ! " The horse was brought ;
In truth he was a noble steed,
A Tartar of the Ukraine breed,
Who look'd as though the speed of thought
Were in his limbs ; but he was wild,
Wild as the wild deer, and untaught,
With spur and bridle undefiled —
  'Twas but a day he had been caught ;
And snorting, with erected mane,
And struggling fiercely, but in vain,
In the full foam of wrath and dread
To me the desert-born was led ;
They bound me on, that menial throng,
Upon his back with many a thong ;
Then loosed him with a sudden lash
Away ! — away ! — and on we dash ! —
Torrents less rapid and less rash !

Away ! — away ! — my breath was gone :
I saw not where he hurried on :
'Twas scarcely yet the break of day,
And on he foam'd — away ! — away ! —
The last of human sounds which rose,
As I was darted from my foes,
Was the wild shout of savage laughter,
Which on the wind came roaring after
A moment from that rabble rout :
With sudden wrath I wrench'd my head,

And snapp'd the cord which to the mane
Had bound my neck in lieu of rein,
And, writhing half my form about,
Howl'd back my curse; but midst the tread,
The thunder of my courser's speed,
Perchance they did not hear nor heed:
It vexes me — for I would fain
Have paid their insult back again.
I paid it well in after days:
There is not of that castle-gate,
Its drawbridge and portcullis' weight,
Stone, bar, moat, bridge, or barrier left;
Nor of its field a blade of grass,
   Save what grows on a ridge of wall,
   Where stood the hearthstone of the hall;
And many a time ye there might pass,
Nor dream that e'er that fortress was:
I saw its turrets in a blaze,
Their crackling battlements all cleft,
   And the hot lead pour down like rain
From off the scorch'd and blackening roof,
Whose thickness was not vengeance-proof.
   They little thought that day of pain,
When launch'd, as on the lightning's flash,
They bade me to destruction dash,
   That one day I should come again,
With twice five thousand horse, to thank
   The Count for his uncourteous ride.
They play'd me then a bitter prank,
   When, with the wild horse for my guide,
They bound me to his foaming flank:
At length I play'd them one as frank —

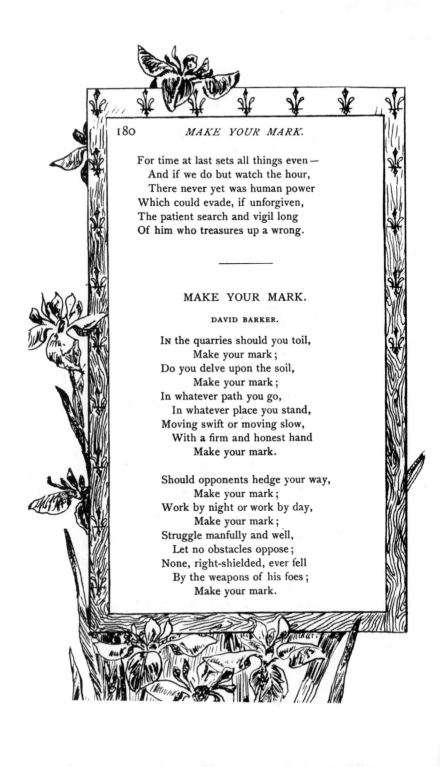

For time at last sets all things even —
And if we do but watch the hour,
There never yet was human power
Which could evade, if unforgiven,
The patient search and vigil long
Of him who treasures up a wrong.

MAKE YOUR MARK.

DAVID BARKER.

In the quarries should you toil,
   Make your mark ;
Do you delve upon the soil,
   Make your mark ;
In whatever path you go,
   In whatever place you stand,
Moving swift or moving slow,
   With a firm and honest hand
   Make your mark.

Should opponents hedge your way,
   Make your mark ;
Work by night or work by day,
   Make your mark ;
Struggle manfully and well,
   Let no obstacles oppose ;
None, right-shielded, ever fell
   By the weapons of his foes ;
   Make your mark.

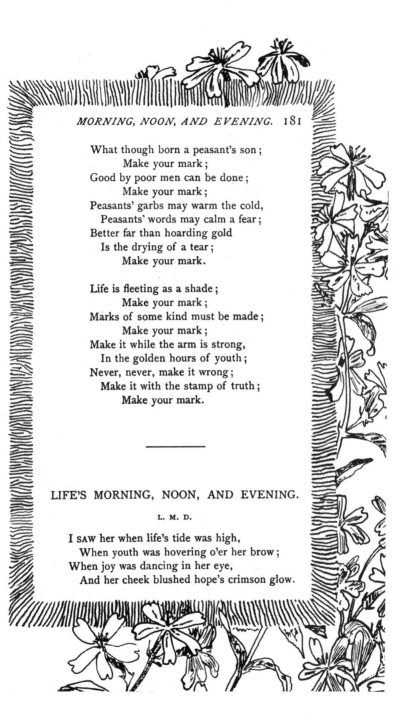

What though born a peasant's son;
   Make your mark;
Good by poor men can be done;
   Make your mark;
Peasants' garbs may warm the cold,
   Peasants' words may calm a fear;
Better far than hoarding gold
   Is the drying of a tear;
   Make your mark.

Life is fleeting as a shade;
   Make your mark;
Marks of some kind must be made;
   Make your mark;
Make it while the arm is strong,
   In the golden hours of youth;
Never, never, make it wrong;
   Make it with the stamp of truth;
   Make your mark.

LIFE'S MORNING, NOON, AND EVENING.

L. M. D.

I SAW her when life's tide was high,
   When youth was hovering o'er her brow;
When joy was dancing in her eye,
   And her cheek blushed hope's crimson glow.

I saw her mid a fairy throng;
  She seemed the gayest of the gay;
I saw her lightly glide along,
  'Neath beauty's smile and pleasure's lay.

I saw her in her bridal robe;
  The blush of joy was mounting high;
I marked her bosom's heaving throb,
  I marked her dark and downcast eye.

I saw her when a mother's love
  Asked at her hand a mother's care;
She looked an angel from above,
  Hovering around a cherub fair.

I saw her not till, cold and pale,
  She slumbered on Death's icy arm;
The rose had faded on her cheek,
  Her lip had lost its power to charm.

That eye was dim which brightly shone,
  That brow was cold, that heart was still;
The witcheries of that form had flown,
  The lifeless clay had ceased to feel.

I saw her wedded to the grave;
  Her bridal robes were weeds of death;
And o'er her pale, cold brow was hung
  The damp, sepulchral, icy wreath.

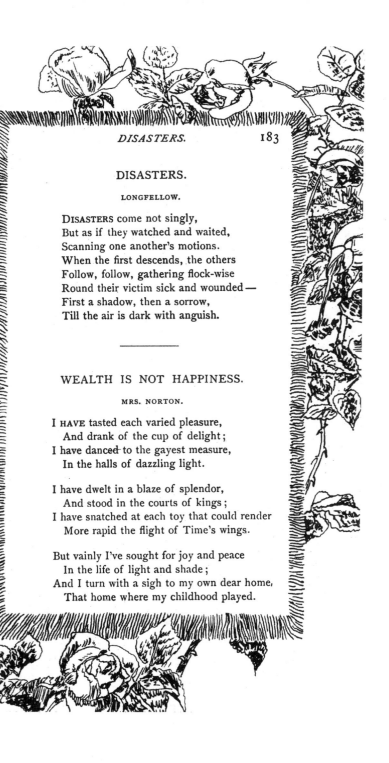

DISASTERS.

LONGFELLOW.

DISASTERS come not singly,
But as if they watched and waited,
Scanning one another's motions.
When the first descends, the others
Follow, follow, gathering flock-wise
Round their victim sick and wounded —
First a shadow, then a sorrow,
Till the air is dark with anguish.

WEALTH IS NOT HAPPINESS.

MRS. NORTON.

I HAVE tasted each varied pleasure,
  And drank of the cup of delight;
I have danced to the gayest measure,
  In the halls of dazzling light.

I have dwelt in a blaze of splendor,
  And stood in the courts of kings;
I have snatched at each toy that could render
  More rapid the flight of Time's wings.

But vainly I've sought for joy and peace
  In the life of light and shade;
And I turn with a sigh to my own dear home,
  That home where my childhood played.

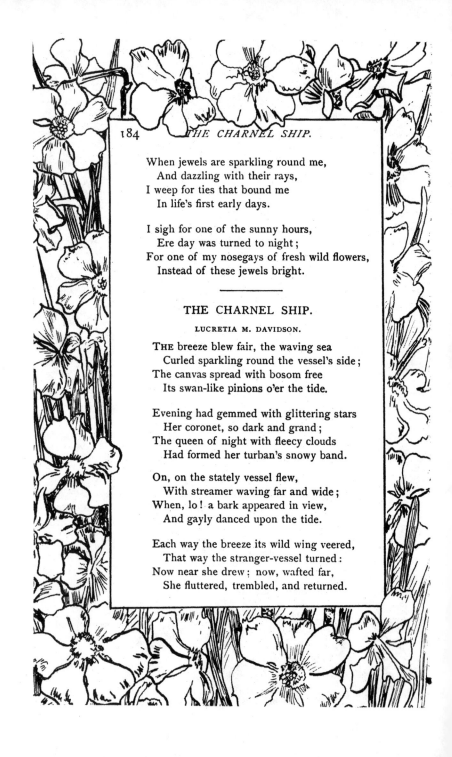

When jewels are sparkling round me,
  And dazzling with their rays,
I weep for ties that bound me
  In life's first early days.

I sigh for one of the sunny hours,
  Ere day was turned to night;
For one of my nosegays of fresh wild flowers,
  Instead of these jewels bright.

THE CHARNEL SHIP.

LUCRETIA M. DAVIDSON.

THE breeze blew fair, the waving sea
  Curled sparkling round the vessel's side;
The canvas spread with bosom free
  Its swan-like pinions o'er the tide.

Evening had gemmed with glittering stars
  Her coronet, so dark and grand;
The queen of night with fleecy clouds
  Had formed her turban's snowy band.

On, on the stately vessel flew,
  With streamer waving far and wide;
When, lo! a bark appeared in view,
  And gayly danced upon the tide.

Each way the breeze its wild wing veered,
  That way the stranger-vessel turned:
Now near she drew; now, wafted far,
  She fluttered, trembled, and returned.

" It is the pirate's curséd bark !
  The villains linger to decoy ;
Thus bounding o'er the waters dark,
  They seek to lure, and then destroy.

" Perchance those strange and wayward signs
  May be the signals of distress,"
The captain cried ; " for, mark ye, now,
  Her sails are flapping wide and loose."

And now the stranger-vessel came
  Near to that gay and gallant bark ;
It seemed a wanderer, fair and lone,
  Upon life's wave, so deep and dark.

And not a murmur, not a sound,
  Came from that lone and dreary ship ;
The icy chains of silence bound
  Each rayless eye and pallid lip.

For Death's wing had been waving there ;
  The cold dew hung on every brow,
And sparkled there, like angel tears,
  Shed o'er the silent crew below.

Onward that ship was gayly flying,
  Its bosom the sailor's grave ;
The breeze, 'mid the shrouds, in low notes sighing
  Their requiem over the brave.

Fly on, fly on, thou lone vessel of death,
  Fly on with thy desolate crew ;
For mermaids are twining a sea-weed wreath
  'Mong the red coral groves for you.

A HOME TO REST IN.

MORFORD.

THE world, dear John, as the old folks told us,
  Is a world of trouble and care;
Many a cloud of grief will enfold us,
  And the sunshine of joy is but rare.
But there's something yet to be bright and blest in,
  No matter how humble the lot;
The world still gives us a home to rest in,
  Its holiest, happiest spot.

Sweet home! dear home! on the northern heather,
  On the sunniest southern plain;
The Lapland hut in its wintry weather,
  The tent of the Indian main;
Be it gorgeous wealth that our temple is drest in,
  Be it poor and of little worth,
O home, *our* home — a home to rest in —
  Is the dearest thing on earth.

But time, dear John, is using us badly;
  Our homes crumble day by day,
And we're laying our dear ones, swiftly and sadly,
  In the dust of the valley away.
There's a death robe soon for us both to rest in,
  A place for us under the sod;
Be heaven at last the home we shall rest in,
  The rest for the children of God!

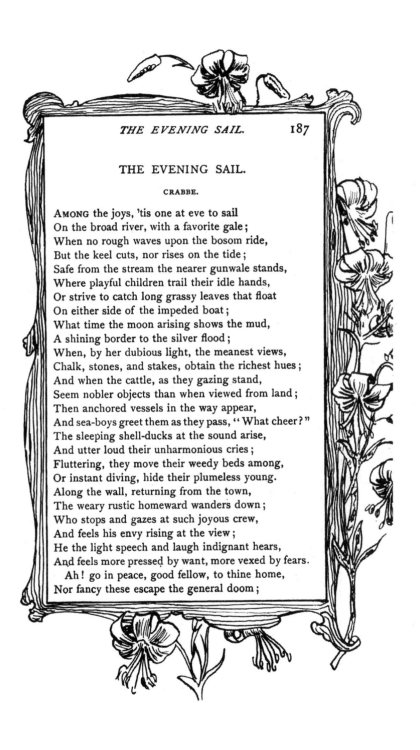

THE EVENING SAIL.

CRABBE.

AMONG the joys, 'tis one at eve to sail
On the broad river, with a favorite gale;
When no rough waves upon the bosom ride,
But the keel cuts, nor rises on the tide;
Safe from the stream the nearer gunwale stands,
Where playful children trail their idle hands,
Or strive to catch long grassy leaves that float
On either side of the impeded boat;
What time the moon arising shows the mud,
A shining border to the silver flood;
When, by her dubious light, the meanest views,
Chalk, stones, and stakes, obtain the richest hues;
And when the cattle, as they gazing stand,
Seem nobler objects than when viewed from land;
Then anchored vessels in the way appear,
And sea-boys greet them as they pass, "What cheer?"
The sleeping shell-ducks at the sound arise,
And utter loud their unharmonious cries;
Fluttering, they move their weedy beds among,
Or instant diving, hide their plumeless young.
Along the wall, returning from the town,
The weary rustic homeward wanders down;
Who stops and gazes at such joyous crew,
And feels his envy rising at the view;
He the light speech and laugh indignant hears,
And feels more pressed by want, more vexed by fears.
  Ah! go in peace, good fellow, to thine home,
Nor fancy these escape the general doom;

Gay as they seem, be sure with them are hearts
With sorrow tried; there's sadness in their parts:
If thou couldst see them when they think alone,
Mirth, music, friends, and those amusements gone;
Couldst thou discover every secret ill
That pains their spirit, or resists their will;
Couldst thou behold forsaken Love's distress,
Or Envy's pang at glory and success,
Or Beauty, conscious of the spoils of Time,
Or Guilt alarmed when Memory shows the crime;
All that gives sorrow, terror, grief, and gloom;
Content would cheer thee trudging to thine home.
　There are, 'tis true, who lay their cares aside,
And bid some hours in calm enjoyment glide;
Perchance some fair one to the sober night
Adds (by the sweetness of her song) delight;
And as the music on the water floats,
Some bolder shore returns the softened notes;
Then, youth, beware, for all around conspire
To banish caution and to wake desire;
The day's amusement, feasting, beauty, wine,
These accents sweet and this soft hour combine,
When most unguarded, then to win that heart of thine
But see, they land! the fond enchantment flies,
And in its place life's common views arise.

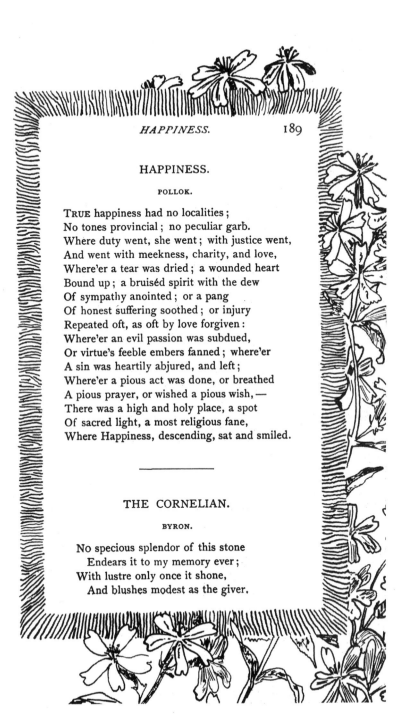

HAPPINESS.

POLLOK.

TRUE happiness had no localities;
No tones provincial; no peculiar garb.
Where duty went, she went; with justice went,
And went with meekness, charity, and love,
Where'er a tear was dried; a wounded heart
Bound up; a bruiséd spirit with the dew
Of sympathy anointed; or a pang
Of honest suffering soothed; or injury
Repeated oft, as oft by love forgiven:
Where'er an evil passion was subdued,
Or virtue's feeble embers fanned; where'er
A sin was heartily abjured, and left;
Where'er a pious act was done, or breathed
A pious prayer, or wished a pious wish, —
There was a high and holy place, a spot
Of sacred light, a most religious fane,
Where Happiness, descending, sat and smiled.

THE CORNELIAN.

BYRON.

No specious splendor of this stone
   Endears it to my memory ever;
With lustre only once it shone,
   And blushes modest as the giver.

THE CORNELIAN.

Some, who can sneer at friendship's ties,
  Have for my weakness oft reproved me;
Yet still the simple gift I prize,
  For I am sure the giver loved me.

He offered it with downcast look,
  As fearful that I might refuse it;
I told him, when the gift I took,
  My only fear should be to lose it.

This pledge attentively I viewed,
  And sparkling as I held it near,
Methought one drop the stone bedewed,
  And ever since I've loved a tear.

Still to adorn his humble youth,
  Nor wealth nor birth their treasures yield;
But he who seeks the flowers of truth
  Must quit the garden for the field.

'Tis not the plant upreared in sloth
  Which beauty shows, and sheds perfume;
The flowers which yield the most of both
  In Nature's wild luxuriance bloom.

Had Fortune aided Nature's care,
  For once forgetting to be blind,
His would have been an ample share;
  If well-proportioned to his mind.

But had the goddess clearly seen,
  His form had fixed her fickle breast,
Her countless hoards would his have been,
  And none remained to give the rest.

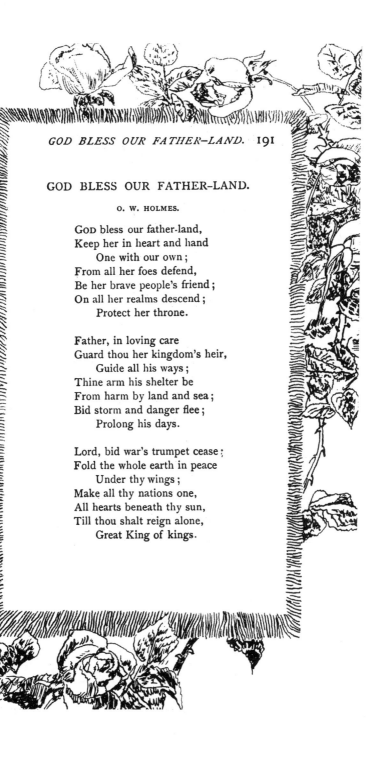

GOD BLESS OUR FATHER-LAND.

O. W. HOLMES.

GOD bless our father-land,
Keep her in heart and hand
   One with our own;
From all her foes defend,
Be her brave people's friend;
On all her realms descend;
   Protect her throne.

Father, in loving care
Guard thou her kingdom's heir,
   Guide all his ways;
Thine arm his shelter be
From harm by land and sea;
Bid storm and danger flee;
   Prolong his days.

Lord, bid war's trumpet cease;
Fold the whole earth in peace
   Under thy wings;
Make all thy nations one,
All hearts beneath thy sun,
Till thou shalt reign alone,
   Great King of kings.

ONLY ONE LIFE.

ANON.

'Tis not for man to trifle: life is brief,
　　And sin is here.
Our age is but the falling of a leaf,
　　A dropping tear.
We have no time to sport away the hours;
All must be earnest in a world like ours.

Not *many* lives, but only *one* have we;
　　One, only one.
How sacred should that one life ever be—
Day after day filled up with blessed toil,
Hour after hour still bringing in new spoil!

THE MAY QUEEN.

ALFRED TENNYSON.

PART FIRST.

You must wake and call me early, call me early,
　　mother dear;
To-morrow 'ill be the happiest time of all the glad
　　new year;
Of all the glad new year, mother, the maddest,
　　merriest day;
For I'm to be Queen o' the May, mother, I'm to be
　　Queen o' the May.

I sleep so sound all night, mother, that I shall never
    wake,
If you do not call me loud, when the day begins to
    break;
But I must gather knots of flowers, and buds and
    garlands gay,
For I'm to be Queen o' the May, mother, I'm to be
    Queen o' the May.

.   .   .

Little Effie shall go with me to-morrow to the green,
And you'll be there too, mother, to see me made the
    Queen;
For the shepherd lads on every side 'ill come from
    far away,
And I'm to be Queen o' the May, mother, I'm to be
    Queen o' the May.

.   .   .

All the valley, mother, 'ill be fresh, and green, and still,
And the cowslip and the crowfoot are over all the hill,
And the rivulet in the flowery dale 'ill merrily glance
    and play,
For I'm to be Queen o' the May, mother, I'm to be
    Queen o' the May.

So you must wake and call me early, call me early,
    mother dear;
To-morrow 'ill be the happiest time of all the glad
    new year;
To-morrow 'ill be of all the year the maddest, merriest
    day,
For I'm to be Queen o' the May, mother, I'm to be
    Queen o' the May.

PART SECOND — NEW YEAR'S EVE.

If you're waking, call me early, call me early, mother
dear;
For I would see the sun rise upon the glad new year;
It is the last new year that I shall ever see;
Then you may lay me low i' the mould, and think no
more of me.

To-night I saw the sun set; he set and left behind
The good old year, the dear old time, and all my
peace of mind;
And the new year's coming up, mother, but I shall
never see
The blossom on the blackthorn, the leaf upon the tree.

. . .

There's not a flower on all the hills; the frost is on
the pane;
I only wish to live till the snowdrops come again;
I wish the snow would melt, and the sun come out
on high;
I long to see a flower so before the day I die.

The building rook 'ill caw from the windy, tall elm-tree,
And the tufted plover pipe along the fallow lea,
And the swallow 'ill come back again with summer
o'er the wave,
But I shall lie alone, mother, within the mouldering
grave.

. . .

When the flowers come again, mother, beneath the
waning light,
You'll never see me more in the long, gray fields at
night;

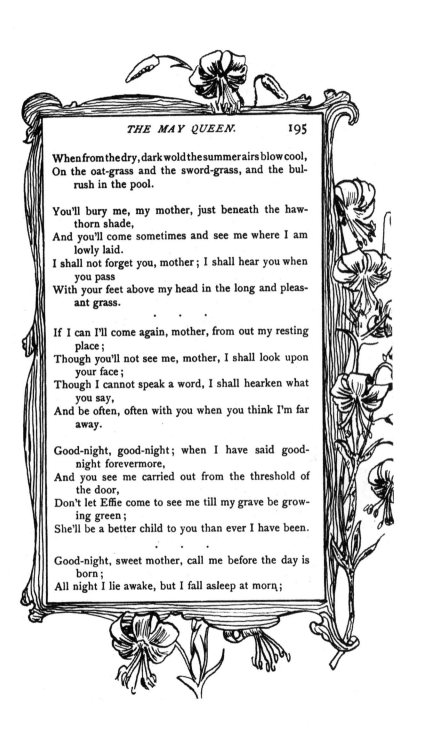

When from the dry, dark wold the summer airs blow cool,
On the oat-grass and the sword-grass, and the bul-
rush in the pool.

You'll bury me, my mother, just beneath the haw-
thorn shade,
And you'll come sometimes and see me where I am
lowly laid.
I shall not forget you, mother; I shall hear you when
you pass
With your feet above my head in the long and pleas-
ant grass.

. . .

If I can I'll come again, mother, from out my resting
place;
Though you'll not see me, mother, I shall look upon
your face;
Though I cannot speak a word, I shall hearken what
you say,
And be often, often with you when you think I'm far
away.

Good-night, good-night; when I have said good-
night forevermore,
And you see me carried out from the threshold of
the door,
Don't let Effie come to see me till my grave be grow-
ing green;
She'll be a better child to you than ever I have been.

. . .

Good-night, sweet mother, call me before the day is
born;
All night I lie awake, but I fall asleep at morn;

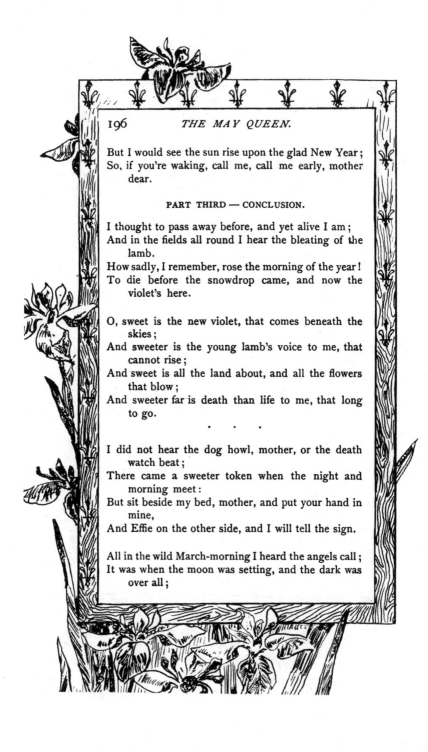

But I would see the sun rise upon the glad New Year;
So, if you're waking, call me, call me early, mother
dear.

PART THIRD — CONCLUSION.

I thought to pass away before, and yet alive I am;
And in the fields all round I hear the bleating of the
lamb.
How sadly, I remember, rose the morning of the year!
To die before the snowdrop came, and now the
violet's here.

O, sweet is the new violet, that comes beneath the
skies;
And sweeter is the young lamb's voice to me, that
cannot rise;
And sweet is all the land about, and all the flowers
that blow;
And sweeter far is death than life to me, that long
to go.

.   .   .

I did not hear the dog howl, mother, or the death
watch beat;
There came a sweeter token when the night and
morning meet:
But sit beside my bed, mother, and put your hand in
mine,
And Effie on the other side, and I will tell the sign.

All in the wild March-morning I heard the angels call;
It was when the moon was setting, and the dark was
over all;

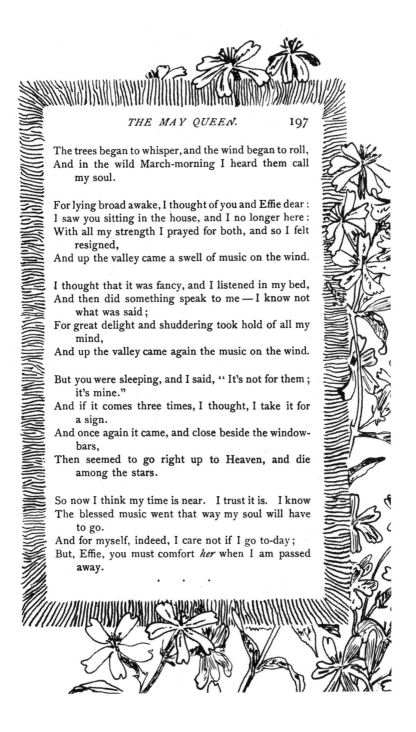

The trees began to whisper, and the wind began to roll,
And in the wild March-morning I heard them call
　　my soul.

For lying broad awake, I thought of you and Effie dear:
I saw you sitting in the house, and I no longer here;
With all my strength I prayed for both, and so I felt
　　resigned,
And up the valley came a swell of music on the wind.

I thought that it was fancy, and I listened in my bed,
And then did something speak to me — I know not
　　what was said;
For great delight and shuddering took hold of all my
　　mind,
And up the valley came again the music on the wind.

But you were sleeping, and I said, "It's not for them;
　　it's mine."
And if it comes three times, I thought, I take it for
　　a sign.
And once again it came, and close beside the window-
　　bars,
Then seemed to go right up to Heaven, and die
　　among the stars.

So now I think my time is near. I trust it is. I know
The blessed music went that way my soul will have
　　to go.
And for myself, indeed, I care not if I go to-day;
But, Effie, you must comfort *her* when I am passed
　　away.

　　　　　　．　　．　　．

O, look! the sun begins to rise, the heavens are in a
    glow;
He shines upon a hundred fields, and all of them I
    know;
And there I move no longer now, and there his light
    may shine, —
Wild flowers in the valley, for other hands than mine.

O, sweet and strange it seems to me, that ere this
    day is done,
The voice that now is speaking may be beyond the
    sun —
Forever and forever with those just souls and true:
And what is life, that we should moan? Why make
    we such ado?

Forever and forever, all in a blessed home,
And there to wait a little while till you and Effie
    come —
To lie within the light of God, as I lie upon your
    breast,
And the wicked cease from troubling, and the weary
    are at rest.

BONDS OF AFFECTION.

LANDON.

THERE is in life no blessing like affection;
It soothes, it hallows, elevates, subdues,
And bringeth down to earth its native heaven.

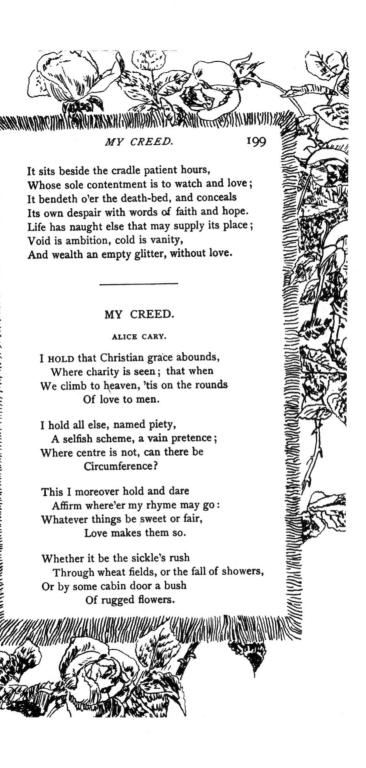

It sits beside the cradle patient hours,
Whose sole contentment is to watch and love;
It bendeth o'er the death-bed, and conceals
Its own despair with words of faith and hope.
Life has naught else that may supply its place;
Void is ambition, cold is vanity,
And wealth an empty glitter, without love.

MY CREED.

ALICE CARY.

I HOLD that Christian grace abounds,
    Where charity is seen; that when
We climb to heaven, 'tis on the rounds
    Of love to men.

I hold all else, named piety,
    A selfish scheme, a vain pretence;
Where centre is not, can there be
    Circumference?

This I moreover hold and dare
    Affirm where'er my rhyme may go:
Whatever things be sweet or fair,
    Love makes them so.

Whether it be the sickle's rush
    Through wheat fields, or the fall of showers,
Or by some cabin door a bush
    Of rugged flowers.

'Tis not the wide phylactery,
  Nor stubborn fast, nor stated prayers,
That makes us saints; we judge the tree
    By what it bears.

And when a man can live apart
  From works, on theologic trust,
I know the blood about his heart
    Is dry as dust.

———

THE ROSE BY THE WAYSIDE.

D. A. DROWN.

A LITTLE rose bloomed in the way
In which I roamed one sunny day;
    It looked so fair,
I wondered why alone it grew,
And why so long concealed from view
    While nestling there.

Its blushing petals, wide outspread,
A richer perfume quickly shed,
    Dripping with dew,
Which seemed in whispered tones to say,
As soon I put the thorns away,
    " I bloomed for you.

" The sunshine kissed my lips at morn,
Soon as I peeped to hail the dawn,
    With blushes red;

I was content through day to day;
No roaming footsteps passed this way
    By beauty led."

I claimed the treasure, pure and fair,
As all mine own; with special care
    I kept it long;
I said sweet sayings o'er and o'er:
But one bright morn it spoke no more;
    Its leaves were gone.

Thus in the varied paths of life,
Amid its cares, its toils, its strife,
    We often roam;
Then some sweet memories charm us here,
Some holy thoughts dispel all fear,
    And guide us home.

And when earth's charms, like withered flowers,
Amid affliction's darkest hours
    No longer cheer,
A holy peace, a quiet joy,
Which unbelief can ne'er destroy,
    Brings Heaven near.

LOVE AND REASON.

MOORE.

'Twas in the summer time so sweet,
  When hearts and flowers are both in season,
That — who, of all the world, should meet,
  One early dawn, but Love and Reason!

Love told his dream of yesternight,
  While Reason talked about the weather;
The morn, in sooth, was fair and bright,
  And on they took their way together.

The boy in many a gambol flew,
  While Reason, like a Juno, stalked,
And from her portly figure threw
  A lengthened shadow as she walked.

No wonder Love, as on they passed,
  Should find that sunny morning chill;
For still the shadow Reason cast
  Fell on the boy, and cooled him still.

In vain he tried his wings to warm,
  Or find a pathway not so dim,
For still the maid's gigantic form
  Would pass between the sun and him!

"This must not be," said little Love —
  "The sun was made for more than you."
So, turning through a myrtle grove,
  He bade the portly nymph adieu.

Now gladly roves the laughing boy
   O'er many a mead, by many a stream,
In every breeze inhaling joy,
   And drinking bliss in every beam.

From all the gardens, all the bowers,
   He culled the many sweets they shaded,
And ate the fruits, and smelled the flowers,
   Till taste was gone and odor faded.

But now the sun, in pomp of noon,
   Looked blazing o'er the parchéd plains;
Alas! the boy grew languid soon,
   And fever thrilled through all his veins;

The dew forsook his baby brow,
   No more with vivid bloom he smiled;
O, where was tranquil Reason now,
   To cast her shadow o'er the child?

Beneath a green and aged palm,
   His foot, at length, for shelter turning,
He saw the nymph reclining calm,
   With brow as cool as his was burning.

"O, take me to that bosom cold,"
   In murmurs at her feet he said;
And Reason oped her garment's fold,
   And flung it round his fevered head.

He felt her bosom's icy touch,
   And soon it lulled his pulse to rest;
For, ah! the chill was quite too much,
   And Love expired on Reason's breast.

THE BRIDE'S FAREWELL.

MRS. HEMANS.

WHY do I weep? to leave the vine
  Whose clusters o'er me bend, —
The myrtle — yet, O call it mine,
  The flowers I loved to tend.
A thousand thoughts of all things dear
  Like shadows o'er me sweep,
To leave my sunny childhood here;
  O, therefore let me weep.

I leave thee, sister; we have played
  Through many a joyous hour,
Where the silvery green of the olive shade
  Hung dim o'er fount and bower;
Yes, thou and I, by stream, by shore,
  In song, in prayer, in sleep,
Have been as we may be no more;
  Kind sister, let me weep.

I leave thee, father; eve's bright moon
  Must now light other feet,
With the gathered grapes, and the lyre in tune,
  Thy homeward step to greet,
Thou in whose voice, to bless thy child,
  Rang tones of love so deep,
Whose eye o'er all my youth hath smiled,
  I leave thee; let me weep.

Mother, I leave thee; on thy breast,
  Pouring out joy and woe,
I have found that holy place of rest
  Still changeless — yet I go.
Lips that have lulled me with your strain,
  Eyes that have watched my sleep,
Will earth give love like yours again?
  Sweet mother, let me weep.

THE DAYS OF YORE.

DOUGLAS THOMPSON.

You see the slender spire that peers
  Above the trees that skirt the stream;
'Twas there I passed those early years
  Which now seem like some happy dream.
You see the vale that bounds the view:
  'Twas there my father's mansion stood,
Before the grove, whose varied hue
  Is mirrored in the tranquil flood.

There's not a stone remaining there,
  A relic of that fine old hall;
For strangers came the spot to share,
  And bade the stately structure fall!
But now, if Fortune proves my friend,
  And gives me what may yet remain,
In that dear spot my days to end,
  I'll build a mansion there again.

THE PATH OF INDEPENDENCE.

ANON.

An easy task it is to tread
  The path the multitude will take;
  But independence dares the stake
If but by fair conviction led.

Then haste, truth-seeker, on thy way,
  Nor heed the worldling's smile or frown,
  The brave alone shall wear the crown
The noble only clasp the bay.

Go, worker of the public weal;
  When knaves combine, and plot and plan,
  Assert the dignity of man,
Teach the dishonest hearts to feel.

Still keep thy independence whole;
  Let nothing warp thee from thy course,
  And thou shalt wield a giant's force,
And wrong before thy foot shall roll.

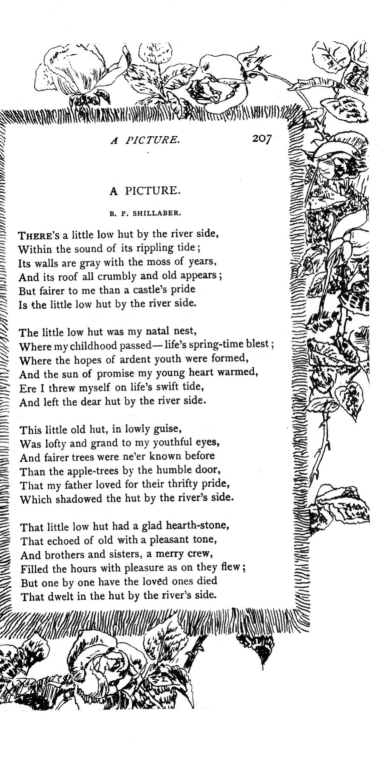

A PICTURE.

B. P. SHILLABER.

THERE'S a little low hut by the river side,
Within the sound of its rippling tide;
Its walls are gray with the moss of years,
And its roof all crumbly and old appears;
But fairer to me than a castle's pride
Is the little low hut by the river side.

The little low hut was my natal nest,
Where my childhood passed—life's spring-time blest;
Where the hopes of ardent youth were formed,
And the sun of promise my young heart warmed,
Ere I threw myself on life's swift tide,
And left the dear hut by the river side.

This little old hut, in lowly guise,
Was lofty and grand to my youthful eyes,
And fairer trees were ne'er known before
Than the apple-trees by the humble door,
That my father loved for their thrifty pride,
Which shadowed the hut by the river's side.

That little low hut had a glad hearth-stone,
That echoed of old with a pleasant tone,
And brothers and sisters, a merry crew,
Filled the hours with pleasure as on they flew;
But one by one have the loved ones died
That dwelt in the hut by the river's side.

A PICTURE.

The father and the children gay
The grave and the world have called away;
But quietly all alone there sits
By the pleasant window in summer, and knits,
An aged woman, long years allied
With the little old hut by the river's side.

That little old hut to the lonely wife
Is the cherished stage of her active life;
Each scene is recalled in memory's beam,
As she sits by the window in pensive dream,
And joys and woes roll back like a tide,
In that little old hut by the river's side.

My mother!—alone, by the river side,
She waits for the flood of the heavenly tide,
And the voice that shall thrill her heart with its call
To meet once more with the dear ones all,
And form, in region beautified,
The band that first met by the river's side.

That dear old hut by the river's side
With the warmest pulse of my heart is allied,
And a glory is over its dark walls thrown
That statelier fabrics have never known;
And I shall still love, with a fonder pride,
That little old hut by the river's side.

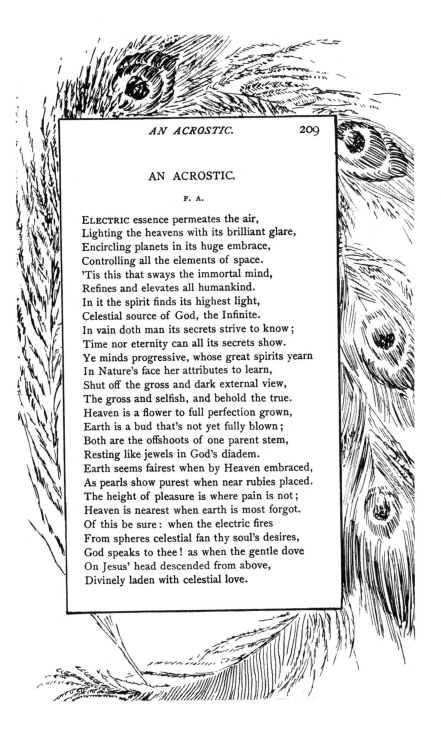

AN ACROSTIC.

F. A.

ELECTRIC essence permeates the air,
Lighting the heavens with its brilliant glare,
Encircling planets in its huge embrace,
Controlling all the elements of space.
'Tis this that sways the immortal mind,
Refines and elevates all humankind.
In it the spirit finds its highest light,
Celestial source of God, the Infinite.
In vain doth man its secrets strive to know;
Time nor eternity can all its secrets show.
Ye minds progressive, whose great spirits yearn
In Nature's face her attributes to learn,
Shut off the gross and dark external view,
The gross and selfish, and behold the true.
Heaven is a flower to full perfection grown,
Earth is a bud that's not yet fully blown;
Both are the offshoots of one parent stem,
Resting like jewels in God's diadem.
Earth seems fairest when by Heaven embraced,
As pearls show purest when near rubies placed.
The height of pleasure is where pain is not;
Heaven is nearest when earth is most forgot.
Of this be sure: when the electric fires
From spheres celestial fan thy soul's desires,
God speaks to thee! as when the gentle dove
On Jesus' head descended from above,
Divinely laden with celestial love.

FROM THE MERCHANT OF VENICE.

SHAKESPEARE.

LORENZO.

How sweet the moonlight sleeps upon this bank!
Here will we sit, and let the sounds of music
Creep in our ears; soft stillness, and the night,
Become the touches of sweet harmony.
Sit, Jessica: look, how the floor of heaven
Is thick inlaid with patines of bright gold;
There's not the smallest orb which thou behold'st
But in his motion like an angel sings,
Still quiring to the young-eyed cherubins:
Such harmony is in immortal souls;
But, whilst this muddy vesture of decay
Doth grossly close it in, we cannot hear it.
                              [*Enter Musicians.*
Come, ho, and wake Diana with a hymn;
With sweetest touches pierce your mistress' ear,
And draw her home with music.

JESSICA.

I am never merry when I hear sweet music.
                                        [*Music.*

LORENZO.

The reason is, your spirits are attentive;
For do but note a wild and wanton herd,
Or race of youthful and unhandled colts,
Fetching mad bounds, bellowing and neighing loud,
Which is the hot condition of their blood;

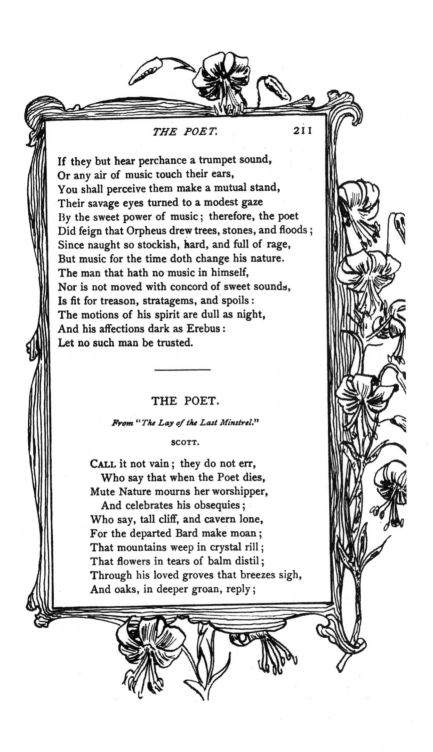

If they but hear perchance a trumpet sound,
Or any air of music touch their ears,
You shall perceive them make a mutual stand,
Their savage eyes turned to a modest gaze
By the sweet power of music; therefore, the poet
Did feign that Orpheus drew trees, stones, and floods;
Since naught so stockish, hard, and full of rage,
But music for the time doth change his nature.
The man that hath no music in himself,
Nor is not moved with concord of sweet sounds,
Is fit for treason, stratagems, and spoils:
The motions of his spirit are dull as night,
And his affections dark as Erebus:
Let no such man be trusted.

THE POET.

From "The Lay of the Last Minstrel."

SCOTT.

CALL it not vain; they do not err,
  Who say that when the Poet dies,
Mute Nature mourns her worshipper,
  And celebrates his obsequies;
Who say, tall cliff, and cavern lone,
For the departed Bard make moan;
That mountains weep in crystal rill;
That flowers in tears of balm distil;
Through his loved groves that breezes sigh,
And oaks, in deeper groan, reply;

And rivers teach their rushing wave
To murmur dirges round his grave.

Not that, in sooth, o'er mortal urn
Those things inanimate can mourn;
But that the stream, the wood, the gale,
Is vocal with the plaintive wail
Of those who, else forgotten long,
Lived in the poet's faithful song;
And, with the poet's parting breath,
Whose memory feels a second death.
The maid's pale shade, who wails her lot,
That love, true love, should be forgot,
From rose and hawthorn shakes the tear
Upon the gentle Minstrel's bier;
The phantom Knight, his glory fled,
Mourns o'er the field he heaped with dead;
Mounts the wild blast that sweeps amain,
And shrieks along the battle-plain.
The Chief, whose antique crownlet long
Still sparkled in the feudal song,
Now, from the mountain's misty throne,
Sees, in the thanedom once his own,
His ashes undistinguished lie,
His place, his power, his memory die;
His groans the lonely caverns fill;
His tears of rage impel the rill:
All mourn the minstrel's harp unstrung,
Their name unknown, their praise unsung.

ILLUSTRATION OF A PICTURE.

A Spanish Girl in Reverie.

O. W. HOLMES.

SHE twirled the string of golden beads
    That round her neck was hung —
My grandsire's gift; the good old man
    Loved girls when he was young;
And, bending lightly o'er the chord,
    And turning half away,
With something like a youthful sigh,
    Thus spoke the maiden gay: —

"Well, one may trail her silken robe,
    And bind her locks with pearls;
And one may wreathe the woodland rose
    Among her floating curls;
And one may tread the dewy grass,
    And one the marble floor,
Nor half-hid bosom heave the less,
    Nor broidered corset more!

"Some years ago, a dark-eyed girl,
    Was sitting in the shade, —
There's something brings her to my mind
    In that young dreaming maid, —
And in her hand she held a flower,
    A flower whose speaking hue
Said, in the language of the heart,
    Believe the giver true.

"And as she looked upon its leaves,
  The maiden made a vow
To wear it when the bridal wreath
  Was woven for her brow;
She watched the flower, as, day by day
  The leaflets curled and died;
But he who gave it never came
  To claim her for his bride.

"O, many a summer's morning glow
  Has leant the rose its ray,
And many a winter's drifting snow
  Has swept its bloom away;
But she has kept that faithless pledge
  To this her winter hour,
And keeps it still, herself alone,
  And wasted like the flower."

Her pale lip quivered, and the light
  Gleamed in her moistening eyes.
I asked her how she liked the tints
  In those Castilian skies:
"She thought them misty — 'twas perhaps
  Because she stood too near."
She turned away, and as she turned,
  I saw her wipe a tear.

THE DIVER.

MRS. HEMANS.

THOU hast been where the rocks of coral grow;
　Thou hast fought with eddying waves;
Thy cheek is pale and thy heart beats low,
　Thou searcher of ocean's caves.

Thou hast looked on the gleaming wealth of old,
　And wrecks where the brave have striven;
The deep is a strong and fearful hold,
　But thou its bar hast riven!

A wild and weary life is thine,
　A wasting task and lone,
Though treasure-grots for thee may shine
　To all beside unknown.

A weary life; but a swift decay
　Soon, soon shall set thee free;
Thou'rt passing fast from thy toils away,
　Thou wrestler with the sea!

In thy dim eye, on thy hollow cheek,
　Well are the death-signs read—
Go! for the pearl in its cavern seek,
　Ere hope and power be fled.

And bright in beauty's coronal
　That glistening gem shall be,
A star to all in the festive hall;
　But who will think on thee?

None; as it gleams from the queen-like head,
  Not one midst throngs will say : —
" A life hath been like a rain-drop shed
  For that pale, quivering ray."

Woe for the wealth thus dearly bought!
  And are not those like thee,
Who win for earth the gems of thought?
  O wrestler with the sea!

Down to the gulfs of the soul they go,
  Where the passion-fountains burn,
Gathering the jewels far below
  From many a buried urn; —

Wringing from lava veins the fire
  That o'er bright words is poured ;
Learning deep sounds, to make the lyre
  A spirit in each chord.

But O, the price of bitter tears,
  Paid for the lonely power
That throws at last o'er desert years
  A darkly glorious dower!

Like flower seeds, by the wild wind spread,
  So radiant thoughts are strewed ;
The soul whence those high gifts are shed
  May faint in solitude.

And who will think, when the strain is sung
  Till a thousand hearts are stirred,

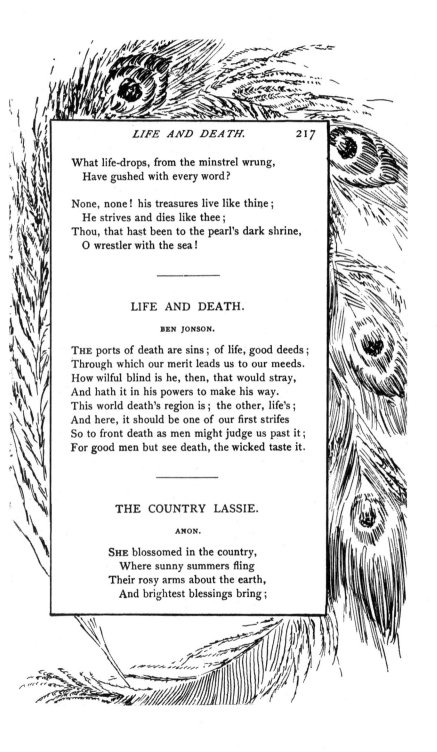

What life-drops, from the minstrel wrung,
　Have gushed with every word?

None, none! his treasures live like thine;
　He strives and dies like thee;
Thou, that hast been to the pearl's dark shrine,
　O wrestler with the sea!

————————

LIFE AND DEATH.

BEN JONSON.

THE ports of death are sins; of life, good deeds;
Through which our merit leads us to our meeds.
How wilful blind is he, then, that would stray,
And hath it in his powers to make his way.
This world death's region is; the other, life's;
And here, it should be one of our first strifes
So to front death as men might judge us past it;
For good men but see death, the wicked taste it.

————————

THE COUNTRY LASSIE.

ANON.

SHE blossomed in the country,
　Where sunny summers fling
Their rosy arms about the earth,
　And brightest blessings bring;

Health was her sole inheritance,
　And grace her only dower;
I never dreamed the wildwood
　Contained so sweet a flower.

Far distant from the city,
　And inland from the sea,
My lassie bloomed in goodness,
　As pure as pure could be;
She caught her dewy freshness
　From hill and mountain bower;
I never dreamed the wildwood
　Contained so sweet a flower.

The rainbow must have lent her
　Some of its airy grace,
The wild rose parted with a blush
　That nestled on her face;
The sunbeam got entangled in
　The long waves of her hair,
For she had grown to be
　So modest and so fair.

The early birds had taught her
　Their joyous matin song,
And some of their soft innocence,
　She's been with them so long;
And for her now, if need be,
　I'd part with wealth and power;
I never dreamed the wildwood
　Contained so sweet a flower.

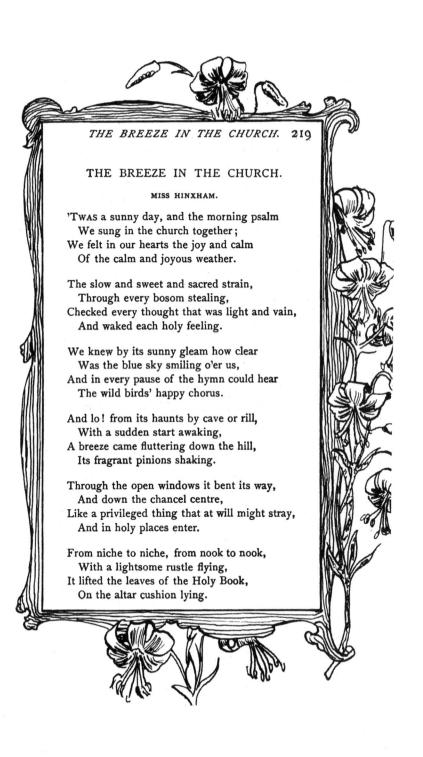

THE BREEZE IN THE CHURCH.

MISS HINXHAM.

'Twas a sunny day, and the morning psalm
  We sung in the church together;
We felt in our hearts the joy and calm
  Of the calm and joyous weather.

The slow and sweet and sacred strain,
  Through every bosom stealing,
Checked every thought that was light and vain,
  And waked each holy feeling.

We knew by its sunny gleam how clear
  Was the blue sky smiling o'er us,
And in every pause of the hymn could hear
  The wild birds' happy chorus.

And lo! from its haunts by cave or rill,
  With a sudden start awaking,
A breeze came fluttering down the hill,
  Its fragrant pinions shaking.

Through the open windows it bent its way,
  And down the chancel centre,
Like a privileged thing that at will might stray,
  And in holy places enter.

From niche to niche, from nook to nook,
  With a lightsome rustle flying,
It lifted the leaves of the Holy Book,
  On the altar cushion lying.

It fanned the old clerk's hoary hair,
  And the children's bright young faces;
Then vanished, none knew how or where,
  Leaving its pleasant traces.

It left sweet thoughts of summer hours
  Spent on the quiet mountains;
And the church seemed full of the scent of flowers,
  And the trickling fall of fountains.

The image of scenes so still and fair
  With our music sweetly blended,
While it seemed their whispered hymn took share
  In the praise that to Heaven ascended.

We thought of Him who had poured the rills
  And through the green mountains led them;
Whose hand, when he piled the enduring hills,
  With a mantle of beauty spread them.

And a purer passion was borne above,
  In a louder anthem swelling,
As we bowed to the visible spirit of love
  On those calm summits dwelling.

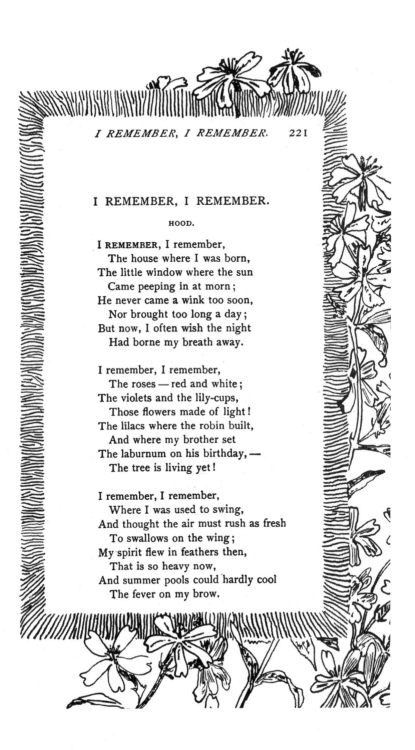

I REMEMBER, I REMEMBER.

HOOD.

I REMEMBER, I remember,
　The house where I was born,
The little window where the sun
　Came peeping in at morn;
He never came a wink too soon,
　Nor brought too long a day;
But now, I often wish the night
　Had borne my breath away.

I remember, I remember,
　The roses — red and white;
The violets and the lily-cups,
　Those flowers made of light!
The lilacs where the robin built,
　And where my brother set
The laburnum on his birthday, —
　The tree is living yet!

I remember, I remember,
　Where I was used to swing,
And thought the air must rush as fresh
　To swallows on the wing;
My spirit flew in feathers then,
　That is so heavy now,
And summer pools could hardly cool
　The fever on my brow.

I remember, I remember,
  The fir-trees dark and high;
I used to think their slender tops
  Were close against the sky.
It was a childish ignorance;
  But now 'tis little joy
To know I'm farther off from heaven
  Than when I was a boy.

THE TOAST.

SCOTT.

The feast is o'er! Now brimming wine
In lordly cup is seen to shine
  Before each eager guest;
And silence fills the crowded hall,
As deep as when the herald's call
  Thrills in the royal breast.

Then up arose the noble host,
And smiling cried: — "A toast, a toast,
  To all our ladyes fair.
Here, before all, I pledge the name
Of Staunton's proud and beauteous dame,
  The Ladye Gundamere."

Then to his feet each gallant sprung,
And joyous was the shout that rung
  As Stanley gave the word:
And every cup was raised on high,
Nor ceased the loud and gladsome cry,
  Till Stanley's voice was heard.

" Enough, enough," he smiling said,
And lowly bent his haughty head.
  " That all may have their due,
Now each in turn must play his part,
And pledge the ladye of his heart,
    Like gallant knight and true."

Then one by one each guest sprung up,
And drained in turn the brimming cup,
    And named the loved one's name;
And each, as hand on high he raised,
His ladye's grace or beauty praised,
    Her constancy and fame.

'Tis now St. Leon's turn to rise;
On him are fixed those countless eyes;
    A gallant knight is he;
Envied by some, admired by all,
Far-famed in ladye's bower and hall,
    The flower of chivalry.

St. Leon raised his kindling eye,
And lifts the sparkling cup on high.
    " I drink to one," he said,
" Whose image never may depart,
Deep graven on this grateful heart,
    Till memory be dead.

To one whose love for me shall last
When lighter passions long have passed,
    So holy 'tis and true;
To one whose love hath longer dwelt,
More deeply fixed, more keenly felt,
    Than any pledged by you,"

Each guest upstarted at the word,
And laid a hand upon his sword,
    With fury-flashing eye;
And Stanley said: — "We crave the name,
Proud knight, of this most peerless dame,
    Whose love you count so high."

St. Leon paused, as if he would
Not breathe her name in careless mood,
    Thus lightly to another;
Then bent his noble head, as though
To give that word the reverence due,
    And gently said, "My Mother!"

TIME.

YOUNG.

THE bell strikes one; we take no note of time,
But from its loss. To give it, then, a tongue
Is wise in man. As if an angel spoke,
I feel the solemn sound. If heard aright,
It is the knell of my departed hours.
Where are they? With the years beyond the flood.
It is the signal that demands despatch;
How much is to be done.

THE HEART'S FINE GOLD.

W. O. BOURNE.

I SAW a little girl
    That shivered by my side,
And the sparkling snow, with a whiff and a whirl,
Wove a frosty wreath in her hanging curl,
    As she pushed her hair aside.

I saw her tearful eye,
    That spoke in tender power,
And the throbbing heart, with a throe and a sigh,
Were the speaking tongue, that assured me why
    She came in that chilly hour.

I asked what brought her there.
    In accents low and sad,
She asked for some food, for crust was the fare,
Of mother and babe, mid the heart's despair;
    In rags they were thinly clad.

Her father with the dead
    Had gone to take his rest;
He had struggled long with the toil and dread
Of the life in which the laborers tread,
    And had always done his best.

Her simple tale I heard,
    Nor did she speak in vain;
For the prayerful tone, and the sigh, and the word
Of the pale, thin lips, all my pity stirred,
    As she spoke in tears again.

Her wants I well supplied
    With such as I could spare ;
And the poor girl wept in her soul's grateful tide,
For her heart was full, and she vainly tried
    To utter its promptings there.

My heart grew rich that day,
    My soul more noble grew,
For her tears that fell were pearls in the ray
Of the great love sun that shall chase away
    The night and its gloom-born dew.

I would that I could spend
    My life in joys like this ;
I would gather gems, and the gold with them blend
Of a thousand hearts, till my life should end
    In a heaven of love's pure bliss.

THE OLD FOLKS' ROOM.

ANON.

THE old man sat by the chimney side ;
    His face was wrinkled and wan ;
And he leaned both hands on his stout oak cane,
    As if all work were done.

His coat was of good old-fashioned gray ;
    The pockets were deep and wide,

Where his " specs " and his steel tobacco box
  Lay snugly side by side.

The old man liked to stir the fire,
  So near him the tongs were kept;
Sometimes he mused as he gazed at the coals,
  Sometimes he sat and wept.

What saw he in the embers there?
  Ah! pictures of other years;
And now and then they wakened smiles,
  But oftener started tears.

His good wife sat on the other side,
  In a high-back, flag-seat chair;
I see 'neath the pile of her muslin cap
  The sheen of her silvery hair.

There's a happy look on her aged face,
  As she busily knits for him,
And Nillie takes up the stitches dropped,
  For grandmother's eyes are dim.

Their children come and read the news
  To pass the time, each day;
How it stirs the blood in an old man's heart
  To hear of the world away!

'Tis a homely scene, — I told you so, —
  But pleasant it is to view;
At least I thought it so myself,
  And sketched it down for you.

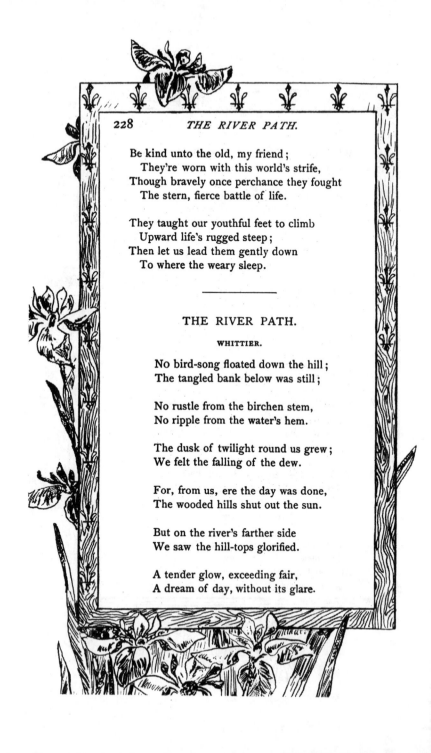

Be kind unto the old, my friend;
  They're worn with this world's strife,
Though bravely once perchance they fought
  The stern, fierce battle of life.

They taught our youthful feet to climb
  Upward life's rugged steep;
Then let us lead them gently down
  To where the weary sleep.

THE RIVER PATH.

WHITTIER.

No bird-song floated down the hill;
The tangled bank below was still;

No rustle from the birchen stem,
No ripple from the water's hem.

The dusk of twilight round us grew;
We felt the falling of the dew.

For, from us, ere the day was done,
The wooded hills shut out the sun.

But on the river's farther side
We saw the hill-tops glorified.

A tender glow, exceeding fair,
A dream of day, without its glare.

With us the damp, the chill, the gloom;
With them the sunset's rosy bloom;

While dark, through willowy vistas seen,
The river rolled in shade between.

From out the darkness where we trod
We gazed upon those hills of God,

Whose light seemed not of moon or sun;
We spake not, but our thought was one.

We paused, as if from that bright shore
Beckoned our dear ones gone before;

And still our beating hearts to hear
The voices lost to mortal ear!

Sudden our pathway turned from night;
The hills swung open to the light;

Through their green gates the sunshine showed
A long slant splendor downward flowed.

Down glade and glen and bank it rolled;
It bridged the shady stream with gold;

And, borne on piers of mist, allied
The shadowy with the sunlit side!

" So," prayed we, " when our feet draw near
The river dark, with mortal fear,

"And the night cometh chill with dew,
O Father! let thy light break through!

" So let the hills of doubt divide,
So bridge with faith the sunless tide!

" So let the eyes that fail on earth
On thy eternal hills look forth!

"And in thy beckoning angels know
The dear ones whom we loved below."

THE BANQUET.

LANDON.

THERE was a feast that night,
And colored lamps sent forth their odorous light
Over gold carving, and the purple fall
Of tapestry; and around each stately hall
Were statues pale, and delicate, and fair,
As all of Beauty, save her blush, were there;
And, like light clouds, floating around each room
The censers sent their breathings of perfume;
And scented waters mingled with the breath
Of flowers that died as they rejoiced in death;
The tulip, with its globe of rainbow light;
The red rose, as it languished with delight;
The bride-like hyacinth, drooping as with shame;
And the anemone, whose cheek of flame

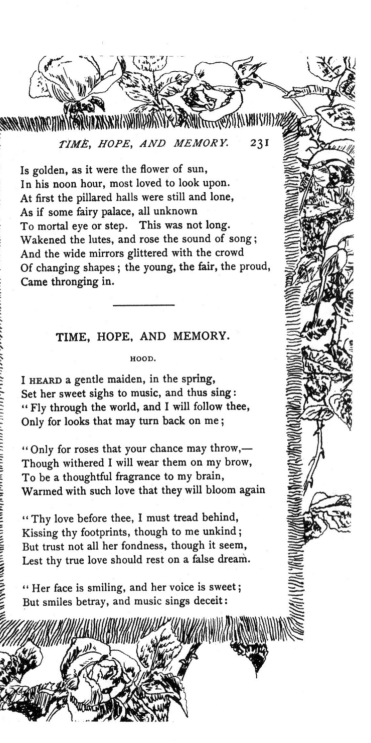

Is golden, as it were the flower of sun,
In his noon hour, most loved to look upon.
At first the pillared halls were still and lone,
As if some fairy palace, all unknown
To mortal eye or step.   This was not long.
Wakened the lutes, and rose the sound of song;
And the wide mirrors glittered with the crowd
Of changing shapes; the young, the fair, the proud,
Came thronging in.

TIME, HOPE, AND MEMORY.

HOOD.

I HEARD a gentle maiden, in the spring,
Set her sweet sighs to music, and thus sing:
" Fly through the world, and I will follow thee,
Only for looks that may turn back on me;

"Only for roses that your chance may throw,—
Though withered I will wear them on my brow,
To be a thoughtful fragrance to my brain,
Warmed with such love that they will bloom again

" Thy love before thee, I must tread behind,
Kissing thy footprints, though to me unkind;
But trust not all her fondness, though it seem,
Lest thy true love should rest on a false dream.

" Her face is smiling, and her voice is sweet;
But smiles betray, and music sings deceit:

And words speak false ; — yet, if they welcome prove,
I'll be their echo, and repeat their love.

" Only, if wakened to sad truth at last,
The bitterness to come, and sweetness past,
When thou art vext, then turn again, and see
Thou hast loved Hope, but Memory loved thee."

LITTLE ROSE.

Blackwood's Magazine.

SHE comes with fairy footsteps ;
　Softly their echoes fall ;
And her shadow plays, like a summer shade,
　Across the garden wall.
The golden light is dancing bright
　Mid the mazes of her hair,
And her fair young locks are waving free
　To the wooing of the air.

Like a sportive fawn she boundeth
　So gleefully along ;
As a wild young bird she caroleth
　The burden of a song.
The summer birds are clustering thick
　Around her dancing feet,
And on her cheek the clustering breeze
　Is breaking soft and sweet.

The very sunbeams seem to linger
  Above that holy head,
And the wild flowers at her coming
  Their richest fragrance shed.
And O, how lovely light and fragrance
  Mingle in the life within!
O, how fondly do they nestle
  Round the soul that knows no sin!

She comes, the spirit of our childhood, —
  A thing of mortal birth,
Yet beareth still a breath of heaven,
  To redeem her from the earth.
She comes in bright-robed innocence,
  Unsoiled by blot or blight,
And passeth by our wayward path
  A gleam of angel light.

O, blessed things are children!
  The gifts of heavenly love;
They stand betwixt our heavenly hearts
  And better things above.
They link us with the spirit world
  By purity and truth,
And keep our hearts still fresh and young
  With the presence of their youth.

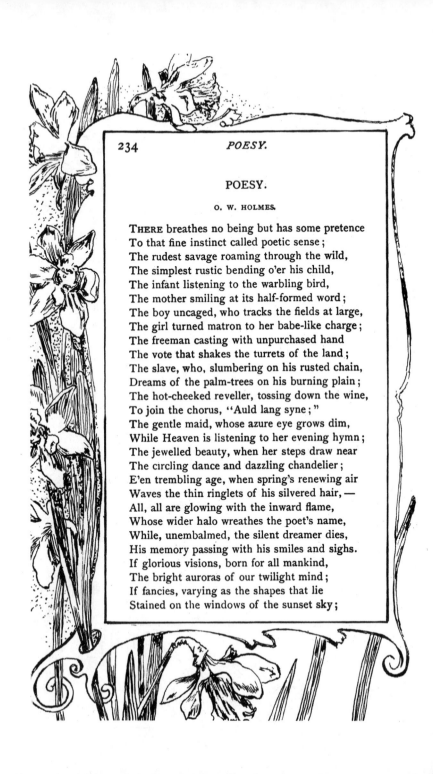

POESY.

O. W. HOLMES.

THERE breathes no being but has some pretence
To that fine instinct called poetic sense;
The rudest savage roaming through the wild,
The simplest rustic bending o'er his child,
The infant listening to the warbling bird,
The mother smiling at its half-formed word;
The boy uncaged, who tracks the fields at large,
The girl turned matron to her babe-like charge;
The freeman casting with unpurchased hand
The vote that shakes the turrets of the land;
The slave, who, slumbering on his rusted chain,
Dreams of the palm-trees on his burning plain;
The hot-cheeked reveller, tossing down the wine,
To join the chorus, "Auld lang syne;"
The gentle maid, whose azure eye grows dim,
While Heaven is listening to her evening hymn;
The jewelled beauty, when her steps draw near
The circling dance and dazzling chandelier;
E'en trembling age, when spring's renewing air
Waves the thin ringlets of his silvered hair, —
All, all are glowing with the inward flame,
Whose wider halo wreathes the poet's name,
While, unembalmed, the silent dreamer dies,
His memory passing with his smiles and sighs.
If glorious visions, born for all mankind,
The bright auroras of our twilight mind;
If fancies, varying as the shapes that lie
Stained on the windows of the sunset sky;

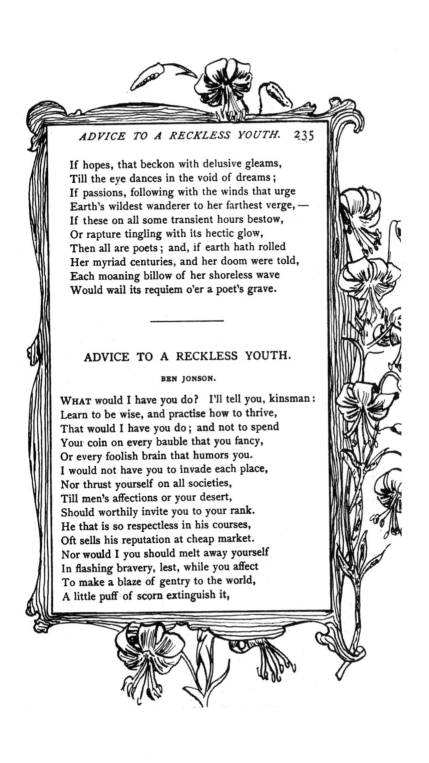

If hopes, that beckon with delusive gleams,
Till the eye dances in the void of dreams;
If passions, following with the winds that urge
Earth's wildest wanderer to her farthest verge, —
If these on all some transient hours bestow,
Or rapture tingling with its hectic glow,
Then all are poets; and, if earth hath rolled
Her myriad centuries, and her doom were told,
Each moaning billow of her shoreless wave
Would wail its requiem o'er a poet's grave.

ADVICE TO A RECKLESS YOUTH.

BEN JONSON.

WHAT would I have you do? I'll tell you, kinsman:
Learn to be wise, and practise how to thrive,
That would I have you do; and not to spend
Your coin on every bauble that you fancy,
Or every foolish brain that humors you.
I would not have you to invade each place,
Nor thrust yourself on all societies,
Till men's affections or your desert,
Should worthily invite you to your rank.
He that is so respectless in his courses,
Oft sells his reputation at cheap market.
Nor would I you should melt away yourself
In flashing bravery, lest, while you affect
To make a blaze of gentry to the world,
A little puff of scorn extinguish it,

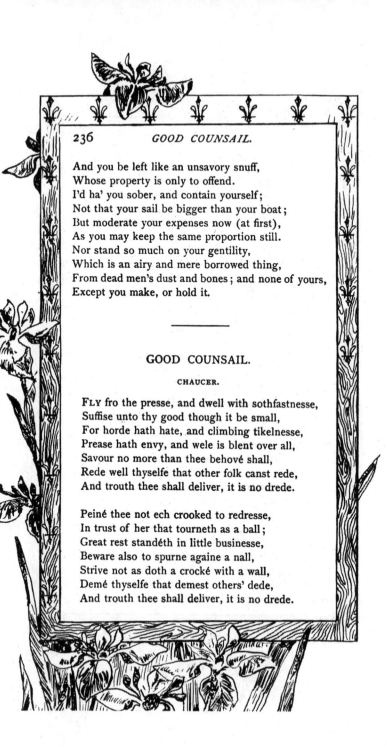

And you be left like an unsavory snuff,
Whose property is only to offend.
I'd ha' you sober, and contain yourself;
Not that your sail be bigger than your boat;
But moderate your expenses now (at first),
As you may keep the same proportion still.
Nor stand so much on your gentility,
Which is an airy and mere borrowed thing,
From dead men's dust and bones; and none of yours,
Except you make, or hold it.

GOOD COUNSAIL.

CHAUCER.

FLY fro the presse, and dwell with sothfastnesse,
Suffise unto thy good though it be small,
For horde hath hate, and climbing tikelnesse,
Prease hath envy, and wele is blent over all,
Savour no more than thee behové shall,
Rede well thyselfe that other folk canst rede,
And trouth thee shall deliver, it is no drede.

Peiné thee not ech crooked to redresse,
In trust of her that tourneth as a ball;
Great rest standéth in little businesse,
Beware also to spurne againe a nall,
Strive not as doth a crocké with a wall,
Demé thyselfe that demest others' dede,
And trouth thee shall deliver, it is no drede.

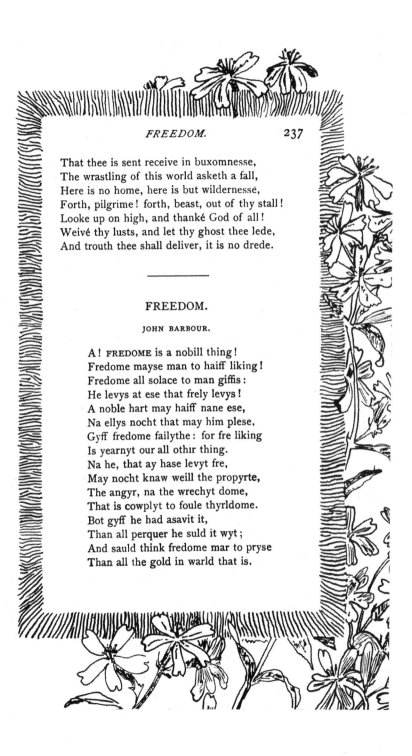

That thee is sent receive in buxomnesse,
The wrastling of this world asketh a fall,
Here is no home, here is but wildernessé,
Forth, pilgrime! forth, beast, out of thy stall!
Looke up on high, and thanké God of all!
Weivé thy lusts, and let thy ghost thee lede,
And trouth thee shall deliver, it is no drede.

FREEDOM.

JOHN BARBOUR.

A! FREDOME is a nobill thing!
Fredome mayse man to haiff liking!
Fredome all solace to man giffis:
He levys at ese that frely levys!
A noble hart may haiff nane ese,
Na ellys nocht that may him plese,
Gyff fredome failythe: for fre liking
Is yearnyt our all othir thing.
Na he, that ay hase levyt fre,
May nocht knaw weill the propyrte,
The angyr, na the wrechyt dome,
That is cowplyt to foule thyrldome.
Bot gyff he had asavit it,
Than all perquer he suld it wyt;
And sauld think fredome mar to pryse
Than all the gold in warld that is,

JOHN ANDERSON, MY JO.

ROBERT BURNS.

JOHN ANDERSON, my jo, John,
  When we were first acquent,
Your locks were like the raven,
  Your bonie brow was brent;
But now your brow is beld, John,
  Your locks are like the snow:
But blessings on your frosty pow,
  John Anderson, my jo.

John Anderson, my jo, John,
  We clamb the hill thegither,
And monie a canty day, John,
  We've had wi' ane anither;
Now we maun totter down, John,
  But hand in hand we'll go,
And sleep thegither at the foot,
  John Anderson, my jo.

———

THE PLEASURES OF HEAVEN.

BEN JONSON.

THERE all the happy souls that ever were,
Shall meet with gladness in one theatre;
And each shall know there one another's face,
By beatific virtue of the place.

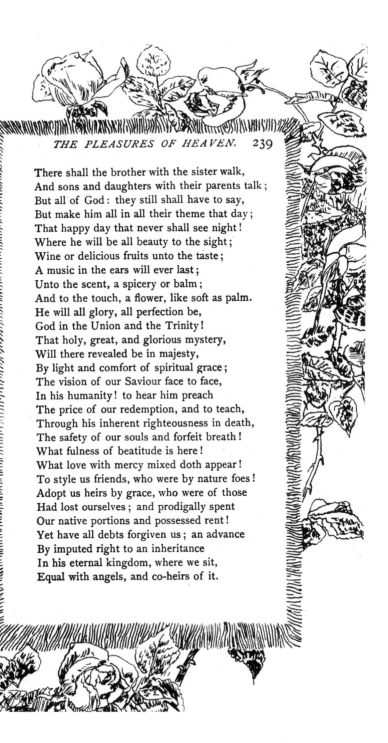

There shall the brother with the sister walk,
And sons and daughters with their parents talk;
But all of God: they still shall have to say,
But make him all in all their theme that day;
That happy day that never shall see night!
Where he will be all beauty to the sight;
Wine or delicious fruits unto the taste;
A music in the ears will ever last;
Unto the scent, a spicery or balm;
And to the touch, a flower, like soft as palm.
He will all glory, all perfection be,
God in the Union and the Trinity!
That holy, great, and glorious mystery,
Will there revealed be in majesty,
By light and comfort of spiritual grace;
The vision of our Saviour face to face,
In his humanity! to hear him preach
The price of our redemption, and to teach,
Through his inherent righteousness in death,
The safety of our souls and forfeit breath!
What fulness of beatitude is here!
What love with mercy mixed doth appear!
To style us friends, who were by nature foes!
Adopt us heirs by grace, who were of those
Had lost ourselves; and prodigally spent
Our native portions and possessed rent!
Yet have all debts forgiven us; an advance
By imputed right to an inheritance
In his eternal kingdom, where we sit,
Equal with angels, and co-heirs of it.

TO BLOSSOMS.

ROBERT HERRICK.

FAIR pledges of a fruitful tree,
    Why do you fall so fast?
    Your date is not so past,
But you may stay yet here awhile,
    To blush and gently smile,
      And go at last.

What! were ye born to be,
    An hour or half's delight,
    And so to bid good-night?
'Tis pity nature brought ye forth
Merely to show your worth,
    And lose you quite.

But you are lovely leaves, where we
    May read how soon things have
    Their end, though ne'er so brave:
And after they have shown their pride,
    Like you awhile, they glide
      Into the grave.

———

VERTUE.

GEORGE HERBERT.

SWEET day, so cool, so calm, so bright,
The bridall of the earth and skie:
The dew shall weep thy fall to-night,
    For thou must die.

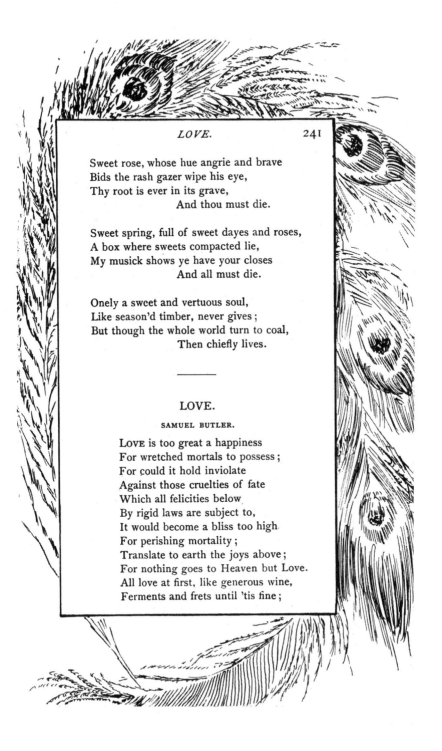

Sweet rose, whose hue angrie and brave
Bids the rash gazer wipe his eye,
Thy root is ever in its grave,
      And thou must die.

Sweet spring, full of sweet dayes and roses,
A box where sweets compacted lie,
My musick shows ye have your closes
      And all must die.

Onely a sweet and vertuous soul,
Like season'd timber, never gives ;
But though the whole world turn to coal,
      Then chiefly lives.

LOVE.

SAMUEL BUTLER.

LOVE is too great a happiness
For wretched mortals to possess ;
For could it hold inviolate
Against those cruelties of fate
Which all felicities below
By rigid laws are subject to,
It would become a bliss too high
For perishing mortality ;
Translate to earth the joys above ;
For nothing goes to Heaven but Love.
All love at first, like generous wine,
Ferments and frets until 'tis fine ;

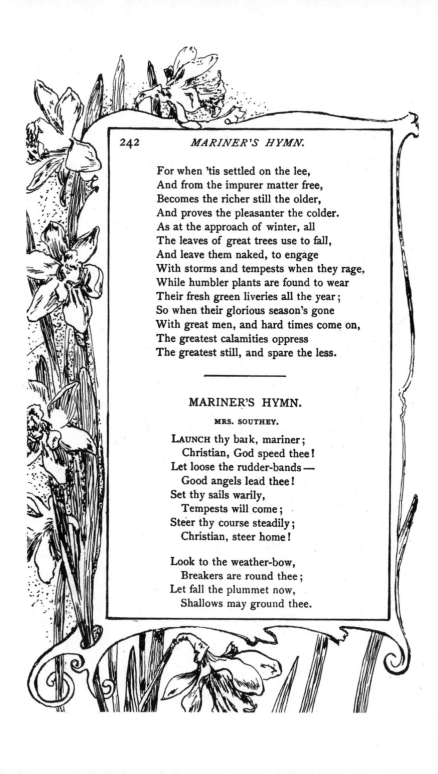

For when 'tis settled on the lee,
And from the impurer matter free,
Becomes the richer still the older,
And proves the pleasanter the colder.
As at the approach of winter, all
The leaves of great trees use to fall,
And leave them naked, to engage
With storms and tempests when they rage,
While humbler plants are found to wear
Their fresh green liveries all the year;
So when their glorious season's gone
With great men, and hard times come on,
The greatest calamities oppress
The greatest still, and spare the less.

MARINER'S HYMN.

MRS. SOUTHEY.

LAUNCH thy bark, mariner;
   Christian, God speed thee!
Let loose the rudder-bands —
   Good angels lead thee!
Set thy sails warily,
   Tempests will come;
Steer thy course steadily;
   Christian, steer home!

Look to the weather-bow,
   Breakers are round thee;
Let fall the plummet now,
   Shallows may ground thee.

Reef in the foresail there;
  Hold the helm fast!
So — let the vessel wear —
  There swept the blast.

" What of the night, watchman?
  What of the night? "
" Cloudy — all quiet —
  No land yet — all's right."
Be wakeful, be vigilant —
  Danger may be
At an hour when all seemeth
  Securest to thee.

How! gains the leak so fast?
  Clean out the hold —
Hoist up thy merchandise,
  Heave out the gold;
There — let the ingots go —
  Now the ship rights;
Hurrah! the harbor's near —
  Lo! the red lights!

Slacken not sail yet
  At inlet or island;
Straight for the beacon steer,
  Straight for the high land.
Crowd all thy canvas on,
  Cut through the foam —
Christian! cast anchor now —
  Heaven is thy home!

PEACE.

GEORGE HERBERT.

SWEET Peace, where dost thou dwell?   I humbly
crave,
Let me once know.
I sought thee in a secret cave,
And ask'd, if Peace were there.
A hollow winde did seem to answer, No;
Go seek elsewhere.

I did; and going did a rainbow note:
Surely, thought I,
This is the lace of Peace's coat:
I will search out the matter.
But while I lookt the clouds immediately
Did break and scatter.

Then went I to a garden and did spy
A gallant flower,
The crown Imperiall: Sure, said I,
Peace at the root must dwell.
But when I digg'd, I saw a worm devoure
What show'd so well.

At length I met a rev'rend good old man;
Whom when for Peace
I did demand, he thus began:
There was a Prince of old
At Salem dwelt, who liv'd with good increase
Of flock and fold.

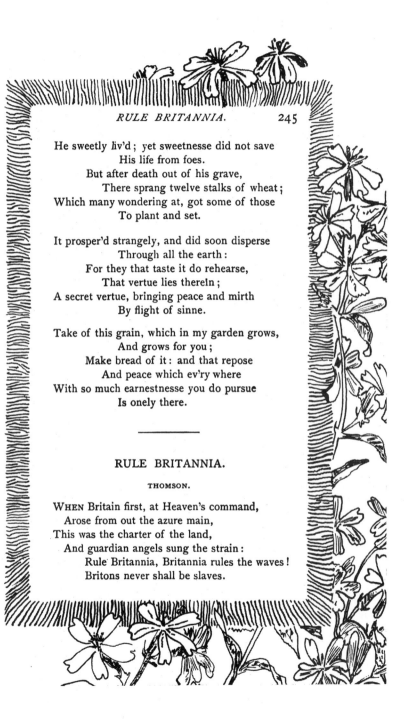

He sweetly liv'd; yet sweetnesse did not save
    His life from foes.
But after death out of his grave,
    There sprang twelve stalks of wheat;
Which many wondering at, got some of those
    To plant and set.

It prosper'd strangely, and did soon disperse
    Through all the earth:
For they that taste it do rehearse,
    That vertue lies therein;
A secret vertue, bringing peace and mirth
    By flight of sinne.

Take of this grain, which in my garden grows,
    And grows for you;
Make bread of it: and that repose
    And peace which ev'ry where
With so much earnestnesse you do pursue
    Is onely there.

————

RULE BRITANNIA.

THOMSON.

WHEN Britain first, at Heaven's command,
    Arose from out the azure main,
This was the charter of the land,
    And guardian angels sung the strain:
      Rule Britannia, Britannia rules the waves!
      Britons never shall be slaves.

The nations not so blest as thee
  Must in their turn to tyrants fall,
Whilst thou shalt flourish great and free,
  The dread and envy of them all.
      Rule Britannia, etc.

Still more majestic shalt thou rise,
  More dreadful from each foreign stroke;
As the loud blast that tears the skies
  Serves but to root thy native oak.
      Rule Britannia, etc.

Thee haughty tyrants ne'er shall tame;
  All their attempts to bend thee down
Will but arouse thy generous flame,
  And work their woe and thy renown.
      Rule Britannia, etc.

To thee belongs the rural reign;
  Thy cities shall with commerce shine;
All shall be subject to the main,
  And every shore it circles thine,
      Rule Britannia, etc.

The muses, still with freedom found,
  Shall to thy happy coast repair;
Blest isle, with matchless beauty crowned,
  And manly hearts to guard the fair.
      Rule Britannia, etc.

THE MAID'S LAMENT.

LANDOR.

I LOVED him not; and yet, now he is gone,
    I feel I am alone.
I checked him while he spoke; yet could he speak,
    Alas! I would not check.
For reasons not to love him once I sought,
    And wearied all my thought
To vex myself and him: I now would give
    My love could he but live
Who lately lived for me, and when he found
    'Twas vain, in holy ground
He hid his face amid the shades of death!
    I waste for him my breath
Who wasted his for me; but mine returns,
    And this lone bosom burns
With stifling heat, heaving it up in sleep,
    And waking me to weep
Tears that had melted his soft heart: for years
    Wept he as bitter tears!
"Merciful God!" such was his latest prayer,
    "These may she never share!"
Quieter is his breath, his breast more cold,
    Than daisies in the mould,
Where children spell athwart the churchyard gate
    His name and life's brief date.
Pray for him, gentle souls, whoe'er ye be,
    And O! pray, too, for me!

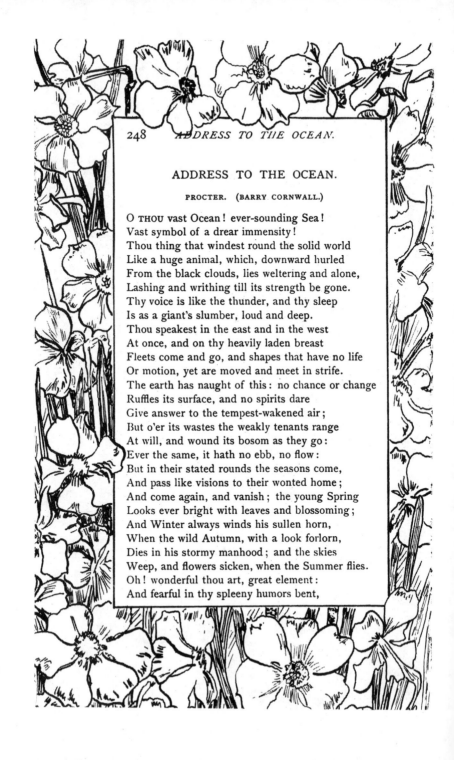

ADDRESS TO THE OCEAN.

PROCTER. (BARRY CORNWALL.)

O THOU vast Ocean! ever-sounding Sea!
Vast symbol of a drear immensity!
Thou thing that windest round the solid world
Like a huge animal, which, downward hurled
From the black clouds, lies weltering and alone,
Lashing and writhing till its strength be gone.
Thy voice is like the thunder, and thy sleep
Is as a giant's slumber, loud and deep.
Thou speakest in the east and in the west
At once, and on thy heavily laden breast
Fleets come and go, and shapes that have no life
Or motion, yet are moved and meet in strife.
The earth has naught of this : no chance or change
Ruffles its surface, and no spirits dare
Give answer to the tempest-wakened air ;
But o'er its wastes the weakly tenants range
At will, and wound its bosom as they go :
Ever the same, it hath no ebb, no flow :
But in their stated rounds the seasons come,
And pass like visions to their wonted home ;
And come again, and vanish ; the young Spring
Looks ever bright with leaves and blossoming ;
And Winter always winds his sullen horn,
When the wild Autumn, with a look forlorn,
Dies in his stormy manhood ; and the skies
Weep, and flowers sicken, when the Summer flies.
Oh! wonderful thou art, great element :
And fearful in thy spleeny humors bent,

And lovely in repose ; thy summer form
Is beautiful ; and when thy silver waves
Make music in earth's dark and winding caves,
I love to wander on thy pebbled beach,
Marking the sunlight at the evening hour,
And hearken to the thoughts thy waters teach —
Eternity — Eternity — and Power.

JEANIE MORRISON.

WILLIAM MOTHERWELL.

I'VE wandered east, I've wandered west,
   Through many a weary way ;
But never, never can forget
   The love of life's young day ;
The fire that's blawn on Beltane e'en,
   May weel be black gin Yule ;
But blacker fa' awaits the heart
   Where first fond love grows cool.

O dear, dear Jeanie Morrison,
   The thochts o' bygane years
Still fling their shadows owre my path,
   And blind my een wi' tears !
They blind my een wi' saut, saut tears,
   And sair and sick I pine,
As memory idly summons up
   The blythe blinks o' langsyne.

'Twas then we loved ilk ither weel,
　'Twas then we twa did part;
Sweet time! — sad time! — twa bairns at
　　schule,
　Twa bairns, and but ae heart!
'Twas then we sat on ae laigh bink,
　To lear ilk ither lear;
And tones, and looks, and smiles were shed,
　Remembered ever mair.

I wonder, Jeanie, aften yet,
　When sitting on that bink,
Cheek touchin' cheek, loof locked in loof,
　What our wee heads could think.
When baith bent down owre ae braid page,
　Wi' ae buik on our knee,
Thy lips were on thy lesson, but
　My lesson was in thee.

O mind ye how we hung our heads,
　How cheeks brent red wi' shame,
Whene'er the schule-weans, laughin', said,
　We cleek'd thegither hame?
And mind ye o' the Saturdays —
　The schule then skaled at noon —
When we ran aff to speel the braes —
　The broomy braes o' June?

The throssil whistled in the wood,
　The burn sung to the trees,
And we with Nature's heart in tune
　Concerted harmonies;

And on the knowe aboon the burn,
　For hours thegither sat
In the silentness o' joy, till baith
　Wi' very gladness grat!

Aye, aye, dear Jeanie Morrison,
　Tears trinkled doun your cheek,
Like dew-beads on a rose, yet nane
　Had ony power to speak!
That was a time, a blessed time,
　When hearts were fresh and young,
When freely gushed all feelings forth,
　Unsyllabled — unsung!

THE EXILE'S SONG.

ROBERT GILFILLAN.

Oh! why left I my hame?
　Why did I cross the deep?
Oh! why left I the land
　Where my forefathers sleep?
I sigh for Scotia's shore,
　And I gaze across the sea,
But I canna get a blink
　O' my ain countrie!

The palm-tree waveth high,
　And fair the myrtle springs;
And, to the Indian maid,
　The bulbul sweetly sings.

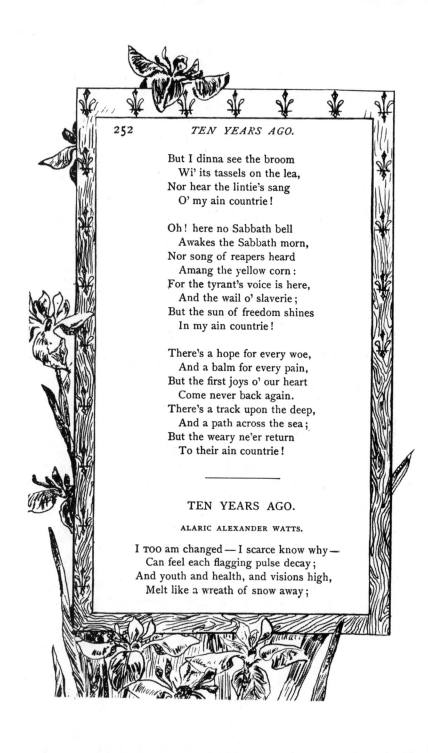

But I dinna see the broom
　Wi' its tassels on the lea,
Nor hear the lintie's sang
　O' my ain countrie!

Oh! here no Sabbath bell
　Awakes the Sabbath morn,
Nor song of reapers heard
　Amang the yellow corn:
For the tyrant's voice is here,
　And the wail o' slaverie;
But the sun of freedom shines
　In my ain countrie!

There's a hope for every woe,
　And a balm for every pain,
But the first joys o' our heart
　Come never back again.
There's a track upon the deep,
　And a path across the sea;
But the weary ne'er return
　To their ain countrie!

TEN YEARS AGO.

ALARIC ALEXANDER WATTS.

I TOO am changed — I scarce know why —
　Can feel each flagging pulse decay;
And youth and health, and visions high,
　Melt like a wreath of snow away;

Time cannot sure have wrought the ill;
  Though worn in this world's sickening strife,
In soul and form, I linger still
  In the first summer month of life;
Yet journey on my path below,
Oh! how unlike — ten years ago!

But look not thus: I would not give
  The wreck of hopes that thou must share,
To bid those joyous hours revive
  When all around me seemed so fair.
We've wandered on in sunny weather,
  When winds were low, and flowers in bloom,
And hand in hand have kept together,
  And still will keep, mid storm and gloom;
Endeared by ties we could not know
When life was young — ten years ago!

Has Fortune frowned? Her frowns were vain,
  For hearts like ours she could not chill;
Have friends proved false? Their love might wane,
  But ours grew fonder, firmer still.
Twin barks on this world's changing wave,
  Steadfast in calms, in tempests tried;
In concert still our fate we'll brave,
  Together cleave life's fitful tide;
Nor mourn, whatever winds may blow,
Youth's first wild dreams — ten years ago!

WE MET.

THOMAS HAYNES BAYLY.

WE met — 'twas in a crowd — and I thought he
    would shun me;
He came — I could not breathe, for his eye was
    upon me;
He spoke — his words were cold, and his smile was
    unaltered;
I knew how much he felt, for his deep-toned voice
    falter'd.
I wore my bridal robe, and I rivall'd its whiteness;
Bright gems were in my hair, how I hated their
    brightness!
He called me by my name, as the bride of another —
Oh, thou hast been the cause of this anguish, my
    mother!

And once again we met, and a fair girl was near him:
He smiled, and whispered low — as I once used to
    hear him.
She leant upon his arm — once 'twas mine, and mine
    only —
I wept, for I deserved to feel wretched and lonely.
And she will be his bride! at the altar he'll give her
The love that was too pure for a heartless deceiver.
The world may think me gay, for my feelings I
    smother —
Oh, thou hast been the cause of this anguish, my
    mother!

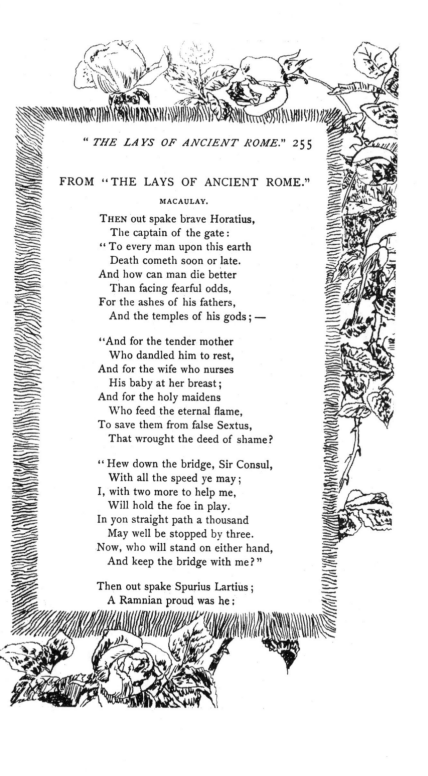

FROM "THE LAYS OF ANCIENT ROME."

MACAULAY.

THEN out spake brave Horatius,
　The captain of the gate:
" To every man upon this earth
　Death cometh soon or late.
And how can man die better
　Than facing fearful odds,
For the ashes of his fathers,
　And the temples of his gods; —

"And for the tender mother
　Who dandled him to rest,
And for the wife who nurses
　His baby at her breast;
And for the holy maidens
　Who feed the eternal flame,
To save them from false Sextus,
　That wrought the deed of shame?

" Hew down the bridge, Sir Consul,
　With all the speed ye may;
I, with two more to help me,
　Will hold the foe in play.
In yon straight path a thousand
　May well be stopped by three.
Now, who will stand on either hand,
　And keep the bridge with me?"

Then out spake Spurius Lartius;
　A Ramnian proud was he:

" Lo, I will stand at thy right hand,
    And keep the bridge with thee."
And out spake strong Herminius ;
    Of Titian blood was he :
" I will abide on thy left side,
    And keep the bridge with thee."

" Horatius," quoth the Consul,
    " As thou say'st, so let it be."
And straight against that great array
    Forth went the dauntless three ;
For Romans in Rome's quarrel
    Spared neither land nor gold,
Nor son nor wife, nor limb nor life,
    In the brave days of old.

Then none was for a party ;
    Then all were for the state ;
Then the great men helped the poor,
    And the poor man loved the great ;
Then lands were fairly portioned ;
    Then spoils were fairly sold ;
The Romans were like brothers
    In the brave days of old.

Now Roman is to Roman
    More hateful than a foe,
And the tribunes beard the high,
    And the fathers grind the low.
As we wax hot in faction,
    In battle we wax cold :
Wherefore men fight not as they fought
    In the brave days of old.

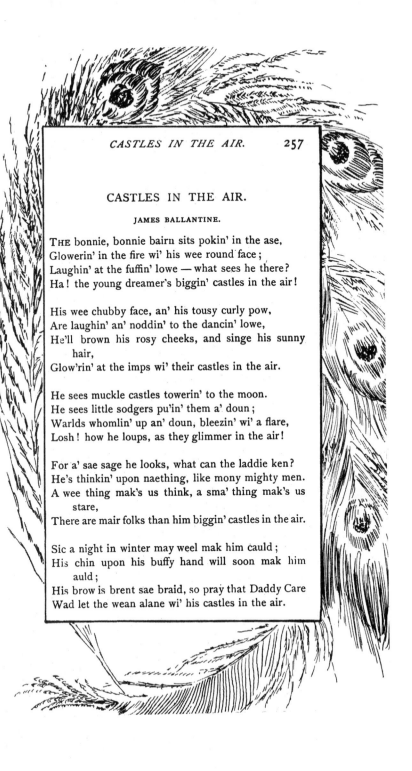

CASTLES IN THE AIR.

JAMES BALLANTINE.

THE bonnie, bonnie bairn sits pokin' in the ase,
Glowerin' in the fire wi' his wee round face;
Laughin' at the fuffin' lowe — what sees he there?
Ha! the young dreamer's biggin' castles in the air!

His wee chubby face, an' his tousy curly pow,
Are laughin' an' noddin' to the dancin' lowe,
He'll brown his rosy cheeks, and singe his sunny
    hair,
Glow'rin' at the imps wi' their castles in the air.

He sees muckle castles towerin' to the moon.
He sees little sodgers pu'in' them a' doun;
Warlds whomlin' up an' doun, bleezin' wi' a flare,
Losh! how he loups, as they glimmer in the air!

For a' sae sage he looks, what can the laddie ken?
He's thinkin' upon naething, like mony mighty men.
A wee thing mak's us think, a sma' thing mak's us
    stare,
There are mair folks than him biggin' castles in the air.

Sic a night in winter may weel mak him cauld;
His chin upon his buffy hand will soon mak him
    auld;
His brow is brent sae braid, so pray that Daddy Care
Wad let the wean alane wi' his castles in the air.

He'll glower at the fire, and he'll keek at the light;
But mony sparkling stars are swallow'd up by Night;
Aulder een than his are glamour'd by a glare,
Hearts are broken — heads are turned — wi' castles
  in the air.

THE MEN OF OLD.

R. M. MILNES.

I KNOW not that the men of old
  Were better than men now,
Of heart more kind, of hand more bold
  Of more ingenuous brow:
I heed not those who pine for force
  A ghost of time to raise,
As if they thus could check the course
  Of these appointed days.

Still is it true, and over-true,
  That I delight to close
This book of life self-wise and new,
  And let my thoughts repose
On all that humble happiness
  The world has since foregone —
The daylight of contentedness
  That on those faces shone!

With rights, though not too closely scanned,
  Enjoyed, as far as known —
With will, by no reverse unmanned —
  With pulse of even tone —

They from to-day and from to-night
  Expected nothing more
Than yesterday and yesternight
  Had proffered them before.

A man's best things are nearest him,
  Lie close about his feet;
It is the distant and the dim
  That we are sick to greet:
For flowers that grow our hands beneath
  We struggle and aspire —
Our hearts must die, except they breathe
  The air of fresh desire.

CLEAR THE WAY.

CHARLES MACKAY.

MEN of thought! be up, and stirring
      Night and day:
Sow and seed — withdraw the curtain —
      Clear the way!
Men of action, aid and cheer them,
      As ye may!
There's a fount about to stream,
There's a light about to beam,
There's a warmth about to glow,
There's a flower about to blow;
There's a midnight blackness changing
      Into gray;
Men of thought and men of action,
      Clear the way!

Once the welcome light has broken,
    Who shall say
What the unimagined glories
    Of the day?
What the evil that shall perish
    In its ray?
Aid the dawning, tongue and pen;
Aid it, hopes of honest men;
Aid it, paper — aid it, type —
Aid it, for the hour is ripe,
And our earnest must not slacken
    Into play.
Men of thought and men of action,
    Clear the way!

Lo! a cloud's about to vanish
    From the day;
And a brazen wrong to crumble
    Into clay.
Lo! the Right's about to conquer;
    Clear the way!
With the Right shall many more
Enter smiling at the door;
With the giant Wrong shall fall
Many others, great and small,
That for ages long have held us
    For their prey.
Men of thought and men of action,
    Clear the way!

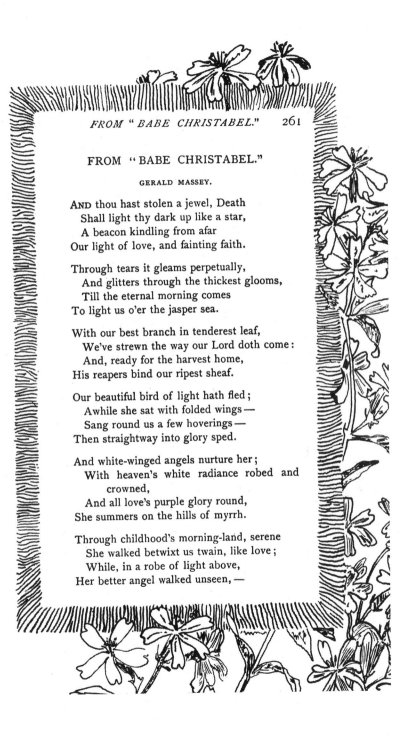

FROM "BABE CHRISTABEL."

GERALD MASSEY.

AND thou hast stolen a jewel, Death
   Shall light thy dark up like a star,
   A beacon kindling from afar
Our light of love, and fainting faith.

Through tears it gleams perpetually,
   And glitters through the thickest glooms,
   Till the eternal morning comes
To light us o'er the jasper sea.

With our best branch in tenderest leaf,
   We've strewn the way our Lord doth come :
   And, ready for the harvest home,
His reapers bind our ripest sheaf.

Our beautiful bird of light hath fled ;
   Awhile she sat with folded wings —
   Sang round us a few hoverings —
Then straightway into glory sped.

And white-winged angels nurture her ;
   With heaven's white radiance robed and
      crowned,
   And all love's purple glory round,
She summers on the hills of myrrh.

Through childhood's morning-land, serene
   She walked betwixt us twain, like love ;
   While, in a robe of light above,
Her better angel walked unseen, —

Till life's highway broke bleak and wild;
  Then, lest her starry garments trail
  In mire, heart bleed, and courage fail,
The angel's arms caught up the child.

Her wave of life hath backward rolled
  To the great ocean; on whose shore
  We wander up and down, to store
Some treasures of the times of old : —

And aye we seek and hunger on
  For precious pearls and relics rare,
  Strewn on the sands for us to wear
At heart for love of her that's gone.

O weep no more ! there yet is balm
  In Gilead ! Love doth ever shed
  Rich healing where it nestles — spread
O'er desert pillows some green palm !

Strange glory streams through life's wild rents,
  And through the open door of death
  We see the heaven that beckoneth
To the beloved going hence.

God's ichor fills the hearts that bleed ;
  The best fruit loads the broken bough ;
  And in the wounds our sufferings plough,
Immortal love sows sovereign seed.

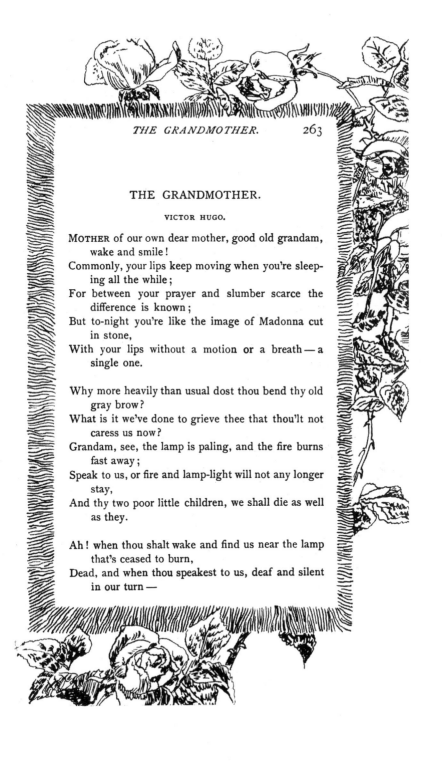

THE GRANDMOTHER.

VICTOR HUGO.

MOTHER of our own dear mother, good old grandam,
    wake and smile!
Commonly, your lips keep moving when you're sleep-
    ing all the while;
For between your prayer and slumber scarce the
    difference is known;
But to-night you're like the image of Madonna cut
    in stone,
With your lips without a motion **or** a breath — a
    single one.

Why more heavily than usual dost thou bend thy old
    gray brow?
What is it we've done to grieve thee that thou'lt not
    caress us now?
Grandam, see, the lamp is paling, and the fire burns
    fast away;
Speak to us, or fire and lamp-light will not any longer
    stay,
And thy two poor little children, we shall die as well
    as they.

Ah! when thou shalt wake and find us near the lamp
    that's ceased to burn,
Dead, and when thou speakest to us, deaf and silent
    in our turn —

Then how great will be thy sorrow! then thou'lt cry
    for us in vain,
Call upon thy saint and patron for a long, long time,
    and fain,
And a long, long time embrace us ere we come to
    life again!

Only feel how warm our hands are; wake and place
    thy hands in ours;
Wake, and sing us some old ballad of the wandering
    troubadours.
Tell us of those knights whom fairies used to help to
    love and fame:
Knights who brought, instead of posies, spoils and
    trophies to their dame,
And whose war-cry in the battle was a lady's gentle
    name.

Tell us what's the sacred token wicked shapes and
    sprites to scare!
And of Lucifer — who was it saw him flying through
    the air?
What's the gem that's on the forehead of the King
    of Gnomes displayed?
Does Archbishop Turpin's psalter, or Roland's enor-
    mous blade,
Daunt the great black King of Evil? — say, which
    makes him most afraid?

Or thy large old Bible reach us, with its pictures
    bright and blue,
Heaven all gold, and saints a-kneeling, and the infant
    Jesus too,

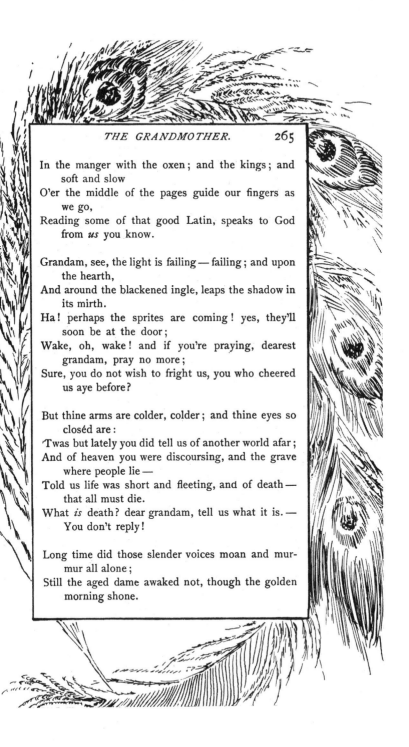

In the manger with the oxen; and the kings; and
soft and slow
O'er the middle of the pages guide our fingers as
we go,
Reading some of that good Latin, speaks to God
from *us* you know.

Grandam, see, the light is failing — failing; and upon
the hearth,
And around the blackened ingle, leaps the shadow in
its mirth.
Ha! perhaps the sprites are coming! yes, they'll
soon be at the door;
Wake, oh, wake! and if you're praying, dearest
grandam, pray no more;
Sure, you do not wish to fright us, you who cheered
us aye before?

But thine arms are colder, colder; and thine eyes so
closéd are:
'Twas but lately you did tell us of another world afar;
And of heaven you were discoursing, and the grave
where people lie —
Told us life was short and fleeting, and of death —
that all must die.
What *is* death? dear grandam, tell us what it is. —
You don't reply!

Long time did those slender voices moan and mur-
mur all alone;
Still the aged dame awaked not, though the golden
morning shone.

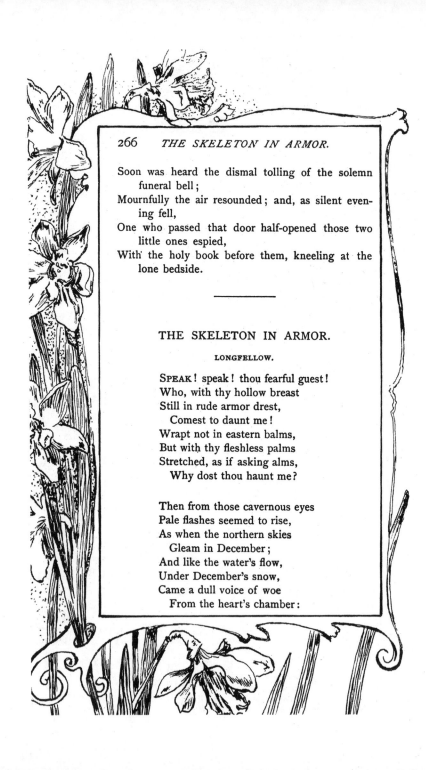

Soon was heard the dismal tolling of the solemn
  funeral bell;
Mournfully the air resounded; and, as silent even-
  ing fell,
One who passed that door half-opened those two
  little ones espied,
With the holy book before them, kneeling at the
  lone bedside.

THE SKELETON IN ARMOR.

LONGFELLOW.

SPEAK! speak! thou fearful guest!
Who, with thy hollow breast
Still in rude armor drest,
  Comest to daunt me!
Wrapt not in eastern balms,
But with thy fleshless palms
Stretched, as if asking alms,
  Why dost thou haunt me?

Then from those cavernous eyes
Pale flashes seemed to rise,
As when the northern skies
  Gleam in December;
And like the water's flow,
Under December's snow,
Came a dull voice of woe
  From the heart's chamber:

" I was a Viking old!
My deeds, though manifold,
No Skald in song has told!
　No Saga taught thee!
Take heed that in thy verse
Thou dost the tale rehearse,
Else dread a dead man's curse!
　For this I sought thee.

" Far in the Northern land,
By the wide Baltic's strand,
I, with my childish hand,
　Tamed the gerfalcon;
And, with my skates fast bound,
Skimmed the half-frozen Sound,
That the poor whimpering hound
　Trembled to walk on.

" Oft to his frozen lair
Tracked I the grisly bear,
While from my path the hare
　Fled like a shadow;
Oft through the forest dark
Followed the were-wolf's bark,
Until the soaring lark
　Sang from the meadow.

" But when I older grew,
Joining a corsair's crew,
O'er the dark sea I flew
　With the marauders.

Wild was the life we led;
Many the souls that sped,
Many the hearts that bled,
 By our stern orders.

" Many a wassail-bout
Wore the long winter out;
Often our midnight shout
 Set the cocks crowing,
As we the Berserk's tale
Measured in cups of ale,
Draining the oaken pail
 Filled to o'erflowing.

" Once as I told in glee
Tales of the stormy sea,
Soft eyes did gaze on me,
 Burning, yet tender;
And, as the white stars shine
On the dark Norway pine,
On that dark heart of mine
 Fell their soft splendor.

" I wooed the blue-eyed maid,
Yielding, yet half afraid,
And in the forest's shade
 Our vows were plighted.
Under its loosened vest
Fluttered her little breast,
Like birds within their nest
 By the hawk frighted.

" Bright in her father's hall
Shields gleamed upon the wall,
Loud sang the minstrels all,
  Chanting his glory;
When of old Hildebrand
I asked his daughter's hand,
Mute did the minstrels stand
  To hear my story.

" While the brown ale he quaffed,
Loud then the champion laughed,
And, as the wind-gusts waft
  The sea-foam brightly,
So the loud laugh of scorn,
Out of those lips unshorn,
From the deep drinking-horn
  Blew the foam lightly.

" She was a Prince's child,
I but a Viking wild,
And though she blushed and smiled,
  I was discarded!
Should not the dove so white
Follow the sea-mew's flight?
Why did they leave that night
  Her nest unguarded?

" Scarce had I put sea,
Bearing the maid with me —
Fairest of all was she
  Among the Norsemen! —

When, on the white sea-strand,
Waving his arméd hand,
Saw we old Hildebrand,
  With twenty horsemen,

'' Then launched they to the blast;
Bent like a reed each mast;
Yet we were gaining fast,
  When the wind failed us;
And with a sudden flaw
Came round the gusty Skaw,
So that our foe we saw
  Laugh as he hailed us.

'' And as, to catch the gale,
Round veered the flapping sail,
Death was the helmsman's hail
  Death without quarter!
Mid-ships, with iron keel
Struck we her ribs of steel;
Down her black hulk did reel
  Through the black water!

''As with his wings aslant,
Sails the fierce cormorant,
Seeking some rocky haunt,
  With his prey laden,
So toward the open main
Beating to sea again,
Through the wild hurricane
  Bore I the maiden.

" Three weeks we westward bore,
And when the storm was o'er,
Cloud-like we saw the shore
   Stretching to leeward;
There, for my lady's bower,
Built I the lofty tower
Which, to this very hour,
   Stands looking seaward.

" There lived we many years;
Time dried the maiden's tears;
She had forgot her fears,
   She was a mother.
Death closed her mild blue eyes;
Under that tower she lies;
Ne'er shall the sun arise
   On such another!

" Still grew my bosom then,
Still as a stagnant fen!
Hateful to me were men —
   The sunlight hateful!
In the vast forest here,
Clad in my warlike gear,
Fell I upon my spear,
   O, death was grateful!

" Thus, seamed with many scars,
Bursting its prison bars,
Up to its native stars
   My soul ascended!

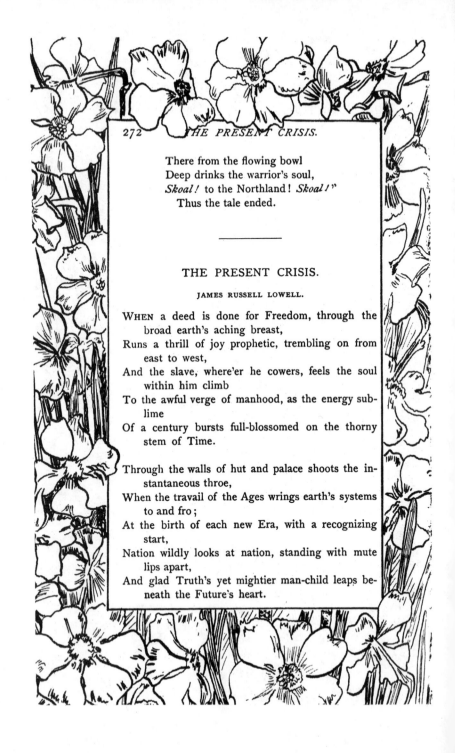

There from the flowing bowl
Deep drinks the warrior's soul,
Skoal! to the Northland! *Skoal!*"
Thus the tale ended.

THE PRESENT CRISIS.

JAMES RUSSELL LOWELL.

WHEN a deed is done for Freedom, through the
broad earth's aching breast,
Runs a thrill of joy prophetic, trembling on from
east to west,
And the slave, where'er he cowers, feels the soul
within him climb
To the awful verge of manhood, as the energy sub-
lime
Of a century bursts full-blossomed on the thorny
stem of Time.

Through the walls of hut and palace shoots the in-
stantaneous throe,
When the travail of the Ages wrings earth's systems
to and fro;
At the birth of each new Era, with a recognizing
start,
Nation wildly looks at nation, standing with mute
lips apart,
And glad Truth's yet mightier man-child leaps be-
neath the Future's heart.

So the Evil's triumph sendeth, with a terror and a
    chill,
Under continent to continent, the sense of coming
    ill,
And the slave, where'er he cowers, feels his sympa-
    thies with God
In hot tear-drops ebbing earthward, to be drunk up
    by the sod,
Till a corpse crawls round unburied, delving in the
    nobler clod !

For mankind are one in spirit, and an instinct bears
    along,
Round the earth's electric circle, the swift flash of
    right or wrong ;
Whether conscious or unconscious, yet Humanity's
    vast frame
Through its ocean-sundered fibres feels the gush of
    joy or shame ; —
In the gain or loss of one race all the rest have equal
    claim.

Once to every man and nation comes the moment to
    decide,
In the strife of Truth with Falsehood, for the good
    or evil side ;
Some great cause, God's new Messiah, offering each
    the bloom or blight,
Parts the goats upon the left-hand, and the sheep
    upon the right, —
And the choice goes by for ever 'twixt that darkness
    and that light !

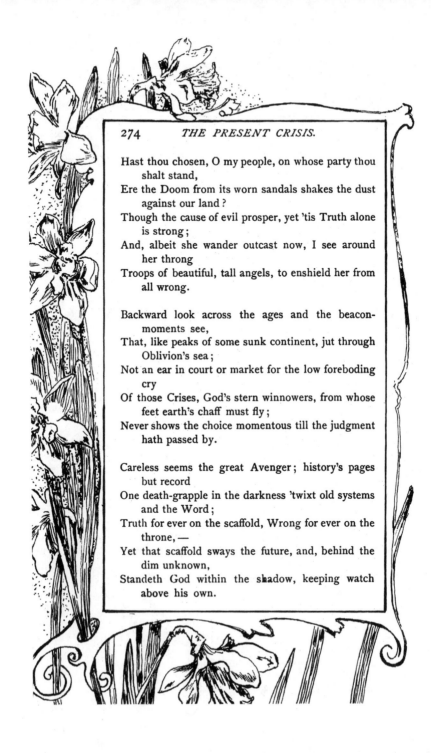

Hast thou chosen, O my people, on whose party thou
shalt stand,
Ere the Doom from its worn sandals shakes the dust
against our land?
Though the cause of evil prosper, yet 'tis Truth alone
is strong;
And, albeit she wander outcast now, I see around
her throng
Troops of beautiful, tall angels, to enshield her from
all wrong.

Backward look across the ages and the beacon-
moments see,
That, like peaks of some sunk continent, jut through
Oblivion's sea;
Not an ear in court or market for the low foreboding
cry
Of those Crises, God's stern winnowers, from whose
feet earth's chaff must fly;
Never shows the choice momentous till the judgment
hath passed by.

Careless seems the great Avenger; history's pages
but record
One death-grapple in the darkness 'twixt old systems
and the Word;
Truth for ever on the scaffold, Wrong for ever on the
throne, —
Yet that scaffold sways the future, and, behind the
dim unknown,
Standeth God within the shadow, keeping watch
above his own.

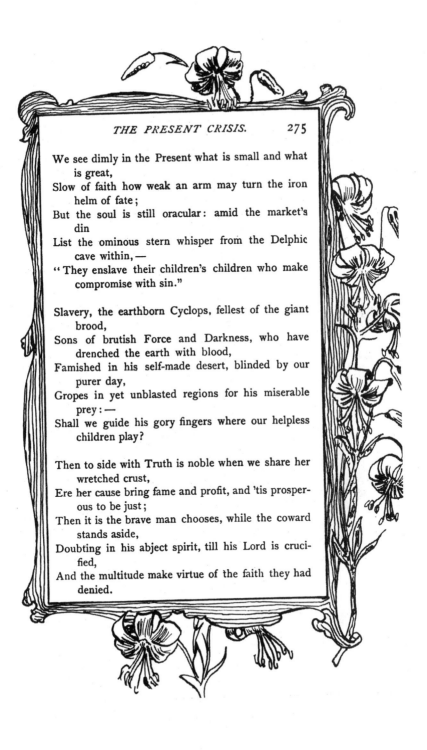

We see dimly in the Present what is small and what
   is great,
Slow of faith how weak an arm may turn the iron
   helm of fate;
But the soul is still oracular: amid the market's
   din
List the ominous stern whisper from the Delphic
   cave within, —
" They enslave their children's children who make
   compromise with sin."

Slavery, the earthborn Cyclops, fellest of the giant
   brood,
Sons of brutish Force and Darkness, who have
   drenched the earth with blood,
Famished in his self-made desert, blinded by our
   purer day,
Gropes in yet unblasted regions for his miserable
   prey : —
Shall we guide his gory fingers where our helpless
   children play?

Then to side with Truth is noble when we share her
   wretched crust,
Ere her cause bring fame and profit, and 'tis prosper-
   ous to be just;
Then it is the brave man chooses, while the coward
   stands aside,
Doubting in his abject spirit, till his Lord is cruci-
   fied,
And the multitude make virtue of the faith they had
   denied.

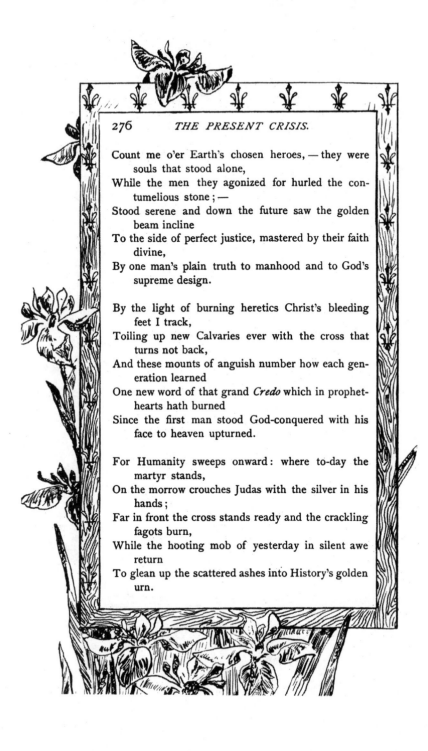

Count me o'er Earth's chosen heroes, — they were
    souls that stood alone,
While the men they agonized for hurled the con-
    tumelious stone ; —
Stood serene and down the future saw the golden
    beam incline
To the side of perfect justice, mastered by their faith
    divine,
By one man's plain truth to manhood and to God's
    supreme design.

By the light of burning heretics Christ's bleeding
    feet I track,
Toiling up new Calvaries ever with the cross that
    turns not back,
And these mounts of anguish number how each gen-
    eration learned
One new word of that grand *Credo* which in prophet-
    hearts hath burned
Since the first man stood God-conquered with his
    face to heaven upturned.

For Humanity sweeps onward: where to-day the
    martyr stands,
On the morrow crouches Judas with the silver in his
    hands ;
Far in front the cross stands ready and the crackling
    fagots burn,
While the hooting mob of yesterday in silent awe
    return
To glean up the scattered ashes into History's golden
    urn.

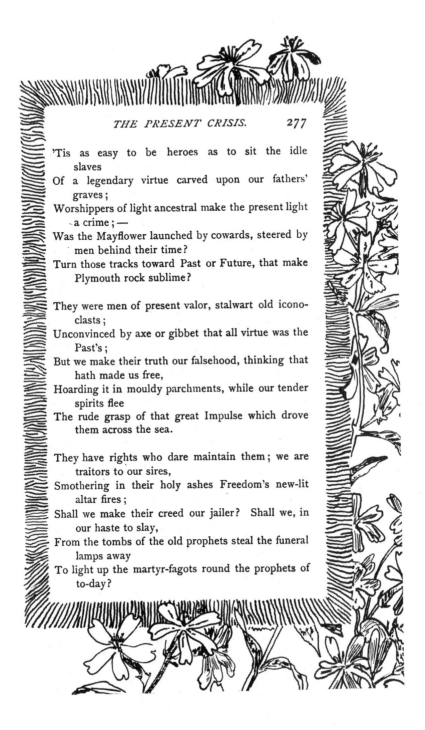

'Tis as easy to be heroes as to sit the idle
    slaves
Of a legendary virtue carved upon our fathers'
    graves ;
Worshippers of light ancestral make the present light
    a crime ; —
Was the Mayflower launched by cowards, steered by
    men behind their time?
Turn those tracks toward Past or Future, that make
    Plymouth rock sublime?

They were men of present valor, stalwart old icono-
    clasts ;
Unconvinced by axe or gibbet that all virtue was the
    Past's ;
But we make their truth our falsehood, thinking that
    hath made us free,
Hoarding it in mouldy parchments, while our tender
    spirits flee
The rude grasp of that great Impulse which drove
    them across the sea.

They have rights who dare maintain them; we are
    traitors to our sires,
Smothering in their holy ashes Freedom's new-lit
    altar fires ;
Shall we make their creed our jailer? Shall we, in
    our haste to slay,
From the tombs of the old prophets steal the funeral
    lamps away
To light up the martyr-fagots round the prophets of
    to-day?

New occasions teach new duties ; Time makes ancient
   good uncouth ;
They must upward still, and onward, who would keep
   abreast of Truth ;
Lo, before us gleam her camp-fires ! we ourselves
   must Pilgrims be,
Launch our Mayflower, and steer boldly through the
   desperate winter sea,
Nor attempt the Future's portal with the Past's blood-
   rusted key.

SONG OF THE STARS

BRYANT.

WHEN the radiant morn of creation broke,
And the world in the smile of God awoke,
And the empty realms of darkness and death
Were moved through their depths by his mighty
   breath,
And orbs of beauty and spheres of flame
From the void abyss by myriads came, —
In the joy of youth as they darted away,
Through the widening wastes of space to play,
Their silver voices in chorus rang,
And this was the song the bright ones sang : —

"Away, away, through the wide, wide sky,
The fair, blue fields that before us lie, —
Each sun, with the worlds that round him roll,
Each planet, poised on her turning pole ;

With her isles of green, and her clouds of white,
And her waters that lie like fluid light.

" For the source of glory uncovers his face,
And the brightness o'erflows unbounded space ;
And we drink as we go the luminous tides
In our ruddy air and our blooming sides :
Lo! yonder the living splendors play ;
Away, on our joyous path, away!

" Look, look, through our glittering ranks afar,
In the infinite azure, star after star,
How they brighten and bloom as they swiftly pass !
How the verdure runs o'er each rolling mass !
And the path of the gentle winds is seen,
Where the small waves dance, and the young woods
    lean.

"And see, where the brighter day-beams pour,
How the rainbows hang in the sunny shower ;
And the morn and eve, with their pomp of hues,
Shift o'er the bright planets, and shed their dews ;
And 'twixt them both, o'er the teeming ground,
With her shadowy cone the night goes round!

"Away, away! in our blossoming bowers,
In the soft air wrapping these spheres of ours,
In the seas and fountains that shine with morn,
See, Love is brooding, and Life is born ;
And breathing myriads are breaking from night,
To rejoice, like us, in motion and light."

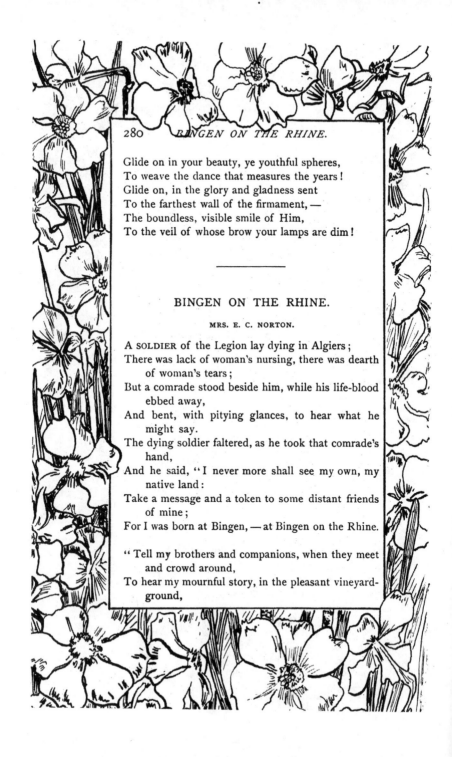

Glide on in your beauty, ye youthful spheres,
To weave the dance that measures the years!
Glide on, in the glory and gladness sent
To the farthest wall of the firmament, —
The boundless, visible smile of Him,
To the veil of whose brow your lamps are dim!

BINGEN ON THE RHINE.

MRS. E. C. NORTON.

A SOLDIER of the Legion lay dying in Algiers;
There was lack of woman's nursing, there was dearth
of woman's tears;
But a comrade stood beside him, while his life-blood
ebbed away,
And bent, with pitying glances, to hear what he
might say.
The dying soldier faltered, as he took that comrade's
hand,
And he said, "I never more shall see my own, my
native land:
Take a message and a token to some distant friends
of mine;
For I was born at Bingen, — at Bingen on the Rhine.

" Tell my brothers and companions, when they meet
and crowd around,
To hear my mournful story, in the pleasant vineyard-
ground,

That we fought the battle bravely, and, when the day
 was done,
Full many a corse lay ghastly pale beneath the set-
 ting sun;
And mid the dead and dying were some grown old
 in wars, —
The death-wound on their gallant breasts, the last of
 many scars;
And some were young, and suddenly beheld life's
 morn decline, —
And one had come from Bingen, — fair Bingen on
 the Rhine.

" Tell my mother that her other son shall comfort
 her old age;
For I was still a truant bird, that thought his home
 a cage;
For my father was a soldier, and even as a child
My heart leaped forth to hear him tell of struggles
 fierce and wild;
And when he died, and left us to divide his scanty
 hoard,
I let them take whate'er they would, — but kept my
 father's sword;
And with boyish love I hung it where the bright light
 used to shine,
On the cottage wall at Bingen, — calm Bingen on the
 Rhine.

" Tell my sister not to weep for me, and sob with
 drooping head,
When the troops come marching home again, with
 glad and gallant tread,

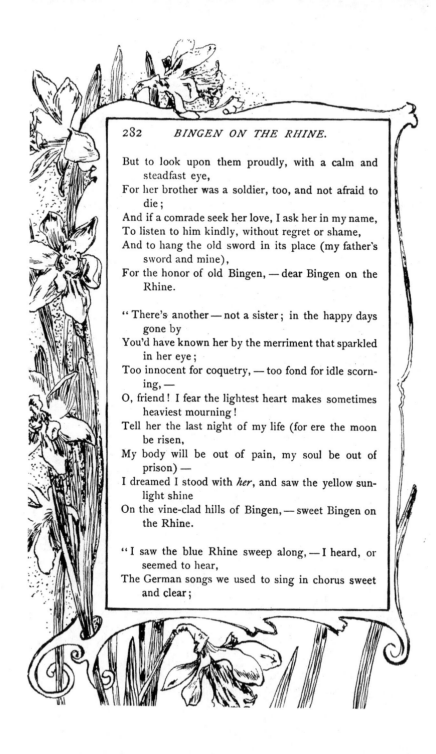

But to look upon them proudly, with a calm and
  steadfast eye,
For her brother was a soldier, too, and not afraid to
  die ;
And if a comrade seek her love, I ask her in my name,
To listen to him kindly, without regret or shame,
And to hang the old sword in its place (my father's
  sword and mine),
For the honor of old Bingen, — dear Bingen on the
  Rhine.

" There's another — not a sister ; in the happy days
  gone by
You'd have known her by the merriment that sparkled
  in her eye ;
Too innocent for coquetry, — too fond for idle scorn-
  ing, —
O, friend ! I fear the lightest heart makes sometimes
  heaviest mourning !
Tell her the last night of my life (for ere the moon
  be risen,
My body will be out of pain, my soul be out of
  prison) —
I dreamed I stood with *her*, and saw the yellow sun-
  light shine
On the vine-clad hills of Bingen, — sweet Bingen on
  the Rhine.

" I saw the blue Rhine sweep along, — I heard, or
  seemed to hear,
The German songs we used to sing in chorus sweet
  and clear ;

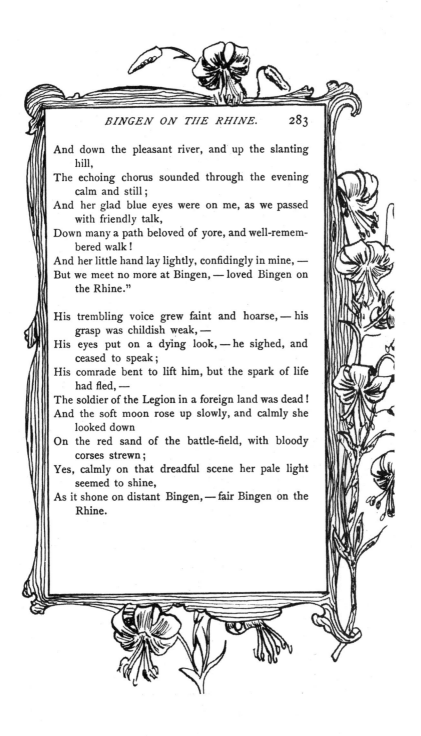

And down the pleasant river, and up the slanting
hill,
The echoing chorus sounded through the evening
calm and still;
And her glad blue eyes were on me, as we passed
with friendly talk,
Down many a path beloved of yore, and well-remem-
bered walk!
And her little hand lay lightly, confidingly in mine, —
But we meet no more at Bingen, — loved Bingen on
the Rhine."

His trembling voice grew faint and hoarse, — his
grasp was childish weak, —
His eyes put on a dying look, — he sighed, and
ceased to speak;
His comrade bent to lift him, but the spark of life
had fled, —
The soldier of the Legion in a foreign land was dead!
And the soft moon rose up slowly, and calmly she
looked down
On the red sand of the battle-field, with bloody
corses strewn;
Yes, calmly on that dreadful scene her pale light
seemed to shine,
As it shone on distant Bingen, — fair Bingen on the
Rhine.

LOVE.

JEAN INGELOW.

From "Songs of Seven."

I LEANED out of window, I smelt the white clover,
  Dark, dark was the garden, I saw not the gate;
"Now if there be footsteps, he comes, my one
    lover —
  Hush, nightingale, hush! O, sweet nightingale,
    wait
        Till I listen and hear
        If a step draweth near;
        For my love, he is late!

"The skies in the darkness stoop nearer and nearer,
  A cluster of stars hangs like fruit on the tree:
The fall of the water comes sweeter, comes clearer; —
  To what art thou listening, and what dost thou see?
        Let the star-clusters glow,
        Let the sweet waters flow,
        And cross quickly to me.

"You night-moths that hover where honey brims
    over
  From sycamore blossoms, or settle, or sleep;
You glow-worms, shine out, and the pathway discover
  To him that comes darkling along the rough steep.
        Ah, my sailor, make haste,
        For the time runs to waste,
        And my love lieth deep —

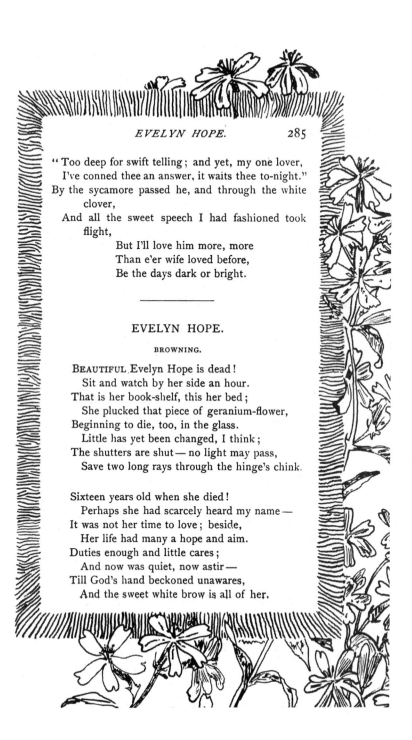

" Too deep for swift telling; and yet, my one lover,
  I've conned thee an answer, it waits thee to-night."
By the sycamore passed he, and through the white
    clover,
And all the sweet speech I had fashioned took
    flight,
        But I'll love him more, more
        Than e'er wife loved before,
        Be the days dark or bright.

EVELYN HOPE.

BROWNING.

BEAUTIFUL Evelyn Hope is dead!
  Sit and watch by her side an hour.
That is her book-shelf, this her bed;
  She plucked that piece of geranium-flower,
Beginning to die, too, in the glass.
  Little has yet been changed, I think;
The shutters are shut — no light may pass,
  Save two long rays through the hinge's chink.

Sixteen years old when she died!
  Perhaps she had scarcely heard my name —
It was not her time to love; beside,
  Her life had many a hope and aim.
Duties enough and little cares;
  And now was quiet, now astir —
Till God's hand beckoned unawares,
  And the sweet white brow is all of her.

Is it too late, then, Evelyn Hope?
  What! your soul was pure and true;
The good stars met in your horoscope,
  Made you of spirit, fire, and dew;
And just because I was thrice as old,
  And our paths in the world diverged so wide,
Each was naught to each, must I be told?
  We were fellow-mortals — naught beside?

No, indeed! for God above
  Is great to grant, as mighty to make,
And creates the love to reward the love;
  I claim you still, for my own love's sake!
Delayed, it may be, for more lives yet,
  Through worlds I shall traverse not a few;
Much is to learn, and much to forget,
  Ere the time be come for taking you.

But the time will come — at last it will —
  When, Evelyn Hope, what meant, I shall say,
In the lower earth — in the years long still —
  That body and soul so pure and gay;
Why your hair was amber I shall divine,
  And your mouth of your own geranium's red —
And what you would do with me, in fine,
  In the new life come in the old one's stead.

I have lived, I shall say, so much since then,
  Given up myself so many times,
Gained me the gains of various men,
  Ransacked the ages, spoiled the climes;

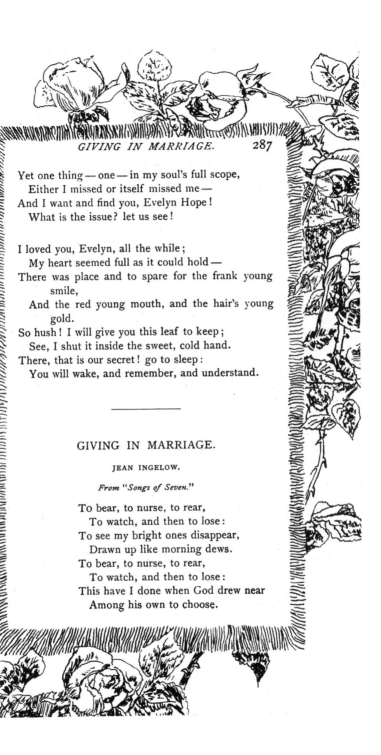

Yet one thing — one — in my soul's full scope,
  Either I missed or itself missed me —
And I want and find you, Evelyn Hope!
  What is the issue? let us see!

I loved you, Evelyn, all the while;
  My heart seemed full as it could hold —
There was place and to spare for the frank young
    smile,
  And the red young mouth, and the hair's young
    gold.
So hush! I will give you this leaf to keep;
  See, I shut it inside the sweet, cold hand.
There, that is our secret! go to sleep:
  You will wake, and remember, and understand.

GIVING IN MARRIAGE.

JEAN INGELOW.

From "Songs of Seven."

To bear, to nurse, to rear,
  To watch, and then to lose:
To see my bright ones disappear,
  Drawn up like morning dews.
To bear, to nurse, to rear,
  To watch, and then to lose:
This have I done when God drew near
  Among his own to choose.

To hear, to heed, to wed,
  And with thy lord depart,
In tears that he, as soon as shed,
  Will let no longer smart.
To hear, to heed, to wed,
  This while thou didst, I smiled;
For now it was not God who said,
  "Mother, give ME thy child."

O fond, O fool and blind,
  To God I gave with tears;
But when a man like grace would find,
  My soul put by her fears.
O fond, O fool and blind:
  God guards in happier spheres;
That man will guard where he did bind
  Is hope for unknown years.

To hear, to heed, to wed,
  Fair lot that maidens choose;
Thy mother's tenderest words are said,
  Thy face no more she views.
Thy mother's lot, my dear,
  She doth it naught accuse:
Her lot to bear, to nurse, to rear,
  To love — and then to lose.

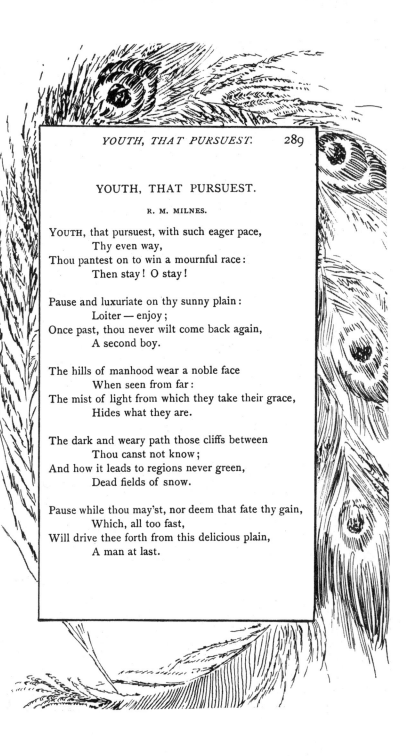

YOUTH, THAT PURSUEST.

R. M. MILNES.

YOUTH, that pursuest, with such eager pace,
    Thy even way,
Thou pantest on to win a mournful race:
    Then stay! O stay!

Pause and luxuriate on thy sunny plain:
    Loiter — enjoy;
Once past, thou never wilt come back again,
    A second boy.

The hills of manhood wear a noble face
    When seen from far:
The mist of light from which they take their grace,
    Hides what they are.

The dark and weary path those cliffs between
    Thou canst not know;
And how it leads to regions never green,
    Dead fields of snow.

Pause while thou may'st, nor deem that fate thy gain,
    Which, all too fast,
Will drive thee forth from this delicious plain,
    A man at last.

AMONG THE BEAUTIFUL PICTURES.

ALICE CARY.

AMONG the beautiful pictures
   That hang on Memory's wall,
Is one of a dim old forest,
   That seemeth best of all ;
Not for its gnarled oaks olden,
   Dark with the mistletoe ;
Not for the violets golden
   That sprinkle the vale below ;

Not for the milk-white lilies
   That lean from the fragrant ledge,
Coquetting all day with the sunbeams,
   And stealing their golden edge ;
Not for the vines on the upland,
   Where the bright red berries rest ;
Nor the pinks, nor the pale, sweet cowslip,
   It seemeth to me the best.

I once had a little brother
   With eyes that were dark and deep ;
In the lap of that old dim forest
   He lieth in peace asleep ;
Light as the down of the thistle,
   Free as the winds that blow,
We roved there the beautiful summers,
   The summers of long ago ;

But his feet on the hills grew weary,
   And one of the autumn eves
I made for my little brother
   A bed of the yellow leaves.
Sweetly his pale arms folded
   My neck in a meek embrace,
As the light of immortal beauty
   Silently covered his face;

And when the arrows of sunset
   Lodged in the tree-tops bright
He fell, in his saint-like beauty,
   Asleep by the gates of light.
Therefore of all the pictures
   That hang on Memory's wall,
The one of the dim old forest
   Seemeth the best of all.

EACH AND ALL

EMERSON.

LITTLE thinks, in the field, yon red-cloaked clown
Of thee from the hill-top looking down;
The heifer that lows in the upland farm,
Far-heard, lows not thine ear to charm;
The sexton, tolling his bell at noon,
Deems not that great Napoleon
Stops his horse, and lists with delight,
Whilst his files sweep round yon Alpine height;

Nor knowest thou what argument
Thy life to thy neighbor's creed has lent.
All are needed by each one —
Nothing is fair or good alone.

I thought the sparrow's note from heaven,
Singing at dawn on the alder-bough;
I brought him home, in his nest, at even;
He sings the song, but it pleases not now;
For I did not bring home the river and sky;
He sang to my ear, — they sang to my eye.

The delicate shells lay on the shore;
The bubbles of the latest wave
Fresh pearls to their enamel gave,
And the bellowing of the savage sea
Greeted their safe escape to me.
I wiped away the weeds and foam —
I fetched my sea-born treasures home;
But the poor, unsightly, noisome things,
Had left their beauty on the shore,
With the sun, and the sand, and the wild uproar.

The lover watched his graceful maid,
As mid the virgin train she strayed;
Nor knew her beauty's best attire
Was woven still by the snow-white choir.
At last she came to his hermitage,
Like the bird from the woodlands to the cage;
The gay enchantment was undone —
A gentle wife, but fairy none.

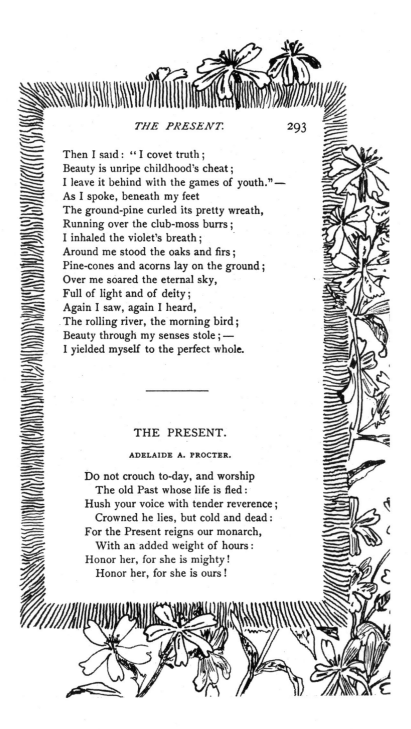

Then I said : " I covet truth ;
Beauty is unripe childhood's cheat ;
I leave it behind with the games of youth."—
As I spoke, beneath my feet
The ground-pine curled its pretty wreath,
Running over the club-moss burrs ;
I inhaled the violet's breath ;
Around me stood the oaks and firs ;
Pine-cones and acorns lay on the ground ;
Over me soared the eternal sky,
Full of light and of deity ;
Again I saw, again I heard,
The rolling river, the morning bird ;
Beauty through my senses stole ; —
I yielded myself to the perfect whole.

THE PRESENT.

ADELAIDE A. PROCTER.

Do not crouch to-day, and worship
    The old Past whose life is fled :
Hush your voice with tender reverence ;
    Crowned he lies, but cold and dead :
For the Present reigns our monarch,
    With an added weight of hours :
Honor her, for she is mighty !
    Honor her, for she is ours !

See, the shadows of his heroes
  Girt around her cloudy throne;
Every day the ranks are strengthened
  By great hearts to him unknown;
Noble things the great Past promised;
  Holy dreams both strange and new;
But the Present shall fulfil them,
  What he promised, she shall do.

She inherits all his treasures,
  She is heir to all his fame;
And the light that lightens round her
  Is the lustre of his name.
She is wise with all his wisdom,
  Living on his grave she stands;
On her brow she bears his laurels,
  And his harvest in her hands.

Coward, can she reign and conquer
  If we thus her glory dim?
Let us fight for her as nobly
  As our fathers fought for him.
God, who crowns the dying ages,
  Bids her rule and us obey:
Bids us cast our lives before her,
  Bids us serve the great To-day.

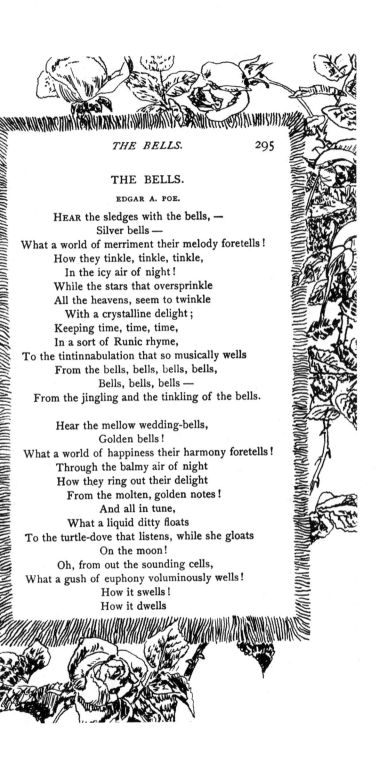

THE BELLS.

EDGAR A. POE.

HEAR the sledges with the bells, —
  Silver bells —
What a world of merriment their melody foretells!
  How they tinkle, tinkle, tinkle,
    In the icy air of night!
  While the stars that oversprinkle
  All the heavens, seem to twinkle
    With a crystalline delight;
  Keeping time, time, time,
  In a sort of Runic rhyme,
To the tintinnabulation that so musically wells
  From the bells, bells, bells, bells,
    Bells, bells, bells —
From the jingling and the tinkling of the bells.

  Hear the mellow wedding-bells,
    Golden bells!
What a world of happiness their harmony foretells!
    Through the balmy air of night
    How they ring out their delight
      From the molten, golden notes!
        And all in tune,
      What a liquid ditty floats
To the turtle-dove that listens, while she gloats
        On the moon!
  Oh, from out the sounding cells,
What a gush of euphony voluminously wells!
        How it swells!
        How it dwells

THE BELLS.

On the Future! how it tells
Of the rapture that impels
To the swinging and the ringing
Of the bells, bells, bells —
Of the bells, bells, bells, bells,
Bells, bells, bells —
To the rhyming and the chiming of the bells!

Hear the loud alarum bells —
Brazen bells!
What a tale of terror now their turbulency tells!
In the startled ear of night
How they scream out their affright!
Too much horrified to speak,
They can only shriek, shriek,
Out of tune,
In a clamorous appealing to the mercy of the fire,
In a mad expostulation with the deaf and frantic fire,
Leaping higher, higher, higher,
With a desperate desire,
And a resolute endeavor,
Now — now to sit or never,
By the side of the pale-faced moon.
Oh, the bells, bells, bells!
What a tale their terror tells
Of despair!
How they clang, and clash, and roar
What a horror they outpour
On the bosom of the palpitating air!
Yet the ear, it fully knows,
By the twanging
And the clanging,

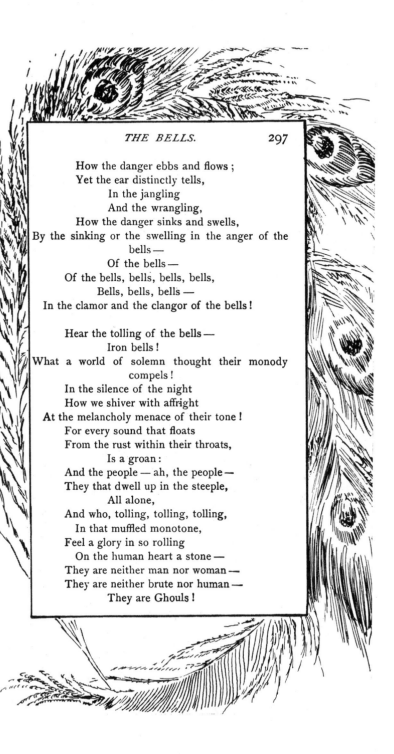

How the danger ebbs and flows ;
Yet the ear distinctly tells,
In the jangling
And the wrangling,
How the danger sinks and swells,
By the sinking or the swelling in the anger of the
bells —
Of the bells —
Of the bells, bells, bells, bells,
Bells, bells, bells —
In the clamor and the clangor of the bells !

Hear the tolling of the bells —
Iron bells !
What a world of solemn thought their monody
compels !
In the silence of the night
How we shiver with affright
At the melancholy menace of their tone !
For every sound that floats
From the rust within their throats,
Is a groan :
And the people — ah, the people —
They that dwell up in the steeple,
All alone,
And who, tolling, tolling, tolling,
In that muffled monotone,
Feel a glory in so rolling
On the human heart a stone —
They are neither man nor woman —
They are neither brute nor human —
They are Ghouls !

And their king it is who tolls;
And he rolls, rolls, rolls, rolls,
　　Rolls a pæan from the bells!
And his merry bosom swells
With the pæan of the bells!
And he dances and he yells;
Keeping time, time, time,
In a sort of Runic rhyme,
　　To the pæan of the bells—
　　　　Of the bells;
Keeping time, time, time,
In a sort Runic rhyme,
　　To the throbbing of the bells—
Of the bells, bells, bells,
　　To the sobbing of the bells;
Keeping time, time, time,
　　As he knells, knells, knells,
In a happy Runic rhyme,
　　To the rolling of the bells—
Of the bells, bells, bells,—
　　To the tolling of the bells,
Of the bells, bells, bells, bells,
　　　　Bells, bells, bells,—
To the moaning and the groaning of the bells.

RAIN IN SUMMER.

LONGFELLOW.

How beautiful is the rain!
After the dust and the heat,
In the broad and fiery street,
In the narrow lane,
How beautiful is the rain!

How it clatters along the roofs,
Like the tramp of hoofs!
How it gushes and struggles out
From the throat of the overflowing spout!

Across the window-pane
It pours and pours;
And swift and wide,
With a muddy tide,
Like a river down the gutter roars
The rain, the welcome rain!

The sick man from his chamber looks
At the twisted brooks;
He can feel the cool
Breath of each little pool;
His fevered brain
Grows calm again,
And he breathes a blessing on the rain.

From the neighboring school
Come the boys,

With more than their wonted noise
And commotion;
And down the wet streets
Sail their mimic fleets,
Till the treacherous pool
Engulfs them in its whirling
And turbulent ocean.

In the country on every side,
Where far and wide,
Like a leopard's tawny and spotted hide
Stretches the plain,
To the dry grass and the drier grain
How welcome is the rain!

In the furrowed land
The toilsome and patient oxen stand;
Lifting the yoke-encumbered head,
With their dilated nostrils spread,
They silently inhale
The clover-scented gale,
And the vapors that arise
From the well-watered and smoking soil.
For this rest in the furrow after toil
Their large and lustrous eyes
Seem to thank the Lord,
More than man's spoken word.

Near at hand,
From under the sheltering trees,
The farmer sees
His pastures and his fields of grain,

As they bend their tops
To the numberless beating drops
Of the incessant rain.
He counts it as no sin
That he sees therein
Only his own thrift and gain.

. . . . . .

ABOU BEN ADHEM AND THE ANGEL.

LEIGH HUNT.

ABOU BEN ADHEM (may his tribe increase!)
Awoke one night from a deep dream of peace,
And saw within the moonlight in his room,
Making it rich, and like a lily in bloom,
An angel writing in a book of gold: —
Exceeding peace had made Ben Adhem bold,
And to the Presence in the room he said,
"What writest thou?"— The vision raised its head,
And, with a look made of all sweet accord,
Answered, "The names of those who love the Lord."
"And is mine one?" said Abou. "Nay, not so,"
Replied the angel. Abou spoke more low,
But cheerly still; and said, "I pray thee, then,
Write me as one that loves his fellow-men."

The Angel wrote and vanished. The next night
It came again with a great wakening light,
And showed the names whom love of God had blessed,
And lo! Ben Adhem's name led all the rest.

THE INCHCAPE ROCK.

R. SOUTHEY.

No stir in the air, no stir in the sea,
The ship was as still as she could be,
Her sails from heaven received no motion
Her keel was steady in the ocean.

Without either sign or sound of their shock
The waves flow'd over the Inchcape Rock ;
So little they rose, so little they fell,
They did not move the Inchcape Bell.

The Abbot of Aberbrothok
Had placed that bell on the Inchcape Rock ;
On a buoy in the storm it floated and swung,
And over the waves its warning rung.

When the Rock was hid by the surges' swell,
The Mariners heard the warning bell ;
And then they knew the perilous Rock,
And blest the Abbot of Aberbrothok.

The sun in heaven was shining gay,
All things were joyful on that day ;
The sea-birds screamed as they wheeled round,
And there was joyance in their sound.

The buoy of the Inchcape Bell was seen
A darker speck on the ocean green ;
Sir Ralph the Rover walked his deck,
And he fixed his eye on the darker speck.

He felt the cheering power of spring,
It made him whistle, it made him sing;
His heart was mirthful to excess,
But the Rover's mirth was wickedness.

His eye was on the Inchcape float;
Quoth he : — " My men, put out the boat,
And row me to the Inchcape Rock,
And I'll plague the Abbot of Aberbrothok."

The boat is lowered, the boatmen row,
And to the Inchcape Rock they go;
Sir Ralph bent over from the boat,
And he cut the bell from the Inchcape float.

Down sunk the bell with a gurgling sound,
The bubbles rose and burst around.
Quoth Sir Ralph :—" The next who comes to the Rock
Won't bless the Abbot of Aberbrothok."

Sir Ralph the Rover sailed away,
He scoured the seas for many a day;
And now grown rich with plundered store,
He steers his course for Scotland's shore.

So thick a haze o'erspreads the sky
They cannot see the sun on high;
The wind hath blown a gale all day,
At evening it hath died away.

On the deck the Rover takes his stand,
So dark it is they see no land.
Quoth Sir Ralph : — " It will be lighter soon,
For there is the dawn of the rising moon."

" Canst hear," said one, " the breakers roar?
For methinks we should be near the shore;
Now where we are I cannot tell,
But I wish I could hear the Inchcape Bell."

They hear no sound; the swell is strong;
Though the wind hath fallen, they drift along,
Till the vessel strikes with a shivering shock:—
"Oh Christ! it is the Inchcape Rock!"

Sir Ralph the Rover tore his hair,
He curst himself in his despair;
The waves rush in on every side,
The ship is sinking beneath the tide.

But even in his dying fear
One dreadful sound could the Rover hear,—
A sound as if with the Inchcape Bell
The fiends below were ringing his knell.

THE RAINBOW.

J. KEBLE.

A FRAGMENT of a rainbow bright
  Through the moist air I see,
All dark and damp on yonder height,
  All bright and clear to me.

An hour ago the storm was here,
  The gleam was far behind,

So will our joys and grief appear,
    When earth has ceased to blind.

Grief will be joy if on its edge
    Fall soft that holiest ray,
Joy will be grief if no faint pledge
    Be there of heavenly day.

ONLY A CURL.

MRS. BROWNING.

FRIENDS of faces unknown, and a land
    Unvisited over the sea,
Who tell me how lonely you stand
With a single gold curl in the hand,
    Held up to be looked at by me, —

While you ask me to ponder and say
    What a father and mother can do
With the bright fellow-locks put away,
Out of reach, beyond kiss, in the clay,
    Where the violets press nearer than you, —

Shall I speak like a poet, or run
    Into weak woman's tears for relief?
Oh, children — I never lost one ;
Yet my arm's round my own little son,
    And Love knows the secret of grief.

And I feel what it must be and is,
  When God draws a new angel so,
Through the house of a man up to His.
With a murmur of music you miss,
  And the rapture of light you forego;

How you think, staring on at the door
  Where the face of your angel flashed in,
That its brightness, familiar before,
Burns off from you ever the more
  For the dark of your sorrow and sin.

"God lent him and takes him," you sigh.
  Nay, there let me break with your pain:
God's generous in giving, say I,
And the thing which he gives, I deny
  That he ever can take back again.

He *gives* what he gives: I appeal
  To all who bear babes; in the hour
When the veil of the body we feel
Rent around us — while torments reveal
  The motherhood's advent in power, —

And the babe cries! — has each of us known
  By apocalypse (God being there
Full in nature) the child is our own,
Life of life, love of love, moan of moan,
  Through all changes, all times, everywhere.

He's ours, and forever.   Believe,
  O father! — O mother, look back
To the first love's assurance!   To give

Means, with God, not to tempt or deceive,
  With a cup thrust in Benjamin's sack.

He gives what he gives. Be content!
  He resumes nothing given — be sure!
God lend? Where the usurers lent
In his temple, indignant he went,
  And scourged away all those impure.

He lends not, but gives to the end,
  As he loves to the end. If it *seem*
That he draws back a gift, comprehend
'Tis to add to it, rather, amend,
  And finish it up to your dream, —

Or keep, as a mother will, toys
  Too costly, though given by herself,
Till the room shall be stiller from noise,
And the children more fit for such joys,
  Kept over their heads on the shelf.

So look up, friends! you who indeed
  Have possessed in your house a sweet piece
Of the heaven which men strive for, must need
Be more earnest than others are — speed
  Where they loiter, persist where they cease

You know how one angel smiles there, —
  Then, courage. 'Tis easy for you
To be drawn by a single gold hair
Of that curl, from earth's storm and despair
  To the safe place above us. Adieu.

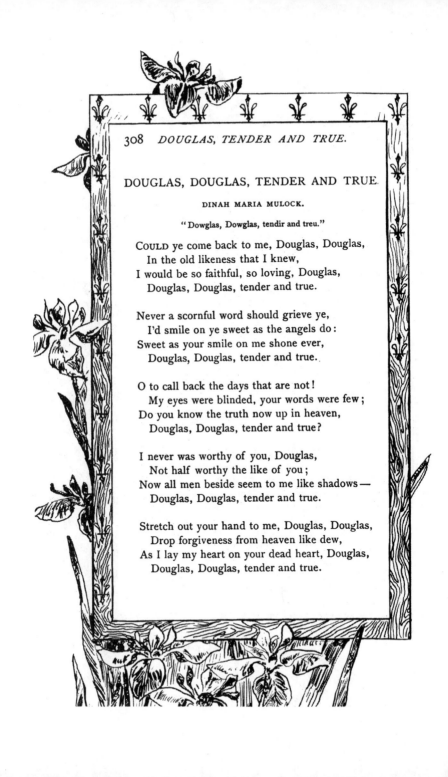

DOUGLAS, DOUGLAS, TENDER AND TRUE.

DINAH MARIA MULOCK.

"Dowglas, Dowglas, tendir and treu."

COULD ye come back to me, Douglas, Douglas,
    In the old likeness that I knew,
I would be so faithful, so loving, Douglas,
    Douglas, Douglas, tender and true.

Never a scornful word should grieve ye,
    I'd smile on ye sweet as the angels do:
Sweet as your smile on me shone ever,
    Douglas, Douglas, tender and true.

O to call back the days that are not!
    My eyes were blinded, your words were few;
Do you know the truth now up in heaven,
    Douglas, Douglas, tender and true?

I never was worthy of you, Douglas,
    Not half worthy the like of you;
Now all men beside seem to me like shadows —
    Douglas, Douglas, tender and true.

Stretch out your hand to me, Douglas, Douglas,
    Drop forgiveness from heaven like dew,
As I lay my heart on your dead heart, Douglas,
    Douglas, Douglas, tender and true.

RING OUT, WILD BELLS.

TENNYSON.

RING out, wild bells, to the wild sky,
  The flying cloud, the frosty light;
  The year is dying in the night —
Ring out, wild bells, and let him die.

Ring out the old, ring in the new —
  Ring, happy bells, across the snow:
  The year is going, let him go;
Ring out the false, ring in the true.

Ring out the grief that saps the mind,
  For those that here we see no more;
  Ring out the feud of rich and poor,
Ring in redress to all mankind.

Ring out a slowly dying cause,
  And ancient forms of party strife;
  Ring in the nobler modes of life,
With sweeter manners, purer laws.

Ring out the want, the care, the sin,
  The faithless coldness of the times;
  Ring out, ring out my mournful rhymes,
But ring the fuller minstrel in.

Ring out false pride in place and blood,
  The civic slander and the spite:
  Ring in the love of truth and right,
Ring in the common love of good.

Ring out old shapes of foul disease,
  Ring out the narrowing lust of gold;
  Ring out the thousand wars of old,
Ring in the thousand years of peace.

Ring in the valiant man and free,
  The larger heart, the kindlier hand;
  Ring out the darkness of the land —
Ring in the Christ that is to be.

STRIVE, WAIT, AND PRAY.

ADELAIDE A. PROCTER.

STRIVE: yet I do not promise
  The prize you dream of to-day
Will not fade when you think to grasp it,
  And melt in your hand away;
But another and holier treasure,
  You would now perchance disdain,
Will come when your toil is over,
  And pay you for all your pain.

Wait: yet I do not tell you
  The hour you long for now
Will not come with its radiance vanished,
  And a shadow upon its brow;
Yet, far through the misty future,
  With a crown of starry light,
An hour of joy you know not
  Is winging her silent flight.

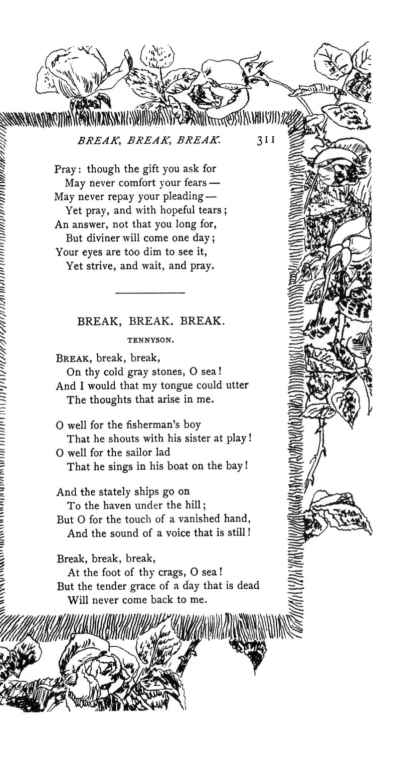

Pray: though the gift you ask for
 May never comfort your fears —
May never repay your pleading —
 Yet pray, and with hopeful tears;
An answer, not that you long for,
 But diviner will come one day;
Your eyes are too dim to see it,
 Yet strive, and wait, and pray.

BREAK, BREAK, BREAK.

TENNYSON.

BREAK, break, break,
 On thy cold gray stones, O sea!
And I would that my tongue could utter
 The thoughts that arise in me.

O well for the fisherman's boy
 That he shouts with his sister at play!
O well for the sailor lad
 That he sings in his boat on the bay!

And the stately ships go on
 To the haven under the hill;
But O for the touch of a vanished hand,
 And the sound of a voice that is still!

Break, break, break,
 At the foot of thy crags, O sea!
But the tender grace of a day that is dead
 Will never come back to me.

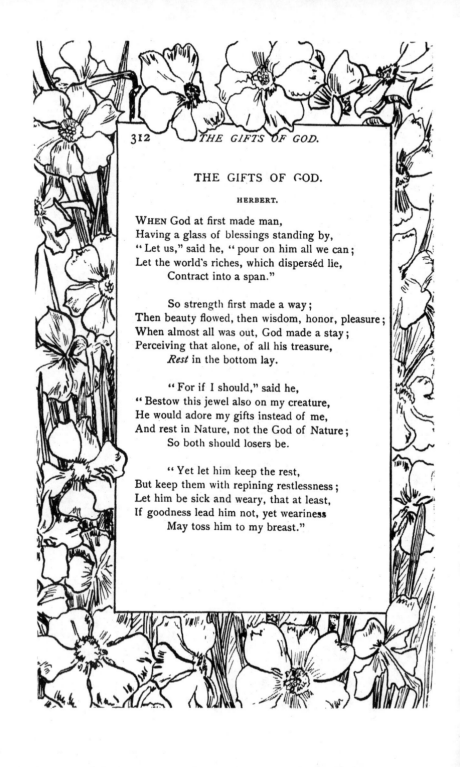

THE GIFTS OF GOD.

HERBERT.

WHEN God at first made man,
Having a glass of blessings standing by,
"Let us," said he, "pour on him all we can;
Let the world's riches, which dispersèd lie,
    Contract into a span."

    So strength first made a way;
Then beauty flowed, then wisdom, honor, pleasure;
When almost all was out, God made a stay;
Perceiving that alone, of all his treasure,
    Rest in the bottom lay.

    "For if I should," said he,
"Bestow this jewel also on my creature,
He would adore my gifts instead of me,
And rest in Nature, not the God of Nature;
    So both should losers be.

    "Yet let him keep the rest,
But keep them with repining restlessness;
Let him be sick and weary, that at least,
If goodness lead him not, yet weariness
    May toss him to my breast."

INCOMPLETENESS.

ADELAIDE A. PROCTER.

NOTHING resting in its own completeness,
   Can have worth or beauty : but alone
Because it leads and tends to further sweetness,
   Fuller, higher, deeper, than its own.

Spring's real glory dwells not in the meaning,
   Gracious though it be, of her blue hours ;
But is hidden in her tender leaning
   Toward the summer's richer wealth of flowers.

Dawn is fair, because her mists fade slowly
   Into day which floods the world with light ;
Twilight's mystery is so sweet and holy,
   Just because it ends in starry night.

Life is only bright when it proceedeth
   Toward a truer, deeper Life above :
Human love is sweetest when it leadeth
   To a more divine and perfect love.

Childhood's smiles unconscious graces borrow
   From strife that in a far-off future lies ;
And angel glances veiled now by life's sorrow,
   Draw our hearts to some belovéd eyes.

Learn the mystery of progression duly :
   Do not call each glorious change decay ;
But know we only hold our treasures truly,
   When it seems as if they passed away.

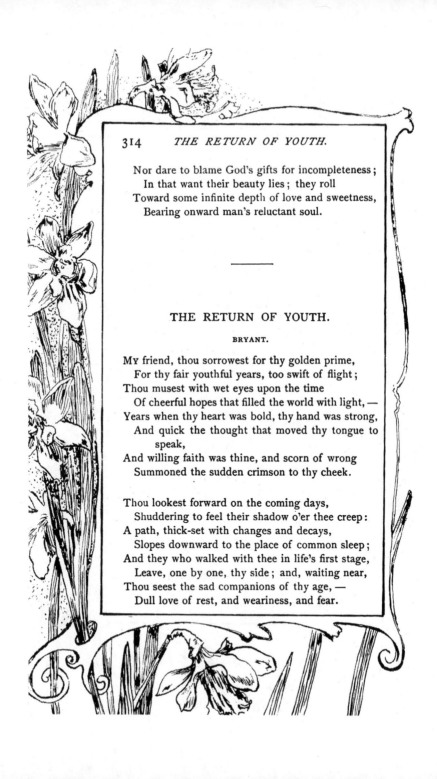

Nor dare to blame God's gifts for incompleteness;
    In that want their beauty lies; they roll
Toward some infinite depth of love and sweetness,
    Bearing onward man's reluctant soul.

THE RETURN OF YOUTH.

BRYANT.

My friend, thou sorrowest for thy golden prime,
    For thy fair youthful years, too swift of flight;
Thou musest with wet eyes upon the time
    Of cheerful hopes that filled the world with light, —
Years when thy heart was bold, thy hand was strong,
    And quick the thought that moved thy tongue to
        speak,
And willing faith was thine, and scorn of wrong
    Summoned the sudden crimson to thy cheek.

Thou lookest forward on the coming days,
    Shuddering to feel their shadow o'er thee creep:
A path, thick-set with changes and decays,
    Slopes downward to the place of common sleep;
And they who walked with thee in life's first stage,
    Leave, one by one, thy side; and, waiting near,
Thou seest the sad companions of thy age, —
    Dull love of rest, and weariness, and fear.

Yet grieve thou not, nor think thy youth is gone,
  Nor deem that glorious season e'er could die;
Thy pleasant youth, a little while withdrawn,
  Waits on the horizon of a brighter sky; —
Waits like the morn, that folds her wing and hides,
  Till the slow stars bring back her dawning hour;
Waits like the vanished Spring, that slumbering bides
  Her own sweet time to waken bud and flower.

There shall he welcome thee, when thou shalt stand
  On his bright morning hills, with smiles more sweet
Than when at first he took thee by the hand,
  Through the fair earth to lead thy tender feet.
He shall bring back, but brighter, broader still,
  Life's early glory to thine eyes again;
Still clothe thy spirit with new strength, and fill
  Thy leaping heart with warmer love than then.

Hast thou not glimpses, in the twilight here,
  Of mountains where immortal morn prevails?
Comes there not through the silence, to thine ear,
  A gentle rustling of the morning gales?
A murmur, wafted from that glorious shore,
  Of streams that water banks forever fair;
And voices of the loved ones gone before,
  More musical in that celestial air?

LABOR AND REST.

DINAH MARIA MULOCK.

Two hands upon the breast,
   And labor's done;
Two pale feet crossed in rest,
   The race is run;
Two eyes with coin-weights shut,
   And all tears cease;
Two lips where grief is mute,
   And wrath at peace! —
So pray we oftentimes, mourning our lot, —
God in his mercy answereth not.

Two hands to work addressed
   Aye for his praise;
Two feet that never rest,
   Walking his ways;
Two eyes that look above,
   Still through all tears;
Two lips that breathe but love,
   Nevermore fears:
So pray we afterward low on our knees; —
   Pardon those erring prayers!
Father, hear these!

THE SANDS O' DEE.

C. KINGSLEY.

"O MARY, go and call the cattle home,
    And call the cattle home,
    And call the cattle home,
  Across the sands o' Dee!"
The western wind was wild and dank with foam,
  And all alone went she.

The creeping tide came up along the sand,
    And o'er and o'er the sand,
    And round and round the sand,
  As far as eye could see;
The blinding mist came down and hid the land —
  And never home came she.

Oh, is it weed, or fish, or floating hair? —
    A tress o' golden hair,
    O' drowned maiden's hair,
  Above the nets at sea.
Was never salmon yet that shone so fair
  Among the stakes on Dee.

They rowed her in across the rolling foam,
    The cruel crawling foam,
    The cruel hungry foam,
  To her grave beside the sea;
But still the boatmen hear her call the cattle home,
  Across the sands o' Dee.

THE WRECK OF THE HESPERUS.

LONGFELLOW.

It was the schooner *Hesperus,*
   That sailed the wintry sea;
And the skipper had taken his little daughter,
   To bear him company.

Blue were her eyes as the fairy flax,
   Her cheeks like the dawn of day,
And her bosom white as the hawthorn buds,
   That ope in the month of May.

The skipper he stood beside the helm,
   His pipe was in his mouth,
And he watched how the veering flaw did blow
   The smoke now west, now south.

Then up and spake an old sailor,
   Had sailed the Spanish Main:
"I pray thee put into yonder port,
   For I fear the hurricane.

"Last night the moon had a golden ring,
   And to-night no moon we see!"
The skipper he blew a whiff from his pipe,
   And a scornful laugh laughed he.

Colder and louder blew the wind,
   A gale from the north-east;
The snow fell hissing in the brine.
   And the billows frothed like yeast.

Down came the storm and smote amain
  The vessel in its strength;
She shuddered and paused like a frighted steed,
  Then leaped her cable's length.

"Come hither! come hither! my little daughter,
  And do not tremble so;
For I can weather the roughest gale
  That ever wind did blow."

He wrapped her warm in his seaman's coat,
  Against the stinging blast;
He cut a rope from a broken spar,
  And bound her to the mast.

"O father! I hear the church-bells ring,
  O say, what may it be?"
"'Tis a fog-bell on a rock-bound coast!"
  And he steered for the open sea.

"O father! I hear the sound of guns,
  O say, what may it be?"
"Some ship in distress that cannot live
  In such an angry sea!"

"O father! I see a gleaming light,
  O say, what may it be?"
But the father answered never a word, —
  A frozen corpse was he.

Lashed to the helm, all stiff and stark,
  With his face turned to the skies,

The lantern gleamed through the gleaming snow
  On his fixed and glassy eyes.

Then the maiden clasped her hands and prayed
  That savéd she might be ;
And she thought of Christ who stilled the waves
  On the Lake of Galilee.

And fast through the midnight dark and drear,
  Through the whistling sleet and snow,
Like a sheeted ghost the vessel swept
  Towards the reef of Norman's Woe.

And ever the fitful gusts between
  A sound came from the land ;
It was the sound of the trampling surf
  On the rocks and the hard sea-sand.

The breakers were right beneath her bows,
  She drifted a dreary wreck,
And a whooping billow swept the crew
  Like icicles from her deck.

She struck where the white and fleecy waves
  Looked soft as carded wool,
But the cruel rocks they gored her sides
  Like the horns of an angry bull.

Her rattling shrouds all sheathed in ice,
  With the masts went by the board ;
Like a vessel of glass she stove and sank,
  Ho ! ho ! the breakers roared.

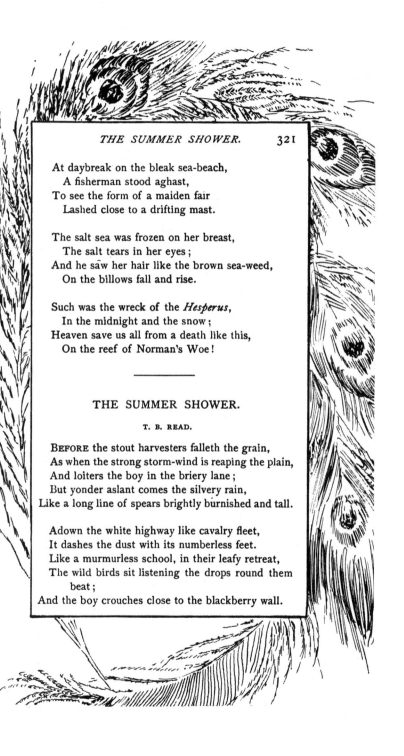

At daybreak on the bleak sea-beach,
  A fisherman stood aghast,
To see the form of a maiden fair
  Lashed close to a drifting mast.

The salt sea was frozen on her breast,
  The salt tears in her eyes;
And he saw her hair like the brown sea-weed,
  On the billows fall and rise.

Such was the wreck of the *Hesperus,*
  In the midnight and the snow;
Heaven save us all from a death like this,
  On the reef of Norman's Woe!

THE SUMMER SHOWER.

T. B. READ.

BEFORE the stout harvesters falleth the grain,
As when the strong storm-wind is reaping the plain,
And loiters the boy in the briery lane;
But yonder aslant comes the silvery rain,
Like a long line of spears brightly burnished and tall.

Adown the white highway like cavalry fleet,
It dashes the dust with its numberless feet.
Like a murmurless school, in their leafy retreat,
The wild birds sit listening the drops round them
    beat;
And the boy crouches close to the blackberry wall.

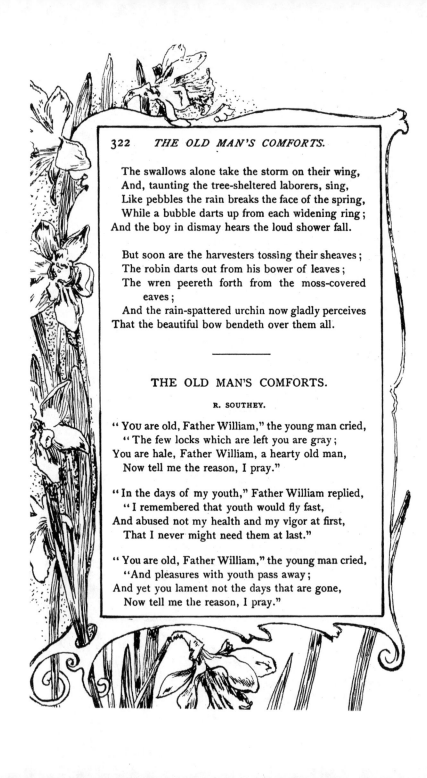

The swallows alone take the storm on their wing,
And, taunting the tree-sheltered laborers, sing,
Like pebbles the rain breaks the face of the spring,
While a bubble darts up from each widening ring;
And the boy in dismay hears the loud shower fall.

But soon are the harvesters tossing their sheaves;
The robin darts out from his bower of leaves;
The wren peereth forth from the moss-covered
    eaves;
And the rain-spattered urchin now gladly perceives
That the beautiful bow bendeth over them all.

THE OLD MAN'S COMFORTS.

R. SOUTHEY.

" You are old, Father William," the young man cried,
    " The few locks which are left you are gray;
You are hale, Father William, a hearty old man,
    Now tell me the reason, I pray."

" In the days of my youth," Father William replied,
    " I remembered that youth would fly fast,
And abused not my health and my vigor at first,
    That I never might need them at last."

" You are old, Father William," the young man cried,
    "And pleasures with youth pass away;
And yet you lament not the days that are gone,
    Now tell me the reason, I pray."

" In the days of my youth," Father William replied,
  " I remembered that youth could not last;
I thought of the future whatever I did,
  That I never might grieve for the past."

" You are old, Father William," the young man cried,
  " And life must be hastening away;
You are cheerful, and love to converse upon death,
  Now tell me the reason, I pray."

" I am cheerful, young man," Father William replied,
  " Let the cause thy attention engage;
In the days of my youth I remembered my God
  And he hath not forgotten my age."

AUTUMN.

P. B. SHELLEY.

THE warm sun is failing, the bleak wind is wailing,
The bare boughs are sighing, the pale flowers are
                dying;
            And the year
On the earth, her death-bed, in a shroud of leaves
                dead,
            Is lying.
        Come, Months, come away,
        From November to May,
        In your saddest array, —
        Follow the bier
        Of the dead cold year,
And like dim shadows watch by her sepulchre.

TO DAFFODILS.

The chill rain is falling, the nipt worm is crawling,
The rivers are swelling, the thunder is knelling
     For the year;
The blithe swallows are flown, and the lizards each
         gone
     To his dwelling.
     Come, Months, come away;
     Put on white, black, and gray;
     Let your light sisters play;
     Ye follow the bier
     Of the dead cold year,
And make her grave green with tear on tear.

TO DAFFODILS.

R. HERRICK.

FAIR daffodils, we weep to see
    You haste away so soon;
As yet the early rising sun
    Has not attained his noon:
     Stay, stay,
    Until the hastening day
     Has run
    But to the even-song;
And having prayed together, we
    Will go with you along.

We have short time to stay, as you ;
　We have as short a spring ;
As quick a growth to meet decay
　As you or any thing :
　　We die,
　As your hours do ; and dry
　　Away
　Like the summer's rain,
Or as the pearls of morning dew,
　Ne'er to be found again.

———

THE FOUNTAIN.

JAMES RUSSELL LOWELL.

INTO the sunshine,
　Full of the light,
Leaping and flashing
　From morn till night !

Into the moonlight,
　Whiter than snow,
Waving so flower-like
　When the winds blow !

Into the starlight,
　Rushing in spray,
Happy at midnight,
　Happy by day !

Ever in motion,
  Blithesome and cheery,
Still climbing heavenward,
  Never aweary;

Glad of all weathers,
  Still seeming best,
Upward or downward
  Motion thy rest;

Full of a nature
  Nothing can tame,
Changed every moment,
  Ever the same;

Ceaseless aspiring,
  Ceaseless content,
Darkness or sunshine
  Thy element;

Glorious fountain!
  Let my heart be
Fresh, changeful, constant,
  Upward like thee!

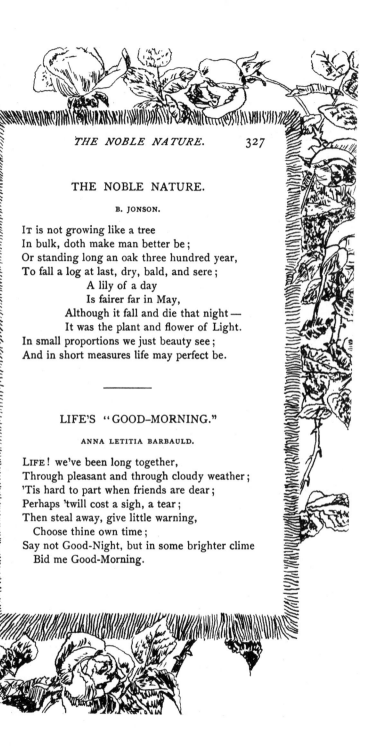

THE NOBLE NATURE.

B. JONSON.

IT is not growing like a tree
In bulk, doth make man better be;
Or standing long an oak three hundred year,
To fall a log at last, dry, bald, and sere;
    A lily of a day
    Is fairer far in May,
    Although it fall and die that night —
    It was the plant and flower of Light.
In small proportions we just beauty see;
And in short measures life may perfect be.

LIFE'S "GOOD-MORNING."

ANNA LETITIA BARBAULD.

LIFE! we've been long together,
Through pleasant and through cloudy weather;
'Tis hard to part when friends are dear;
Perhaps 'twill cost a sigh, a tear;
Then steal away, give little warning,
  Choose thine own time;
Say not Good-Night, but in some brighter clime
  Bid me Good-Morning.

HASTE NOT! REST NOT!

GOETHE.

(Anonymous Translation.)

WITHOUT haste! without rest!
Bind the motto to thy breast;
Bear it with thee as a spell;
Storm or sunshine, guard it well!
Heed not flowers that round thee bloom,
Bear it onward to the tomb!

Haste not! Let no thoughtless deed
Mar for aye the spirit's speed!
Ponder well, and know the right,
Onward then, with all thy might!
Haste not! years can ne'er atone
For one reckless action done.

Rest not! Life is sweeping by,
Go and dare, before you die;
Something mighty and sublime
Leave behind to conquer time!
Glorious 'tis to live for aye,
When these forms have passed away.

Haste not! rest not! calmly wait;
Meekly bear the storms of fate!
Duty be thy polar guide; —
Do the right whate'er betide!
Haste not! rest not! conflicts past,
God shall crown thy work at last.

BRINGING OUR SHEAVES WITH US.

ELIZABETH AKERS.

THE time for toil has passed, and night has come, —
The last and saddest of the harvest eves;
Worn out with labor long and wearisome,
Drooping and faint, the reapers hasten home,
Each laden with his sheaves.

Last of the laborers, thy feet I gain,
Lord of the harvest! and my spirit grieves
That I am burdened, not so much with grain,
As with a heaviness of heart and brain;
Master, behold my sheaves!

Few, light, and worthless, — yet their trifling weight
Through all my frame a weary aching leaves;
For long I struggled with my hopeless fate,
And stayed and toiled till it was dark and late —
Yet these are all my sheaves.

Full well I know I have more tares than wheat —
Brambles and flowers, dry stalks and withered
leaves;
Wherefore I blush and weep, as at thy feet
I kneel down reverently and repeat,
"Master, behold my sheaves!"

I know these blossoms, clustering heavily,
With evening dew upon thy folded leaves,

Can claim no value or utility, —
Therefore shall fragrancy and beauty be
  The glory of my sheaves.

So do I gather strength and hope anew;
  For well I know thy patient love perceives
Not what I did, but what I strove to do, —
And though the full ripe ears be sadly few,
  Thou wilt accept my sheaves.

INDEX TO FIRST LINES.

331

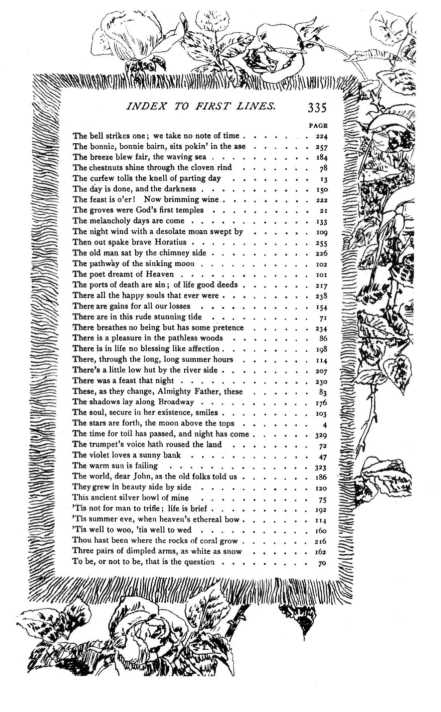